Welcome to this
QuickBreakthrough Edition
of

Truth No One Will Tell You

"Learn the truth and you will have the power to massively improve your life. I love this book!"

David Barron, coauthor of *Power Persuasion* (www.Power-Persuasion.com)

"Hiring Tom as my media and marketing coach has been the most valuable thing I've done in several years. Learn his secrets in this book!"

Dr. JoAnn Dahlkoetter, author of *Your Performing Edge* & coach to Olympians

Praise for Tom Marcoux's other work

"In *[Be Heard & Be Trusted]*, Tom teaches potent tools for finding your voice and powerfully expressing yourself, essential for getting what you want in life."

Marcia Wieder, author of *Making Your Dreams Come True* and PBS celebrity

"Tom's *How to Heal When Life's Too Much*, helps if you are having a rough time. I'd recommend it to clients, colleagues, and friends."

Shannon Seek, Principal, Seek Solutions, author of *Organic Organizing Matrix*

"In *Online Secrets to Build Your Brand*, Tom [gets you] more cash per click."

David Barron, persuasion expert, coauthor of *Power Persuasion*

"Tom's *How Top Salespeople Double Sales in Half the Time*, provides me with new techniques that I use."

Steven Seitz, Sales Manager, Silicon Valley Conference Center

Truth No One Will Tell You

I help people experience enthusiasm, love, and wisdom to fulfill big dreams.

TOM MARCOUX

Personal Mission
Caption

Truth No One Will Tell You

Secrets to Empower Yourself Through an Economic Crisis

Tom Marcoux

America's Communication Coach

&

The Time-Leverage Detective

A QUICKBREAKTHROUGH EDITION

ISBN: 0-9800511-6-9 / 978-0-9800511-6-2

QuickBreakthrough Publishing is an imprint of
Tom Marcoux Media, LLC

More copies are available from the publisher:

Tom Marcoux Media, LLC
(415) 572-6609
TomSuperCoach@gmail.com
www.TomSuperCoach.com

This book was developed and written with care. Names and details were modified to respect privacy where necessary.

Disclaimer: No fiduciary relationship is created hereby between the reader and author or publisher. The author and publisher note that each person's situation is unique and that readers have the responsibility to seek consultations with health, financial, spiritual, and legal professionals when implementing any advice contained herein. The author and publisher make no warranties of any kind, and shall not be liable for any special, consequential, or exemplary damages resulting, in whole or in part, from the reader's use of, or reliance upon, this material.

kunst**+aventur**

Book design, indexing, + photography by

see *Collophon* at rear

Source: Truth No One - Layout - II - 183 October 21, 2009 10:45 AM

Dedication

*this book is dedicated to the
terrific book & film consultant*

JOHANNA MAC LEOD

Acknowledgements

My heartfelt gratitude to all my other team members. Thanks to the guest authors for their voices of great experience. Thanks to Linda L. Chappo, Stacy Diane Horn, and Joan Harrison for editing. Thanks to Amanita Rosenbush for editorial consulting on the R.E.A.C.H. section. Thanks for comments from my father, Al Marcoux. Thanks to my mother, Sumiyo Marcoux, a kind, generous soul. Thanks to Gregg at Kunst+Aventur for the book's cover, design, editing, fact checking, typesetting, indexing, and production logistics. Thanks to Higher Power, our readers, our clients, and our enthusiastic audiences.

Contents

Summary Contents

Detailed Contents

Contents

Part I

Chapter 01

TRUTH NO ONE WILL TELL YOU

Chapter **02**

HOW TO IMPROVE YOUR FINANCIAL SITUATION

Part II

RECESSION-PROOF STRATEGIES

HOW TO FEED YOUR SOUL

SUPPORT YOURSELF

Chapter **06**

OPEN CONNECTION

Chapter **07**

UNLEASH A PLAN

Chapter **08**

LINGER FOR JOY

Part III

Part IV

Chapter **16**

REVEAL OVERCOMING A WEAKNESS

Chapter **17**

ANNOUNCE YOUR STRENGTHS

Chapter **18**

Notice Your Interviewer

Chapter **19**

Devote Yourself to the Job

Chapter **20**

Part IV: Conclusion

Part V

Chapter 21

GET OUT OF DEBT & BACK ON YOUR FEET

Chapter 22

TALK

Chapter 23

UNDERSTAND

Chapter 24

RIGHT-SIZE

Chapter 25

NURTURE

Part VI

Chapter **31**

ENHANCE RELATIONSHIPS

Chapter **32**

SHOW A PERSONAL BRAND

Chapter **33**

STIMULATE PRODUCTIVITY

Chapter **34**

NURTURE YOURSELF

Chapter **35**

OPEN THE TRIGGER-SEQUENCE

Chapter **36**

WIN

Part VII

Chapter **37**

MAKE YOUR IMPOSSIBLE DREAMS COME TRUE

Chapter **38**

DO SOMETHING NOW

Chapter **39**

REACH OUT BY HELPING

Chapter **40**

EMPOWER YOUR TIME PLAN

Chapter **41**

ACT THEN RECOVER

Chapter **42**

MEASURE PROGRESS

Glossary

Bibliography

Index

Part I

1

Truth No One Will Tell You

Empower yourself through an economic crisis

How can you empower yourself to be strong during any crisis? At the time this is being written, American and global markets have been hit with a historic recession. Millions of families and individuals have suffered due to job losses and losing homes to foreclosures. Now what?

On the day he died, Kennedy was scheduled to give a speech. Here is what he intended to say:

> *Leadership and learning are*
> *indispensable to each other.*
>
> JOHN F. KENNEDY

Kennedy's quote gives us the clue that we need in any crisis. True leaders have developed skills to deal with a crisis. How? Many of the best leaders are dedicated life-long learners. Amanda

Ripley,* while studying how people survive disasters, discovered: "Leaders [who help people survive] are knowledgeable, aware of details, and decisive."

What is an effective response when confronted with a crisis? We need to reframe the crisis into a call for us to learn to lead. Lead what and to where? You must lead yourself and others to a state of feeling calm. Do you want to feel better and become stronger? Do you want your life situation to improve? Read on.

You cannot allow the media to lead you. The media in the form of news broadcasts keeps our attention by emphasizing catastrophes. Before every commercial break, you hear negative teasers like: "Hackers are now targeting millions of computers. Yours can be next."

News broadcasts don't emphasize millions of people arriving home from work and kissing their spouse and hugging their children. Instead, broadcasts feature comments about foreclosures and the 14,000 jobs lost at Acme Corporation. For years journalists have said: "If it bleeds, it leads."

Don't be led by the media. You must lead yourself so you feel stronger and take powerful action. And you have already begun. I applaud you for reading this book. You're choosing to impact your mind with positive and inspirational material.

> *Your true freedom flows in your choices*
> *of your own programming.*
>
> TOM MARCOUX

• •

* Amanda Ripley, *The Unthinkable: Who Survives When Disaster Strikes – and Why.*

In fact, you are programming yourself to improve your life situation right now. No one else can do it for you.

Let's Talk About the Truth

The journey to becoming a leader involves discovering your personal truth. This book, *Truth No One Will Tell You*, explores four reasons people fail to express the truth. These include:

1. They don't know the truth.

2. They don't want you to know the truth so they can exploit your weakness.

3. They care about you and want you to avoid getting hurt.

4. They can only guess about what is best for you because your inner truth is only revealed by your answers to effective questions.

An interviewer asked, "Which people are not telling the truth?" Many of us discover that, intentionally or not, the people who do not tell us the truth that could empower us include co-workers, family members, friends, and politicians. Your life is truly in your hands. So we will focus on the L.E.A.D.S. Process,* because you need to be a person who leads.

L – Listen

E – Engage

A – Act

••••••••••••••••••••••••••••••••••••

* I first shared this process in my book *Be Heard & Be Trusted.*

D – Decrease downers

S – Shift to inner sources of happiness

Listen

To keep your job in tough economic times or to gain a new job, you need to be an effective listener. People trust and like individuals who listen well. We confront the myth that to be successful, one needs to be a smooth talker. The truth is that one needs to be an effective listener. To get someone to calm down, you need to make sure they feel that you truly heard him or her.

A manager will often try to retain the people he or she likes during a bad business cycle or crisis. The people who have no rapport with management are the ones who are laid off first. Being an effective listener (and thereby creating a good connection) is also applied when convincing an interviewer that you are an ideal candidate for a new job.

> *People do not care how much you know*
> *until they know how much you care.*
>
> JOHN MAXWELL

To listen well is more than just keeping one's mouth shut.

Effective Listeners

1. Turn their body so that their heart faces the other person's heart.

2. Lean forward.

3. Make listening sounds like "*mm-hmm.*"

4. Mirror feelings by saying things like, "That sounds frustrating."

5. Confirm that they understand by saying "So you want ________. Do I have that about right?"

Also, you must listen well to yourself.

As I mentioned, people can only guess about what is best for you because your inner truth is only revealed by your answers to effective questions. To get to the truth that no one will tell you, you need to provide your own answers to some tough questions, starting with these:

Truth-Revealing Questions

1. What do you really want?

2. What do you want to feel?

3. Where are you grieving?

4. How can you take better care of yourself now?

5. Where are you "contracting"?

6. How can you have some "expansion" in your life?

In your personal journal answer these questions.

What do you really want?

This is where your inner truth begins. Unfortunately, many of us have given up on hoping for something better in life. But you must understand that the past does not determine your future.

Dr. Wayne Dyer emphasizes that the past is merely the wake behind a metaphorical boat. The wake does not drive the boat. The wake (the past) is not the engine of the boat. So put your fears and your preconceptions into a metaphorical drawer for a moment. Just imagine: If the genie from *Aladdin* were next to you, what would you wish for? Write it down.

What do you want to feel?

Cognitive scientists often note that people take certain actions because they think something will yield certain feelings. Why do many people want a relationship? Because they want

illustrated by Tom Marcoux, shaded by Lindsay Morita

to feel loved and have a warm connection. Why settle on an unfulfilling job? Many people have the strong desire to feel safe and secure. Entrepreneurs often have an intense desire to get something done. Such entrepreneurs will endure feelings of uncertainty in order to press on for the accomplishments they crave. Empower yourself by uncovering what you really want to feel. Write your answer to "What do you want to feel?" in your personal journal.

Where are you grieving?

As I mentioned, this book is being written during an extreme recession. Many people are grieving lost jobs, lost retirement funds, and so much more. I can relate to such grieving because I was laid off from two jobs some years ago. In fact, that gave me part of the fuel I needed to build three companies. My advice: Find out where you are grieving then look for the turnaround. The turnaround is a way to reframe the situation so that you have new possibilities. For example, I took the situation "I was laid off" and turned it around to "How can I build a company so that I can earn multiple streams of income?"

How can you take better care of yourself?

This much is certain: The only way to ride out a recession is to take care of yourself day by day. Be sure to get the basics: rest, sleep, exercise, good nutrition, time with friends and loved ones, quiet time, and meditation or prayer. These will also contribute to calm feelings.

Where are you "contracting"?

To contract is to pull back. Have you ever seen a turtle ducking his head back into his shell? The turtle ducks out of fear of being hurt. People also contract when feeling fearful. The problem is that contracting often hurts. It can feel like we're missing out on fun or fulfillment. At present the news media is filled with stories about how consumers are spending less. This makes sense for many families. I hold a powerful phrase in my thoughts:

> *Low overhead equals freedom.*
>
> RAYMOND TELLER
> (of Penn + Teller)

Appropriate "contracting" may include being careful with your budget and choosing a library book over purchasing a book. You may decide to watch a video at home instead of taking family members to a movie theater.

Contracting is natural. But we must pay attention: Contracting can lead us to resent our current circumstances and limitations. And we feel pain. So contracting can actually disrupt any chance you have at getting to calm. And contracting cannot be your sole stance in life. You need some "expansion" in your life.

How can you have some "expansion" in your life?

Here is a crucial distinction: Often, when people complain about how their lives are contracting, they indulge in a cycle of feeling pain, complaining and suffering. Instead, you need to break this cycle so that you can ride out any crisis and get yourself to calm. Find an inexpensive way to have some "expansion" in your life.

The purpose of existence is growth [and] expression.

ROBERT COLLIER

The truth is – we feel happy when we feel hope and we express ourselves creatively. Some people protest that they are not creative. These people need to expand their perception of what creativity truly is. It is creative to help out at a soup kitchen like my friend Linda does. During numerous holiday seasons, she has created good feelings in the people she has helped and, as a by-product, she lifts her own spirits.

Happiness is not a goal, it is a by-product.

ELEANOR ROOSEVELT

Also, many of us find happiness is doing some activity that expresses our unique creativity. I am happy in this moment as I type out these words; I feel expansion occurring in my life experience. No matter what difficulty you may be experiencing in your life, I invite you to find ways to experience expansion on some level. My clients report these activities help them to feel expansion:

- Painting a picture (or another hobby)

- Meditating

- Praying

- Visiting a museum on the "free day" of each month

- Taking a class at a community college or continuing education center

- Taking a yoga, tai chi, or cooking class

- Reading a book

These activities can help your heart feel fulfilled. You may discover that you feel calm-in-the-moment while doing the activity.

> *Our purpose is to look deeply into our*
> *hearts and share what we love.*
>
> SONIA CHOQUETTE

Sonia's quote gives us a springboard to finding ways to have expansion in our lives. For example, if writing and selectively sharing your poetry expresses what you love, then that can brighten and energize your day. My client Valerie writes as she commutes to work on a subway train.

> *Nothing pays better interest than judicious reading.*
>
> ROBERT COLLIER

For example, Rhonda Byrne turned her life around after receiving a book from her daughter. The book, *The Science of Getting Rich,* inspired Rhonda to produce the phenomenal bestselling video *The Secret,* which in turn has influenced millions of people.

Engage

According to *The American Heritage Dictionary*, "engage" is defined (in part) as:

1. "To win over or attract: His smile engages everyone he meets."

2. "To draw into; involve: Engage a shy person in conversation."

One of the most important ways to gain a new job is to hone your personal brand. Your well-developed personal brand will engage the interviewer with whom you're seeking a job. A personal brand is the shortest distance to trust. Imagine which person stands out in a job interview. It's the one with a clear personal brand. A personal brand is your answer to the question: What are you best known for? For those seeking a new job, the personal brand process shows you how to be effective, which can inspire feelings of calm.

The Personal Brand Process

Here are six elements of your personal brand:

1. What are you best known for?

2. Ideally, what do you want to be best known for?

3. What high visibility details of your job are important to your boss, the supervisor above her or him, to the company, CEO or shareholders?

4. Identify two anecdotes.

5. Use a sound bite.

6. Develop a moniker.

What are you best known for?

When I was invited to speak to the Silicon Valley Chapter of the Project Management Institute (a.k.a., PMI Silicon Valley), I asked the meeting planner what the members needed. Here is what I wrote for the announcement to introduce my presentation "Empower Your Personal Brand: Align Yourself for Promotions and Raises."

> Who are you? What extraordinary benefits do you provide for your team and your company? If your supervisor, co-workers, and direct reports don't have a concise answer on the tip of their tongues, you're in trouble! Your Personal Brand is the shortest distance to trust, promotions, and raises. In this tough economic climate, no project manager can risk being a "vague cloud" in the minds of his or her business associates.
>
> This presentation/workshop will give you the opportunity to craft your Personal Brand so people get your strengths fast and remember them. This can translate directly into more income for you!
>
> The top project managers communicate so effectively that people trust them and feel good in cooperating with them. What are their secrets? This workshop by "the Personal Branding Instructor" (reported in the *San Francisco Examiner*) reveals the

techniques and mindset of people who gain success with ease.

By attending this event, professionals will be able to:

- Learn to be heard and be trusted.

- Discover how to get a self-absorbed boss to listen to you and your ideas.

- Get resistance out of the way and get colleagues to buy into what you're proposing.

- Communicate powerfully in high stress situations.

Make your Personal Brand clear, concise and memorable, and career opportunities come to you. Take this vital step forward and align yourself for promotions and raises.

My point is that you need to work on your personal brand over a span of time. It is like feeding a baby. You can't go for a day without taking care of that little one. Similarly, you need to take daily action by keeping a Job Diary and updating your résumé if you have a job right now. Also, pull out your personal journal (for your thoughts and feelings) and write down your best guess to the question: What are you best known for?

What do you ideally want to be best known for?

My client Sarah told me that she is known as a just-in-time project manager. She later realized that she truly wants to be known as the ahead-of-the-game project manager. This is better for Sarah's career because people who are heroes, the ones who get things done just in time, may fail when a team member falls ill. The house of cards tumbles if a project manager fails to put in buffer days and fails to guide team members to get ahead of the game. So write in your personal journal what you really want to be known for.

Which high visibility details matter to superiors?

The supervisor over Sarah's boss says, "During this recession, everything is about budget. Watch your costs, people!" Sarah took note and started strategizing how she could save funds on the budget for her new project.

Let's face this together. Who will a boss hold on to and choose last for any lay off? The person who makes the boss look good to her or his supervisor! Pay close attention to what is most important to the influential people at your workplace – your boss, their supervisor, the company, CEO, and shareholders. You can discover the high visibility details of your job by asking this question: What's most important to you about _____?

Identify two anecdotes

An anecdote is a story with a point. Here is a crucial distinction: It's not real until you tell a story. How is this true? A story inspires an experience for the listener.

We tell stories all the time. Here's a story a client told in one sentence: "Using one of Tom's methods, I got more done in two weeks than in six months." Apparently, she learned to streamline her process. I have posted this endorsement in many places including different Web sites.

Be careful about what stories you tell about yourself and your performance. Tell stories in which your skills and capabilities are clear. I guide clients and graduate students in preparing for job interviews, and I encourage them to have at least two anecdotes per each skill or positive trait they want to highlight when interviewed. An anecdote can include something like: "My client Sarah's face lit up at how fast I turned around the bid. She said that she could always trust me to come through."

Use a sound bite

During a news broadcast, an interviewee may say, "We're looking into the problem now." Then the program cuts back to the announcer. Those six words form a sound bite.

Here's another example of a sound bite: "When a tech problem needs solving – who can? Jan can."

It's true that some people may find this phrase trite. But it is memorable. To this day, I still remember "Coke adds life."

The best sound bite includes words of praise from a supervisor, co-worker, or client. To capture these words keep all e-mails that praise your work. The plan is to be able to say in a job interview: "My supervisor at Acme Company said, 'Joe, I can always count on you to plan ahead for possible delays. You always make sure that we finish products ahead of schedule and with quality.' " Such a sound bite sounds true because someone else (your boss) had said it.

Make sure your sound bite is connected to something that you are both good at and enjoy doing. Write three possible sound bites now:

1. "My supervisor at Acme Company said ______." (A positive comment about you and your work.)

2. "One of my clients said ______."

3. "My co-workers said ______."

Develop a moniker

Have you heard a label like "America's favorite financial adviser"? That's a moniker. Monikers sound like:

- The go-to person for software

- The Tech Wizard of Department M2

- The results coach

- The big jobs manager

A moniker can be a positive nickname. Thirty years later, I still remember the moniker "Superfoot Wallace" that described martial artist Bill Wallace's skill with fast kicks. A moniker can be helpful for your personal brand.

To align ourselves for promotions and raises, we need to be careful about what moniker we get stuck with. We need to come up with a moniker before someone else applies a nickname to us. For example, author Robin Fisher Roffer nearly dropped her drink at a networking event when one of her clients introduced her as "The Sweepstakes Queen of Cable." Robin's client wanted to help her with his introduction. This proves the point that if you are not proactive in placing your personal brand in other people's minds, they'll make their own label (or moniker) for you.

To develop your moniker, listen carefully to how people describe you. For example, my father has often said, "Tom, nothing can stop you [this contributed to my book *Nothing Can Stop You This Year*]." Others have said, "You're unstoppable." At this point, I could incorporate the word "unstoppable" into a moniker.

Once you have a moniker, you can use it in various forms. For example, my client Martha said at a networking event: "My clients often call me The Self-Promotion Master. Now I help people do ..." It takes practice to smoothly incorporate your moniker into your conversations.

Remember, one of the most powerful ways you can engage with a new person is to have your personal brand in fine order.

Act

"You must take action," many of us have heard over our lifetime. But the question is: What action?

> *Power based on love is a thousand times*
> *more effective and permanent than the*
> *one derived from fear of punishment.*

MAHATMA GANDHI

Focus on actions that are positive or expressions of love and kindness.

In this book I provide a number of methods for people to protect their current job or shine in a job interview. People tend to emphasize an outside occurrence like a job loss. The real crisis is fear – whether someone is going through employment trouble or a divorce. It's true that we need to take care of ourselves as we grieve over the loss of a job, retirement funds or something else. But we must focus on: Where do I want to go from here? That's why we need to concentrate on positive actions as we remember Gandhi's quote.

As this is being written, the current extreme recession is giving people punishment 24/7. I noticed for many days in a row that the headlines on my Yahoo.com page included discouraging comments like: "Stock market falls 777 points, 800 points … Asian markets take a beating …" This is not a breakfast of champions. In fact, the most effective Olympic athletes train themselves to focus on positive direction even during the most pressure-filled moments. It is reported that they tell themselves things like, "Run down the track like a gazelle. Explode off the springboard. Glide. Spin. Stick the landing."

Every command is a positive one. In essence, the top Olympic athlete takes action twice: First in her mind, then with her body.

One of the most powerful actions you can take is to bring yourself or someone else to calm. Take these following steps to guide someone to be more cooperative.

The Bring Calm Steps

1. Release your own disquiet.

2. Breathe deeply before seeing or calling the person.

3. Match tone, volume and pacing.

4. In graduated steps, lower your tone and volume … and in graduated steps, slow down your pacing.

Release your own disquiet

As we go through our days, some things happen that disrupt our inner peace. And, unfortunately, we carry them like baggage.

illustrated by Tom Marcoux, shaded by Lindsay Morita

The idea is to release this baggage. The *Write Down, Rip Up Method* begins when you write down the truth about what is bothering you. Then rip up the sheet of paper and place it in your pocket. Do not re-read your agitated comments – that would be like picking up the baggage all over again. Once the upsetting thoughts are down on paper and then ripped up, you will likely discover that you feel lighter and better.

Breathe deeply before meeting the person

If you are scheduled to meet with a troublesome client or an upset manager, make sure that you personally calm down. Many of us find that deep breathing brings calm feelings. Breathe in and allow your stomach area to get "fat." Then breathe out, allowing your stomach area to deflate. This is called belly breathing. You can breathe in for four counts and hold your breath for two counts – and finally breathe out again to four counts. My clients often like to use an affirmation in place of counting. A number of them breathe in with an affirmation like: "Higher Power relaxes me" or "God holds me safe." They then repeat the affirmation while they hold their breath and breathe out again.

Match tone, volume, & pacing

As we speak the sound of our voice can have a pleasing tone like a violin or a grating tone like grinding car gears. To bring another person to calm, we need to meet him or her on the same level. If that person is intense, we can sound intense, too – but we are careful with our words. A salesperson can say with a matching, intense tone: "Yes, you're right, sir. It is an important problem. I'm going to focus on helping you."

We also need to match volume. Replying to a customer's barking voice with syrupy-soft volume and tone will often cause the barking customer to get more agitated. It is better to start by matching tone, volume, and pacing. About pacing: Often we see that someone from New York can do better when talking to someone from the southern United States by slowing down her pace of talking.

In graduated steps, lower tone, volume, & pacing

According to cognitive and neuro-scientists, we have mirror-neurons in our brain. These are the cells that match the energy of someone who is talking to us. As you gradually lower your tone, volume and speed of talking – through mirror-neurons – the other person will often quiet down, too. In this way you bring the other person to calm.

~~~~~~~~~~~~~~~~~~~~

The secret about Act is to focus on actions that provide leverage. Leverage is when you strategically apply a small amount of effort for a big result.

You take effective action when you:

1. Know what you want.

2. Know how to tell when you have what you want.

Knowing these two details makes it easier to decide on a good action – in this moment. This will bring feelings of calm. How? You start to see that you're on track and that you have hope that you can influence your life situation for the better.

Here are guiding ideas for taking action:

You will only get paid by taking action.

MIKE COLLINS
~~~~~~~~~~~~~~~~~~~~

*Your best work is not the triumph of
technique but the purity of purpose.*

TOM MARCOUX

Imperfect action is better than perfect inaction.

HARRY TRUMAN

*Start by doing what's necessary;
then do what's possible;
and suddenly you are doing the impossible.*

ST. FRANCIS OF ASSISI

Decrease Downers

"Downers" are things, activities, or people that drain your energy. We confront the myth: One should be strong enough to put up with a lot of stress. The truth is: No one has time or energy for all things.

We must pick our battles and conserve our energy for what we can truly influence.

Write down what drains your energy. For example, I had to tell a close friend to stop sending me certain cartoons. These cartoons were clever but they brought down my energy. They were filled with complaints. So I told my friend, "Please stop sending me these cartoons. They do not empower me to be good to my clients, my family, nor my students." In this way I decreased (or shut off the flow) of one type of downer.

Reduce the impact of downers in your life and you increase your moments of calm. You will actually feel stronger.

Shift to Inner Sources of Happiness

A crisis is often something outside of our control that knocks us down. It can be a job layoff, a divorce, the loss of a loved one, a severe illness or something else that drains energy and brings great pain. Truly, it's when external sources of happiness are snatched away. Now is the time to build and use internal resources. When the world appears to be crashing down on the outside, we need to shift to inner sources of happiness. In a crisis, two things happen: First, we've lost something so we're grieving. Second, our energy is drained. This tough spot causes many of us to find that we can't implement a life-improving shift of perception because we don't have the energy. Here's a solution: Use a *Low Mood First-Aid Kit* to recover energy. Your kit is a list of activities that you can do on your own to comfort yourself. My clients have reported using:

- A warm bath

- Knitting

- Listening to music

- Playing with pets

- Walking in nature

- Reading a good book

- Writing in a personal journal

- Quiet time for meditation or prayer

Do an activity that makes you feel alive! Focus on the moment. If you're walking in nature with a friend, avoid talking about soaking your aching feet when you get back home. Instead, stay in the moment and focus on the new sights, new aromas, and new sounds. Shift to what you can control: your effort. I guide my clients to separate Effort Goals and Result Goals. You can control your own efforts like making ten marketing phone calls. You cannot control the results. But you can have an inner source of happiness or satisfaction by setting a goal (Effort Goal) and fulfilling it.

My clients report new feelings of calm when they can see that they're making true incremental progress. That's what logging Effort Goal activities provides for you.

Happiness is something to do,
someone to love,
and something to hope for.

CHINESE PROVERB

Effort Goals provide the feelings of hope and calm. My clients log their actions related to attending networking events, sending out résumés, taking quiet time away from cell phones and e-mail, and doing something to enhance personal health.

How to Shift to Inner Sources of Happiness

To improve your mood, what is often the most effective thing to do? – Focus on a question.

*The answer is in the question. Ask better
questions. What am I learning here?
How can we make this better?*

TOM MARCOUX

Try this question, "What am I grateful for?" Write down your
answers.

*Happiness cannot be traveled to, owned, earned, worn,
or consumed. Happiness is the spiritual experience of
living every minute with love, grace, and gratitude.*

DENIS WAITLEY

What are your sources of grace? Prayer? Quiet time? A phone
call with a supportive friend? Focusing on inner sources
of happiness is really about devoting time to your personal
spiritual path.

*The only true security is in Spirit … if our inner
world is lit by love, we are unshakably secure.*

ALAN COHEN

Choose faith, not fear.

JOEL OSTEEN

To choose faith is to focus on things that empower you. Make
a plan and take action. Hold on to the thoughts and intentions
that you are moving forward and through the crisis. Winston
Churchill said, "If you are going through hell, keep going."
Researchers have noted that people who press onward often

exclaim, "I didn't know I could be that strong" and "I learned to have better priorities."

The Truth No One Will Tell You is … You set up your own rules about your own happiness. If you set up conditions, then you will be unhappy more moments of each day. Some people set up the condition: "When I get a new job, I'll be happy" or "When I have a romantic relationship, I'll be happy." Researchers note that human beings adapt to any new situation. It is not about setting conditions; it is about finding the good in the present moment. If you set up expansive opportunities for happiness, then you can enjoy more happy moments.

> *If you want others to be happy, practice compassion.*
> *If you want to be happy, practice compassion.*
>
> THE DALAI LAMA

> *Treat yourself kindly and with compassion.*
> *Happiness is not a destination.*
> *It is a method of life.*
>
> AUSTIN O'MALLEY

So choose to find ways to enjoy this moment. It's up to you.

> *I don't know what your destiny will be, but one thing I do know: the only ones among you who will be really happy are those who have sought and found how to serve.*
>
> ALBERT SCHWEITZER

Life is to be fortified by many friendships.
To love and to be loved is the greatest happiness.

SYDNEY SMITH

Be flexible like a dancer – poised to move in any direction. Dancers are at their best with rest, sleep, good nutrition, time with friends, and opportunities for laughter. Remember, shift to an inner source. Live in this moment.

2

How to Improve Your Financial Situation

At one point, an interviewer asked me, "What are some secrets of making money?" I replied that I have personally used a set of principles that I created for my clients and myself. I'm so concerned about misinformation in general use that I streamlined the principles into the T.R.U.T.H. Process for making money.

> T – Transform to "Yes."
>
> R – Run in better races.
>
> U – Untangle from the money-for-time trade.
>
> T – Take on risk.
>
> H – Hone your persuasion skills.

A great source of feeling calm in turbulent financial times is to have hope. See which of the T.R.U.T.H. Process methods seize your attention and then make an action plan. In this way you will have the hope you need to rise out of any financial rut. As you take baby steps forward, you will begin to feel more hopeful.

Action is the antidote to despair.

JOAN BAEZ

Let's get started …

Transform to "Yes"

Have you noticed that people often have an automatic "no" response to new ideas or new actions? When some new opportunity to earn money comes along, many of us find that "no" rises up. "No, I won't be good enough." "No, they'll reject me and that will feel bad."

Instead, I invite you to transform that "no" to a big "Yes."

- "Yes, I'm going to give this a chance."

- "Yes, I can handle a possible rejection. Instead, I'll call it 'we didn't have a match.'"

As a teenager, I began my work life at a fast food restaurant making minimum wage. I was 15 years old and I washed everything, including floors, windows, and toilets. The first time I earned $400 an hour, I stepped significantly out of my comfort zone. I earned that $400 modeling for an advertisement for a software company.

I was afraid during that photo shoot. For one thing, the position called for an Asian person born and raised in another country. That was not me. I was born and raised in the United States.

In fact, when I walked into the building, the photographer said, "You were born in the U.S., weren't you?" At that point my jangled nerves felt like I wanted to escape out a window.

To make the photo work, I placed my hands together in a reverent manner like I had seen Asian monks do. The photographer took a photo of my head and shoulders. He said, "That's better." Evidently my posture had changed from the hard-charging energy that I usually walked around with. I was playing the role of someone raised in an Asian country.

Here is an important part of Transform to "Yes": Step out of your comfort zone and make the best of a situation.

I remember the first time that I made thousands of dollars through the Internet. I was seized with an idea. At the time I was on a train en route to teaching a graduate level class. I took quick notes. Upon arriving, I got off the train and walked quickly to the university. I went into a side room and quickly typed out two thousand words on my laptop.

My point here is that I said "Yes!" to the idea. I took action and ultimately completed writing a new e-book. People in 12 countries purchased that e-book through the Internet.

When I wrote the first two thousand words of the e-book, I had no idea if what I wrote would work. But I had another "Yes" response.

"Yes, it's all good practice. I'll get better as a writer."

"Yes, I can probably adapt this writing to something else in the future."

Let's move to the second strategy …

Run in Better Races

Years ago I was feeling overwhelmed. I told my sweetheart, "I'm like a racehorse."

"Run in better races," she replied, encouraging me to be more selective.

Good point. I replied, "I need to be in an area where a big payday is possible. "

This proved to be true the first time I earned $1,000 in one hour. At the time I was earning $14 an hour as a marketing assistant.

My question was, *Is there something I can do that comes easy to me, but is hard for other people?*

Write down your own possible answers to this question, which I will repeat: Is there something I can do that comes easy to me, but is hard for other people?

I knew I could study, synthesize information, and convey it in an entertaining way.

Acclaimed television host Johnny Carson said, "People will pay more to be entertained than to be educated." So I earned $1,000 in one hour by speaking to a group on a topic which I had never presented before.

An interviewer commented, "It sounds like it takes chutzpah and courage to try new things and put yourself at risk."

Often, one needs to act with courage. My audiences like my phrase, *Courage is easier when I'm prepared.* The point is that I prepare every day for my next speech, interview or book that I write. In recent years, I have read 108 and 109 books per year, respectively. I prepare by keeping up with my fields of interest.

How does one get into a better race?

It's about your skills in building relationships. And the essence of effective networking (for jobs and more) is building good relationships. So often opportunities that I have enjoyed have come from building business and personal relationships. My first opportunity to be marketed by a speaker bureau at the $5,000 level came from years of building a relationship with the bureau's team members. This is how you get in a better race. You are friendly, trustworthy and helpful in all your dealings with people. Then people bring you opportunities.

The truth about dealing with a financial crisis

Let me tell you about someone I truly admire. Linda had trained as a graphic designer for the hi-tech industry. But when the Silicon Valley Dot-Com Bubble burst, she went through some pain and had to shift gears. Through the years she gained training in a number of fields so that she has multiple ways to bring value to the marketplace. Currently she is one of my editors. She is also a personal chef, author, and weight loss counselor. Formerly she was a hair stylist and hair salon owner. Let's learn from Linda's example: Make sure that you can earn money in many ways. This is called having multiple streams of income. I invite you to follow Linda's example and look for possibilities to use your hidden talents and gain new training for when a crisis arrives.

An interviewer asked: "Does a person need to be assertive?"

It depends on the situation. Would you like to know four sentences that meant $171,543 to me?

After I gave a speech an audience member walked up to me and said, "You should speak for Acme Company." I replied, "Thank you. Who do I talk with? [He told me.] Oh, you have your cell phone? How about we leave her a message now?" Those were the four sentences. The person immediately left a voicemail message and I ultimately closed the deal (that resulted in a number of presentations).

The point here is that I needed to be assertive. First I needed to notice if I had enough rapport with the person who praised me and said, "You should speak for Acme Company." Also, the reason why the four sentences were important is because the man who gave me the compliment was at a peak in his emotional approval of my speaking. That's the reason I wanted him to immediately leave a voicemail message. I knew his enthusiasm would appear on that message.

Let's explore the next technique …

Untangle from the Money-for-Time Trade

Many of us are caught in a real trap: Trading one hour of our time for a certain amount of money. Do you know how I first earned $225 per hour? I asked for it! I realized, though, that there was an upper limit on the hourly wage. But if I could write books … I would do the work once and get paid again and again.

For example, I wrote material for actors and was paid multiple times, including:

- Fees paid for teaching classes.

- Fees paid by students at the classes who chose to purchase the workbook at a cost of $25 each.

- Fees paid in recent years by people who purchased the same material as an e-book entitled *101 Acting Secrets: Tips from A Director for Your Acting, Auditions, Movie Roles, and Self-Promotion.**

Another example: Author Joel Osteen is not in the trap of trading time for money. Joel reportedly earned a $13 million advance fee for his second book. As a pastor he speaks to his in-person congregation of around 40,000 people each Sunday. And millions more view his television broadcasts. As I mentioned earlier, you need to be in an area where a big payday is possible. Joel lives this secret.

An interviewer commented: "Well, that's good for Joel. He has a whole team. His father had built the congregation up to 8,000 people before Joel Osteen took over."

Excellent points! This reminds us that there are no self-made millionaires. Everyone rises to a higher level with the cooperation, help, and guidance of others.

• •

* To get your copy of *101 Acting Secrets: Tips from A Director for Your Acting, Auditions, Movie Roles, and Self-Promotion*, please visit www.TomSuperCoach.com/SpecialOffer.htm.

Five Ways to Stop Trading Time for Money

Write something

If you have some writing talent and you enjoy writing to some measure, consider writing a book, a novel, a screenplay, an audio program, or graphic novel. With writing, a secret is to continually make progress. If you write an article, the material can later appear in an audio program, speech or book. I write some material every day. Some of my clients choose self-publishing and sell their material on the Internet; and other clients go the traditional route of agents and getting a book deal with a major publisher.

This is an "and" universe; that is, you can do one thing and another. A writer can pursue both routes. Some people hesitate because they do not feel like an expert. I alert my clients to the empowering idea that an expert is someone who has devised a system that people like and use. To become an expert may be a lower hurdle than many of us think. Many people start with a personal problem, learn how to solve it, and then train others to solve that problem.

Invent something

Some of us remember the Pet Rock, which was merely a rock with brilliantly witty packaging. Gary Dahl, the man with the idea, offered his graphic designer $50,000 to sell his share of the project. So Gary went on to take the risks and gain the benefits solo. Soon Gary earned $1 million with the Pet Rock.

To find your inspiration, you might read books or watch television shows like "American Inventor." For example, viewers were enthralled when they saw a fireman, Gregg Chavez, propose an idea for a fire safety device called The Guardian Angel. Chavez described his Guardian Angel invention as, "A small, pressurized tank of water, disguised as a Christmas package that is placed under the Christmas tree and attached to a small hose leading to the top of the tree where a fusible link is disguised as an angel. The heat from a fire pops the link and water suppresses the fire."

Close real estate deals

As this is being written, a number of real estate agents express their concerns about how the real estate market has faltered. Let's realize that the real estate business, like a number of other industries, cycles back. For example, a friend recently told me that his real estate agent made $6,000 on the sale of a home. When I mentioned this in an interview, the host said, "Wait a minute. That still sounds like trading time for money." I replied, "I see your point. And, we realize that once a real estate agent acquires the knowledge for closing deals, she can be working on multiple deals at the same time. A number of effective real estate agents have an assistant that does much of the routine office work. This is all about multiplying one's ability to earn large sums in less time. This process is still different from making a set fee of $20 per hour or even $300 per hour."

Sell through the Internet

Millions of people sell items through eBay. Others sell information-related products. For example, my friend author David Barron teamed up with another author (with a large e-subscribers list). David had written and put together a system that guides people to become powerful influencers, and David's share of the profits was $6,000! I have coached clients on how to interview top people in a field, write an article and place it on Web sites. This is how you begin relationships with other authors that can lead to joint, mutually beneficial ventures.

Author and Internet entrepreneur Randy Gage mentions these popular topics that can be written about and sold as an expert's opinion on the Internet: marketing strategies, home-based business, health and wellness, weight loss, sales, crafts, art, wealth building, spiritual enlightenment, finding good employees, relationships, Web site design, gardening, raising a family, nutrition, travel and presentation skills. I would add: ways to live well on a small budget, humor, and pets.

illustrated by Tom Marcoux, shaded by Lindsay Morita

Team up

Some of my audience members say, "I'm not a writer." Don't let that stop you. Years ago, as a ghostwriter, I wrote a speech for a millionaire. And this millionaire had previously sold 1.4 million copies of a (probably ghostwritten) book. Sometimes my clients ask me, "How did you write and publish six books in three years?" I reply that I have a system:

- I write the material.

- I read it out loud to a team member. I revise the material as I hear the spoken words and watch my team member's responses.

- Then I have two editors (one in California and one in Canada) work on the material.

You do not need to be a writer. A client, Marcy, talks into an audio recorder. She has a nephew type up the material. Then she hands the material to a part-time college instructor for revision.

Teaming up is a powerful strategy. For example, I have produced audio programs that have all generated income. But I did not purchase a sound-editing program for my office computer. Why? Because it is more cost effective for me in terms of time and money to go to a veteran sound engineer. He can perform a refinement on the program in 20 seconds when it would take me 20 minutes (of frustration) to do the same function. He has devoted 17 years of his life to his craft of sound engineering and editing. I can walk into his studio, record my material, and step out with a completed master recording within hours! Also, my sound engineer gives me guidance on how I can improve the program as we edit it. This guidance raises the level of quality. Remember to team up.

Constantly prepare for the home run.

TOM MARCOUX

The major principle for gaining sudden profits is to constantly prepare for the home run. That is, on a daily basis, practice and prepare so that when you're in the game you can gain a big, life-improving result. Being in the game may occur when someone says, "You should speak for Acme Company" (an experience I mentioned earlier). Being in the game can also be when you're meeting a friend's sister at a party and it turns out that she needs an employee like you. By the way, use a number of methods of this section so that you feel calm when you're meeting people. A person who experiences some calm and some happiness each day is the person who radiates charisma. People offer charismatic individuals new opportunities. And remember that people tend to like others who listen to them. When you experience calm and some happiness each day, you have more energy to listen to new people you meet.

The point is this – a number of successful people who seem to become an overnight success have been devoting effort over a number of years. They have been continually improving their craft. That is, they constantly prepare for the home run. For example, Jon Stewart (star of *The Daily Show* on Comedy Central) said, "I can't believe how lucky I have been already. And it's *not* in 'Aw, shucks' … I have worked really hard. And I've tried to get better."

I learned something about success when bestselling author Richard Carlson told me his journey when we appeared on a radio show together. Richard said, "*Don't Sweat the Small Stuff* was my tenth book." Richard loved to write and he kept going through nine previous books, each with varying degrees of success.

Richard was perfecting his writing style with every book he wrote. In this way he was constantly preparing for the home run, which became his bestselling book *Don't Sweat the Small Stuff*. Soon, Richard had a bestselling series, including *Don't Sweat the Small Stuff in Love*, *Don't Sweat the Small Stuff with Money*, and others.

Take on Risk

In the section "Conquer Fear," I will introduce the R.E.A.C.H. process to you. Here I want to emphasize that life does not only reward hard work. Big profits often result when someone takes on appropriate risk. A number of people shy away from appropriate risk. That's because they do not have a strategy for risk-taking. Please see "Conquer Fear" for methods that can brighten your life.

> *I will do what others will not do, so in the*
> *future I can do what others cannot do.*
>
> RANDY GAGE

Hone Your Persuasion Skills

What can open the floodgates of financial abundance? It happens when we learn and practice positive persuasion skills. My life changed when I learned that persuasion can have positive outcomes – when I start by focusing on how I can benefit the listener.

Win-win or no deal.

STEPHEN R. COVEY

Positive persuasion is about making sure that a transaction results in benefits for both people – a win-win result. True success is built on positive business and personal relationships. Learn the skills of positive persuasion and gain a whole new world of opportunities.

Comfort can be desirable, but opportunities are fun!

In my books *Be Heard and Be Trusted* and *Nothing Can Stop You This Year*, I go into great depth about positive persuasion skills. Here I will share guidance I give my graduate students who seek to make persuasive speeches and pitches.

I can't persuade you if I don't know you.

TOM MARCOUX

Positive persuasion involves asking gentle questions and listening well. Then you shape your next comments in line with the person's goals and desires.

*The most important persuasion tool you
have in your entire arsenal is integrity.*

ZIG ZIGLAR

*Character may almost be called the most
effective means of persuasion.*

ARISTOTLE

*He that has truth in his heart need never fear
the want of persuasion on his tongue.*

JOHN RUSKIN

It comes down to being credible and trustworthy. To truly persuade someone you need to appeal to emotion. Numerous successful salespeople repeat this adage: people buy on emotion and later justify on fact.

*If you would persuade, you must appeal
to interest rather than intellect.*

BENJAMIN FRANKLIN

Certainly, big decisions require careful thought but a person often starts with a feeling like: I like this house; I want this car; or I look good in this dress. Now, if a salesperson helps the buyer with gentle questions, then a sale can be made. Questions can include:

- Do you want to take advantage of the record low costs of houses during this current recession?

- So where will you be driving this car? Who will see how successful you look?

- This dress is you. Where will you be wearing it?

The successful persuader helps the person see and feel how her own goals will be fulfilled by making a purchase or favorable decision.

~~~~~~~~~~~~~~~~~~

This section, "Truth No One Will Tell You," has been an overview of highlights from my audio programs and presentations. I invite you to read the rest of this book and to seek out my other products for in-depth methods and support in your journey to thrive and empower yourself through any crisis.

Principles:

About the L.E.A.D.S. process: To thrive during a crisis, you need to lead yourself and others to calm.

About the T.R.U.T.H. process: In order to do better financially, you need to stretch and take appropriate risks.

Power Questions:

Which loved one or friend can you invite to practice the Bring Calm Steps? How can you have expansion in your life? Is there something you can do (to earn money) that comes easy to you, but is hard for other people? Where or how can you get additional training so you can have multiple streams of income?*

. . . .

* Here! Get your copy of the *Ultimate Make Money While You Sleep via the Internet System* at www.TomSuperCoach.com/SpecialOffer.htm.
~~~~~~~~~~~~~~~~~~

Conclusion to Part I

In any crisis the truth is: we need to lead ourselves – our thinking, our feelings, and our actions. We cannot wait for anyone else to provide leadership. Fortunately, you will gain cooperation when you begin by focusing on benefits for all involved.

In Part II, "Recession-Proof Strategies," you will learn how to save a business or gain a job during an economic crisis.

Let's move forward. You will strengthen yourself and create better results.

Part II

3

Recession-Proof Strategies

Introduction

What if you just lost your job? How would you find some comfort and reassurance?

Or …

Imagine you saw your business slipping and going under. How could you summon the strength to keep going?

This section provides recession-proof strategies I formulated as I saw a distraught woman interviewed on Oprah Winfrey's television show. The woman was losing her bakery due to the economic recession. My heart went out to her when I saw her in tears and on the verge of a breakdown.

Oprah's guests, who included spiritual advisors, provided insights on how the woman could, at some point, modify her thinking and realize how enduring her pain could become part of her personal growth.

Her trembling face gave the impression of so much pain that it was unlikely that the advisors' comments were sinking in.

I reflected on her pain and her situation.

What if she could save her bakery?

What if she could do something to make her bakery recession-proof?

A phrase came into my mind, The Recession-Proof Cupcake.

The woman needed to consider new options. What if she baked cupcakes that included wise sayings like the ones found in fortune cookies? Perhaps she could form an alliance with local experts and authors to create interesting and thoughtful sayings. Then good fortune would come to everyone through a wise saying on a cupcake. The woman's bakery could gain publicity through the catchy phrase, The Recession-Proof Cupcake. Her business might see a significant rise in sales.

The scenario, the woman's struggle and my next scheduled speech "Thriving in Changing Times" led me to create an audio program *The Recession-Proof Cupcake: How to Feed Your Soul, Save a Business, or Get a Job in a Crisis.* I knew that my next audience would include some people out of work and others trying to save their businesses; and such an audio program could help them beyond the short time together during my speech. This section expands upon that audio program's material.

In this section you will learn the secrets that Albert Einstein, Leonardo da Vinci, Wolfgang Amadeus Mozart, and John F. Kennedy used to maximize their effectiveness. In addition, you'll learn to drop your fears and find your inner calm. You'll discover the flow that serves your deepest needs and creates harmony with your boss, customers, family, romantic partner and all the other valued members in your circle.

I have deep empathy for anyone who suddenly loses a job because years ago I endured being downsized twice. I felt like the ground had crumbed beneath me. The pain of loss hit me in the gut. In this section, I include a number of techniques that I used to recover.

Let's begin the recovery process with a secret from Albert Einstein:

> *You cannot solve a problem on the*
> *level in which it was created.*
>
> ALBERT EINSTEIN

To help you rise to a higher level, this section is designed to give you comfort and insight. As I watched the distraught woman on Oprah's show, I became concerned that many people who are in pain do not have the energy to implement helpful suggestions. The answer is to first feed your soul and recover some energy. When you do, you will be able grieve in parallel with some life-rebuilding activities. We will learn helpful methods to do this in the next chapter when we explore the S.O.U.L. process.

> *We become what we behold.*
>
> MARSHALL MCLUHAN

Part II will inspire you to see the truth behind Marshall's thought. This book, *Truth No One Will Tell You*, reveals the tools, wisdom and inspiration to empower you to become your best self, which can better guide you to handle a crisis with bravery and grace.

Let's take the next step …

In Part III, Chapter 10, "Create Community," you will learn how to save a business by creating a community of people who want you to succeed.

4

How to Feed Your Soul

What if you could bounce back from feeling low and exhausted? In this chapter, we will explore the S.O.U.L. Process:

S – Support yourself

O – Open connection

U – Unleash a plan

L – Linger for joy

We will begin with this secret from Leonardo da Vinci:

I love those who can smile in trouble, who can gather strength from distress, and grow brave by reflection. 'Tis the business of little minds to shrink, but they whose heart is firm, and whose conscience approves their conduct, will pursue their principles unto death.

LEONARDO DA VINCI

To grow brave by reflection is powerful. Often, writing in a personal journal can give us the calm and insight to take a new action to improve a situation. Journaling has helped my clients to make space for themselves and to feel heard. Through journaling, my clients pay attention to their lives and discover how they feel about things. This creates a foundation for building an improved journey through life.

As da Vinci says, to have a firm heart often involves having operating principles. For example, over the years, I have focused on the following: humility is being respectful and grateful; to listen well and to be coachable.

Humility can sometimes be a conscious thought. When confronted with tough times, I ask myself:

- How can I be respectful to all involved?

- What am I grateful for?

- How can I listen even better?

- Can I get coaching for this situation?

When I remember to ask myself these questions, I can develop the calm of a firm heart.

5

Support Yourself

What can you do if you're hit with a surprising loss?
Pause. Pay attention.

Loss saps our energy. It can make us go into a state of shock. We need time to grieve and function.

Often, we do not have the energy to implement helpful suggestions. In fact, we may find ourselves resisting good ideas, and saying, "No. That won't work." A loss can plunge us into negative thinking.

> *Courage consists in the power of self-recovery.*
>
> RALPH WALDO EMERSON

During a crisis, you need courage to act. Also, you need the strength to restrain yourself from harmful, rash decisions. For example, I know a family in which one parent lost a job. The family posted an ad on the Internet to sell a car and received 12 inquiries for it. Unfortunately, they went with the second offer. They did not have the courage to hold out for a better price.

Where do we get such strength?

A first step is to make time to grieve. We need this time. Morrie Schwartz was slowly dying from ALS. His body was shutting down, requiring a nurse and family members to take care of his bodily functions. His friend and former student Mitch Albom chronicled Morrie's journey in *Tuesdays with Morrie*. Morrie said, "There are some mornings when I cry and cry and mourn for myself. Some mornings, I'm so angry and bitter. But it doesn't last too long. Then I get up and say, 'I want to live'"

My clients often find it helpful to release their emotions in a personal journal. If the emotions and thoughts bother you so much, you can rip out the page and burn it so that no one (including you) can ever read it.

Let's learn from the insights of Dr. Elayne Savage on facing and overcoming our fears.

What's Going to Happen to Me?

Facing and overcoming our fears

Elayne Savage, PhD

Fear is in the air and it's contagious.

It's been a bumpy ride and most of us are scared. Dazed. Numbed. Stunned. Immobilized. We go to bed scared and we wake up scared.

Apprehension touches people around us – family, friends and colleagues. One person catches it from another, like a bad cold or mean flu. The anxiety that results can lead to a kind of paralysis. It's hard to think or act.

There's something else in the air. Let's call it helplessness and uncertainty. When these fears are rooted in childhood experiences, a child-like fright takes over.

A small voice asks, "What's going to happen to me?"

When we are all grown up, but again feeling scared and insecure, we may find ourselves experiencing the same fear. And asking the same question. And needing reassurance.

This point is worth remembering. As kids or young adults we may have experienced overwhelming setbacks. We had not yet accumulated the life experience to know that it's not the end of the world. Things do get better. In the midst of present day misfortunes, it's worth trying to remind yourself that things will get better again.

Let's put some of this overwhelm in perspective and take a look at:

- How we are affected by outside events

- Why we are affected and debilitated to this degree

- What steps we can take to overcome it

Looking at loss

As a workplace coach and couples therapist I'm hearing lots of stories about the impact of the economy. Tensions are great. Stress is rampant. Relationships are suffering. But you know all that.

The theme in these experiences is Loss. Loss of jobs is accompanied by loss of income, loss of routine, loss of independence and loss of identity. Loss of homes or savings is permeated with loss of security and loss of well-being. And for some, there is a loss of hope.

And the small voice asks, "What's going to happen to me?"

Coming face to face with loss and the fear of it is difficult. This becomes even more complicated if it reminds you of a painful loss from your early years.

Perhaps a childhood friend moved away. Or you transferred to another school across town or to another state. Or an older brother or sister went away to school, leaving a void.

Maybe it felt like you lost a parent for a while if there was a separation or divorce. Or if there was a serious illness in your family. Or if someone important to you died. These cumulative experiences affect how you cope with present losses.

Disappointments

Disappointments are another form of loss. As a child did you feel disappointed in someone or something? Perhaps someone made a promise they didn't deliver. Or you didn't get that special present you wanted so badly. Or you had your hopes pinned on an 'A.' Or you found out you couldn't count on someone you thought you could trust. These experiences stockpile, just waiting for the next disappointment to occur.

Who among us hasn't believed exaggerated promises or engaged in some wishful thinking or put someone on a pedestal, then watched them tumble off?

Thinking positively and having hope is constructive. However, when our expectations are too big or too unrealistic they come crashing down to reality. Unrealistic expectations are setups for disappointment, disillusionment, and resentment. When we're too invested in a certain outcome, we tend to take disappointment personally.

Loss of trust

Another loss you may be struggling with is loss of trust. This includes the powerful feelings of disloyalty and betrayal. Can you see how losing your job might feel unfair? Or disloyal? If you trusted promises of security, it may even feel like a betrayal.

There's another increasingly frequent occurrence these days: Getting stiffed by someone who owes you money. It's not only the loss of money, but loss of trust as well.

Trust is fragile. When it is violated, it is difficult to restore.

Loss of identity

Layoffs or forced early retirement are happening every day. These sudden shifts in structured time leave large holes in your normal routine.

These sudden losses of employment cause a loss of identity. Work life is a touchstone for how you think of yourself. Losing this identity throws you off-kilter. It leaves a big void in your life. It can be quite a challenge to fill it.

Loss feels like rejection

There's another layer of complexity here. Each of these losses and disappointments can feel like rejection or self-rejection. Rejection is feeling "dissed" in some way: Disrespected for sure. Also dismissed, discarded, dispensable, discounted, or dishonored.

When you are wounded at such a deep place, it's hard not to take it personally. When we take something personally, we perceive ourselves to be a target. We tend to see someone's actions as a personal affront. We feel slighted, or wronged, or attacked.

What a lonely feeling fear can be. Your tendency may be to retreat, lick your wounds and suffer in silence. At times like these it can be difficult to connect with others. But it helps to reach out.

Reaching out

Can you connect with others to talk about these losses and fears? A partner or friend is ideal. A counselor, coach or psychotherapist is another good option. Social networking and forums work, too.

Can you put words to your worries and fears? Then hear yourself say the words out loud. Even if you write in a journal, read your words out loud to yourself. Yes, out loud. It makes all the difference.

When pressure is building it needs to go somewhere. If we don't talk out our feelings, we act them out.

Acting out is one way of releasing tension. It takes many forms. Some of us pick fights, antagonize, fly into rages, or slam doors. Or we might engage in excessive behaviors.

But acting out is not always active. It can be passive as well, such as foot-dragging, "yes, butting," sulking, and giving someone the silent treatment.

All of these behaviors are ways we deal with the anxiety that builds up when we're not able to put words to our feelings, worries and fears.

Respecting different coping styles

Talking to your partner or friend is a good idea that doesn't always work. What if you don't feel supported by the other person? What if you both have different ways of handling upsetting situations? What if you have different coping styles? What if you feel the other person doesn't understand you?

We all have different ways of dealing with stress, anxiety, and fear. We learn our coping skills (or lack of them) from our family and cultural experiences.

- One person may withdraw, experiencing a kind of paralysis, while the other person mobilizes and becomes over-active.

- Another may cocoon, preferring alone time, while the other needs to increase their contact with others.

- Sometimes one is less inclined to talk about feelings and the other talks so much that it's hard to listen anymore.

If either of you feels discounted, you're most likely feeling rejected. Before you know it, someone is taking something personally. Feelings get hurt.

Unless both of you can respect each other's individual styles, misunderstandings and hurt can lead to anger and resentment. Resentment takes up so much space in relationships that there's barely room for connection. And connection is what's so important now.

Tips for coping with fear

- Give yourself permission to be afraid. These are unsettling times. However try not to cross the line into biting the 'fear bait' that gets thrown out by the media and politicians.

- Put a name to your worst fear. Say it out loud.

- Talk it out. Hearing yourself say what you most fear works wonders.

- 'Walk alongside yourself.' Gain some distance from the situation to see it more clearly. Try separating the "now" of the present moment from the "then" of unpleasant childhood experiences. This frees you up from becoming overwhelmed by your feelings.

- This objectivity allows you to choose to make a different response.

- Know that your partner, friends or colleagues may deal with fear differently than you. Don't compare.

- Make a plan. It provides structure and reassurance.

- Try not to take disappointments personally. It takes so much energy. Remind yourself, "This is not about me."

Unblocking energy & moving it around

Here's an image from *Don't Take It Personally! The Art of Dealing with Rejection* which may be helpful:

Visualize a honeycomb. The energy takes the form of warm, thick, sweet, amber-colored liquid, constantly moving through the interconnected tunnels. As the energy flows, a wondrous transformation takes place. Notice how the negative messages of childhood take on new qualities as they flow from space to space.

As the energy changes from life-depleting to life-sustaining, it provides sustenance, allowing room for your needs and wants, and encouraging clear boundaries. Then the energy develops new vitality, permitting choices and enhancing good communication. And it keeps on moving, flowing. Moving and flowing.

Move one finger at a time

Do you find yourself feeling like a scared little child, sitting paralyzed on the sofa, for hours or days? Maybe it seems like you've been living in a cartoon. Things don't seem real to you, you're not a part of time. Sometimes I feel like that myself.

When you're feeling helpless, afraid, immobilized, dazed, numbed, or stunned. When it becomes hard to think or act. Try to move.

Move your fingers or your toes, or your body. Try to get that energy flowing. Once you do even a small amount of movement you are no longer stuck.

If you can remember to move your finger back and forth, then your arm, you have just made a choice to reconnect with your body. Self-soothing works here too. By gently stroking your hand or your arm or your shoulder, you activate energy.

Try pressing the thumb of one hand into the palm of the other. Apply enough pressure to bring yourself back to consciousness, and to your feelings. You have just brought time back into the picture.

Breathe in the colors

My own personal favorite when I'm in a negative place is to take a walk. Releasing those endorphins makes a difference to my feeling of well-being. While I'm walking I breathe in the colors around me; the trees, plants, flowers, buildings, cars. This keeps me present and grounded. And appreciative of my world.

Once you create options for yourself, you don't feel so paralyzed. Once you open up a little, and let the energy flow, you'll be tapping in to a sense of your power.

Watch the energy spread, growing into self-acceptance and creativity. Marvel at how it fills you with a new experience of yourself and new ways of relating to others.

Adapted from Elayne's e-letter/blog: 'Tips from the Queen of Rejection'®

Dr. Elayne Savage is The Queen of Rejection.® This internationally recognized communication and relationship coach is the expert on how not to take rejection so personally. She's a professional speaker and the author of two groundbreaking books published in nine languages: *Don't Take It Personally! The Art of Dealing with Rejection* and *Breathing Room — Creating Space to Be a Couple* (New Harbinger).

www.QueenofRejection.com

Elayne's comments invite us to cope with fear by using methods to nurture ourselves.

> *People are not aware that it is often*
> *empathy they are needing.*
>
> MARSHALL B. ROSENBERG

The central idea of supporting yourself is to give yourself the empathy that you need.

We must learn what will truly soothe ourselves. Let's face it. Some losses can feel even more shocking and painful because they arrive as bad surprises. I once lost a dear friend who committed suicide. Up to that moment, I had never felt deep grief. Following his death, I needed empathy; I needed to hear myself. So I supported myself by writing in my personal journal.

In this economic recession, people are being slammed with loss from every side. People are losing their jobs, retirement funds, set career paths, homes and more. These people can express empathy and kindness to themselves in the form of a Low Mood First Aid Kit. This kit is actually a list of activities you can do to nurture yourself.

Here is a secret from John F. Kennedy:

> *Leadership and learning are indispensable to each other.*

JOHN F. KENNEDY

So learn to take action to soothe yourself. My clients have included these items in their Low Mood First Aid Kit:

- Quiet time with an uplifting book (to help you learn of new possibilities)

- Music

- Prayer

- Meditation

- Writing in a personal journal

- Dancing to a favorite song in my room

- Walking in nature

- Exercise

- Time with a pet

- Belly breathing

Belly breathing is an important tool to bring your focus back to yourself. To do this, breathe in through your nose and allow your belly to inflate to its fullest. Briefly hold in your breath, and then breathe out while your belly deflates. I've heard my audience members comment how this process releases stress from their shoulders, and that they felt calm and even hopeful. I invite you to include belly breathing in your Low Mood First Aid Kit.

> *Where the spirit does not work with*
> *the hand, there is no art.*
>
> **LEONARDO DA VINCI**

You reconnect your spirit to your life when you demonstrate empathy and compassion for yourself. Remember that a sudden loss can put many of us into an emotional shutdown. We must learn to ride out a crisis with bravery and grace, and then nurture ourselves so that we can, in essence, create art out of our lives. Adding in time for meditation or prayer will help make this part of your personal path.

Marc Allen shares a mindset that can help you stay on the path of empowerment.

The Full Half of the Glass & the Benefits in Adversity

Marc Allen

I have a friend who is smart, talented, energetic – and always struggling to pay his rent. One day he asked me a long, rambling question that I summed up this way: "In other words, you're asking me, 'If I'm so smart why aren't I rich yet?'" "Well, yeah," he said. "That's a great question to ask," I said.

I've known him well for years, well enough to know I could tell it to him exactly as I saw it. "Two things immediately come to mind," I said. "On some level – maybe subconsciously – it seems you think you don't really deserve success, for some reason, or maybe you just think it's too hard, or too stressful, to create the life you want ...

"Really look at your deepest beliefs, and come up with an affirmation like, *In an easy and relaxed, healthy and positive way, I am now creating total financial success.* Put in your own words. If you find the right affirmation, it can overcome all kinds of doubts and fears and get you back on course.

"Keep repeating something like this and see what happens: *In an easy and relaxed, healthy and positive way, I am now creating total success.*

"What is total success for you? Of course, it up to you to define it – and the more clearly you define it for yourself, the sooner you'll create it.

"And here's the other thing that comes mind, as long as you asked for it," I said. "You tend to focus so often on the problems, not on the solutions. You spend a lot of time looking at the empty half of the glass. You often say things are harder than they used to be – there's more competition now, blah, blah, blah — which means you think there's less opportunity now than there used to be.

"Our beliefs are not true in themselves but they become true in our experience if we believe they're true.

"You can turn your thinking around. ... Opportunities are everywhere! They've always been everywhere; it's just that we haven't seen them because we haven't been preparing ourselves for them by clearly setting our course.

"You can turn your thinking around by asking yourself, *What are the opportunities, benefits and gifts in the problems I face?*"

He got it – I could tell. He had asked for feedback, and I gave it to him as directly as I could. The next time we talked he added one other good thing. "You know," he said, "as I look back, I can see something else: I've lacked persistence. I gave up too soon on some very good ideas, just because I ran into some obstacles. I'm going to be more persistent – and keep remembering to focus more on opportunities rather than the problems. You're right: There are opportunities everywhere, but we only see them if we look for them."

I've talked to him several times recently and sense a definite positive shift in his energy. The affirmations he has come up with are helping to change those old limiting beliefs. When he catches himself enmeshed with problems, he challenges himself to find the opportunities, benefits, and gifts that are always in the situation as well. And he's being persistent, keeping the same goal in sight until he reaches it.

I have no doubt that sooner or later, he will realize his dreams – as long as he keeps correcting his course, as long as he keeps remembering and doesn't fall back into the old mental habits that weren't supporting his dreams.

Here is a great key to ongoing success, both business and personal. It's something I've known intuitively for a long time, and something I've done my best to put into practice from the very beginning of my career:

The more you live and work in partnership with all, the happier, healthier, and more successful you will be.

This is an excerpt from Marc Allen's book, *The Type Z Guide to Success: A Lazy Person's Manifesto for Wealth and Fulfillment.*

Marc Allen is an internationally renowned author and president and publisher of New World Library, which he co-founded (with Shakti Gawain) in 1977. He has guided the company from a small start-up with no capital to its current position as one of the leading independent publishers in the country. Marc is a well-known musician and composer as well, having produced five albums of music for his label Watercourse Media. His latest book is *The Greatest Secret of All*. His previous book, *The Type-Z Guide to Success*, has been released both in print form and as an innovative multi-media ebook. His most popular book is *The Millionaire Course: A Visionary Plan for Creating the Life of Your Dreams*. It is an entire course, filled with keys to success. He has also published *The Ten Percent Solution: Simple Steps to Improve Our Lives and the World*, and produced a popular audio CD, *Stress Reduction and Creative Meditations*. His books, audios, and workshops have been highly rewarding – even life-changing – experiences for thousands of people, and he has produced a 12-CD audio version of his powerful seminar called *The Success with Ease In-Depth Course*. Marc and his wife Aurilene have founded the Brazil Hope Foundation to help street kids in Brazil.

www.marcallen.com

Marc Allen's comment emphasizes that we need to carefully choose what we focus on, because, he says, that choice will greatly affect what outcomes we experience.

> *A hero is an ordinary individual who finds the strength to persevere and endure in spite of overwhelming obstacles.*

CHRISTOPHER REEVE

Paralyzed and confined to his wheelchair for nine years, Christopher Reeve found a new purpose in speaking up for people suffering with spinal chord injuries. He directed two films from that chair. Chris even coached his son on how to ride a bicycle with his words alone. Christopher Reeve, who was famous for playing Superman, had become a hero in real life.

We learn that heroes take care of themselves so that they can think clearly and do what needs to be done.

> *All our knowledge has its origins in our perceptions.*

LEONARDO DA VINCI

Da Vinci's comment wakes us up to an important point. People who don't take care of themselves are easily susceptible to having false and skewed perceptions. This section on the S.O.U.L. process will give you the tools you need to take care of yourself physically and emotionally.

The truth no one will tell you: Too much of what the media and society tell us is completely built on false and skewed perceptions.

> *If you want to be rich, you cannot be normal.*

NOAH ST. JOHN

Also, if you want to be happy, even during an economic crisis, you cannot be normal. You must take extraordinary care of yourself. And you need access to your inner wisdom.

A Powerful Way to Access Your Inner Wisdom

A secret from Mozart guides us in gaining access to our own wisdom and even inspiration from Higher Power.

> *When I am traveling in a carriage, or walking after a good meal, or during the night when I cannot sleep; it is on such occasions that ideas flow best and most abundantly.*
>
> WOLFGANG AMADEUS MOZART

Mozart's comment reminds us about timing and making space to access our inner wisdom. My clients have pen and paper near their bed and in their pocket or purse to write down helpful ideas whenever they arise. Such helpful ideas can be about how to reach out to customers or how to schedule some downtime away from your business or family members (like having one's sister take the kids on Thursday evenings). This process will help you to feel hopeful, and better able to start to turn things in your favor.

> *Energy and persistence conquer all things.*
>
> BENJAMIN FRANKLIN

In order to persist, you need to support yourself by finding ways to consistently replenish your energy. One of my clients has a list that includes books, music, DVDs (for example, a TV show with no commercials) and humor-filled shows like "Who's Line is it Anyway?"

Be sure to write a list of ways to support yourself. When you take action, you'll have the energy you need to persist.

The Three Elements of Supporting Yourself

The "S" of the S.O.U.L. process stands for support yourself. The truth no one will tell you: You need three things to truly support yourself during the bumpiness of daily life:

1. Take care of yourself

2. Grieve

3. Regain energy

An economic crisis brings loss. The best way I can express this is to share a personal example. When my dear friend (close, like a brother) committed suicide, for the first time I was plunged into deep grief. I hadn't known what grief was before then.

In deep pain, I applied the three elements. I took care of myself by slowing down my schedule. I also told my graduate students the truth: "My friend has died, so I may lose my voice for thirty seconds. But that's okay. We'll flow forward." In this way, when grief surprised me and choked me up, I allowed it to have a place. I also wrote about it in my personal journal.

I did gentle things to guard my energy. I replied to a number of e-mails with: "Please feel comfortable to follow-up with me in two weeks." I continued to exercise and eat nutritious food. I even watched DVDs of favorite shows to give myself brief vacations from thinking of my grief.

Please write in your personal journal how you can: take care of yourself, grieve and regain energy.

Principle:

When hit with a bad surprise, be sure to grieve and to regain energy.

Power Question:

How can you take care of yourself, grieve and regain your energy?

6

Open Connection

Can you remember being in a low mood and spending time with a loved one or friend lifted your spirits?
Connection can fill our hearts and inspire our minds.

It is the time to dare and endure.

WINSTON CHURCHILL

During a crisis, connecting with others can often bring us out of a melancholy place. To be immersed with life can feel renewing.

Playing with a pet can also lighten our feelings. I have seen people spontaneously chuckle or giggle when watching the antics of their furry friends. Playing with a pet places you in the center of the present moment.

Taking action can sometimes be quite difficult. Now Jane Marla Robbins shares methods so that we can nurture and prepare ourselves to be in the present moment during a job interview.

Ace that Job Interview – Use an Acting Technique

Jane Marla Robbins

Everyone wants to look, feel and perform at his or her best for those often uncomfortable, but all too often inescapable, job interviews. Here are some of the techniques that actors have used for centuries to help them look, feel and behave however they want – on a dime.

The very thought of a job interview can make anybody's stress level skyrocket—not what you want if you want to make a good impression. Actors know techniques to eliminate this stress and fear—because it's called "Stage Fright!"

Below I describe an actor's Six Part Preparation, which I recommend doing before any interview. I also describe three other techniques which have helped my clients ace their interviews and get those jobs.

See which techniques in this grab-bag of tricks make you look, feel and perform at your best, so you are as comfortable, powerful, intelligent, charming, or as whatever it is you want or need to be for that interview.

An actor's six-part preparation

I suggest doing at least some version of this Six-Part Preparation before your interview. When I had to perform one of my one-woman plays at Lincoln Center in New York in front of twenty-four hundred people, I did my preparation all day long. I can also do it in two minutes if I have to. Whenever I do it, I know that I have given my psycho-physical "instrument" the best tune-up I can, so that I can be at my very best. The six parts are distilled from the preparations used by actors from Marilyn Monroe to Dustin Hoffman to Sylvester Stallone.

Part I: physical preparation. Just do whatever gets your body moving and feeling alive. Jump, shake, stretch, whatever. When we're scared, we tend to forget we have a strong body, and that it's alive; and people want to hire people who look alive. They themselves hunger to be as alive as they can be. Let them want what you have, and let them hire you for it!

The physical preparation also helps your body know it's strong (and not helpless!). Thinking we're strong lowers our stress, just as fearing we're not strong elevates it. People hire people who they think are strong.

Part II: vocal preparation. Make sounds and feel them vibrating your body. Let "Haaah" resonate your chest bone. Let "Hmmm" vibrate the bones and sinuses of your face cavity. When you do, you'll know, both physically and psychologically, that you're capable of speaking up—effectively and powerfully.

Part III: emotional preparation. Know how you feel before you go into that interview. Otherwise it's likely you'll be not only extremely tense, but also unable to access all the energy you may want or need, since you'll be spending a lot of it keeping yourself from feeling what you're feeling.

I was once angry at a casting director in L.A. for never bringing me in for auditions (even though I'd received raves in New York!). But I didn't know I was angry; it took me many years to know I was even allowed to be angry. When she finally called me into her office, I was so angry and so didn't know it, that I could barely read the words on the little script she had given me!

Knowing and feeling how you feel really helps. Now if I'm angry, I face it and diffuse it, probably by looking at the feelings underneath (usually pain and fear that I might not be good enough).

Part IV: mental preparation. Do some arithmetic in your head, or think of all words starting with the same letter of the alphabet (a, b, c, d, etc.). This actually gets blood flowing in the brain. Just knowing my brain is functioning makes me feel smarter and therefore more relaxed. People want to hire people who are smart.

Part V: spiritual preparation. An experiment at Harvard discovered that even a few minutes of prayer or meditation not only calms your brainwaves but also separates your blood cells so they're not bunched together in an unhealthy way. See if it doesn't calm you down.

Plus isn't it nice to know you know how to keep your blood healthy! People hire people they think are healthy. Plus you might even access some Unlimited source of energy and inspiration.

Part VI: final relaxation. Being relaxed is the opposite of feeling terrified (i.e. stressed), and any technique will do if it works for you. I personally like to invent visual images for various parts of my body. For example, I see my knees as closed flowers opening as if in a time-lapse photograph. Scientific studies have shown that our bodies often respond more profoundly to images from our left brain than to logical words from our right.

Make sure to breathe deeply into the parts of your body that you're relaxing. And make sure you continue breathing fully at that interview, too. If there isn't enough oxygen going to your brain, your ability to think and to communicate is badly compromised. Not good.

Sense memory

If you think you may be intimidated by the person who'll be interviewing you, this technique sometimes does the trick. Here's how it works: You decide on a person, place or thing that you know makes you relaxed, happy and strong, and you allow yourself to remember it with one or more of your senses (sight, sound, touch, etc.).

For example, if seeing crashing waves on ocean rocks gives you energy, makes you feel strong and makes you smile, I suggest you imagine those waves and those rocks behind the person interviewing you. See the waves, feel the salt spray on your face, hear the seagull. Your body will be tricked into thinking those waves and rocks are exactly where you put them.

Why? Because all the sensory realities we have ever experienced are memorized in our cells, and our bodies basically do not know the difference between being with our best friend and merely imagining he or she is there.

Another experiment at Harvard proved how effective and powerful Sense Memory can be. The study followed four groups having operations that required only partial anesthesia, so the patients were awake. Before the procedure, the first group was told by a doctor what he would be doing; the second group was told by a nurse that everything would be alright; the third group was played calming music that would even out their brain waves; and the fourth group was given "guided sensory imagery," modern medicine's name for Sense Memory.

After the operation, this fourth group was found to have shorter hospital stays, lower blood pressure, and needed less anxiety medication and less pain medication than the other three. That's how effective Sense Memory can be!

Marilyn Monroe used Sense Memory to deal with her initial stress on the movie *The Prince and the Showgirl*. For her first scene, she was so intimidated by Sir Laurence Olivier that she basically froze. Her acting coach had her taste an imaginary Coca Cola and sensorially transform Olivier into her boyfriend (Frankie Sinatra). She relaxed right up (to put it mildly).

You too can imagine that the intimidating person in front of you is someone with whom you are comfortable, even, ideally, someone with whom you can be your "best self," as intelligent, relaxed and happy as you want to be. You could see your best friend's hair or hear his or her laugh. Your body will actually respond as if that friend were there. People want to hire people who are happy.

The perfect prop

Many of my clients have been able to find a Perfect Prop to help them get through a challenging interview. Since I loved my Grandma Isabelle very, very much, if I simply feel her locket in my pocket, I feel secure and loved. Feeling secure and loved invariably relaxes you. No one wants to hire someone who is tense. Feeling secure and being in love sometimes makes us shine. Go for it.

Billy Crystal found the Perfect Prop for when he hosted the Academy Awards, a performance probably at least as stressful as any job interview. He chose a toothbrush. He put it in his pocket. He said it made him think he was in the comfort of his own home, where he was relaxed. It sure looked to me as if he breezed through that ceremony.

Inner monologue

An actor's Inner Monologue consists of the thoughts he has decided his character is thinking when he's not speaking aloud. Then the actor recites them silently to himself on stage, usually when another actor is speaking.

For job interviews, my clients create their own perfect Inner Monologue. This is usually a short sentence which helps galvanize them into looking and feeling self-confident. Then they'll repeat it silently to themselves during the interview, whenever they need to.

Sometimes my clients turn their sentences into The Perfect Prop, writing them down on a piece of paper which they put in their pocket, or maybe even into their shoes to make sure they don't forget.

Some of the sentences my clients have found successful for their interviews include:

- I deserve this job.

- I'm allowed to be brilliant (or calm, etc.).

- I'm here to get the job, not to get the interviewer's love.

- I'm allowed to make more money than my father (or mother).

- I will not die if I do not get this job.

- I deserve to be successful.

- I know success is fun.

So go out and have fun and get that job. It may seem daunting, but I figure we might as well have fun, even at a stressful job interview, and these techniques can help you do that. People hire people because they expect they will enjoy working with them. So get out there and have a good time.

> Jane Marla Robbins, a performance coach, actress, and writer, is the author of the book, *Acting Techniques for Everyday Life: Look and Feel Self-Confident in Difficult Real-Life Situations*, now in its fifth printing. Her deck of cue cards, *Perform At Your Best: Acting Techniques for Business, Social, and Personal Success*, won the Gold Axiom Business Book Award. Jane gives workshops at corporations and universities all over the United States, and also coaches privately. The Kennedy Center commissioned her to write and perform the one-woman play, *Reminiscences of Mozart by His Sister*, which she also performed at Lincoln Center in New York. She has starred on Broadway (*Richard III; Morning, Noon and Night*), can be seen in many movies (including *Rocky I, II* and *V; Arachnophobia*) and has appeared on many television shows (including *Murder, She Wrote; E.R.; Beverly Hills 90210*).
>
> You can find out more about Jane through her website, www.janemarlarobbins.com.

Jane demonstrated how we can nurture ourselves and then be positive and active in the present moment during a job interview or some other demanding situation.

> *The secret of health for both mind and body is not to*
> *mourn for the past, nor to worry about the future, but*
> *to live the present moment wisely and earnestly.*
>
> **BUDDHA**

To interact with this present moment, we may find it necessary to say silently: Be here now. Doing so will help you connect with what is true. Numerous authors on spiritual topics discuss how the past is our perception of previous events, and that the truth is taking place only in the present moment.

*Be grateful that you're breathing. That you're not
connected to a machine.*

OPRAH WINFREY

The truth no one will tell you – a large portion of our misery
results from when our focus is too small. You will feel much
better when you switch from a "self-focus" to an "us-focus."

Often we feel more suffering when we're concerned that
things are not going the way we'd prefer. A self-focus can be a
small canvas. We can get caught up in our own pain. Instead,
we can consciously shift our thoughts away from ourselves and
reach out to connect with other people.

For example, I was talking with Raul, a college instructor. He
mentioned how he noticed that his hair was thinning as the years
were going by. Then he switched the direction of his thoughts.
He thought that perhaps, with less hair, he might look more like
an elder and maybe that would be helpful for his students. In an
instant, his personal thought switched to an "us-focus."

If there is a cause you believe in (like raising funds for breast
cancer research), you can discover renewed energy when you
participate with kindred spirits in a united effort. Volunteering
to help someone can feed your soul. My friend Linda volunteers
at a soup kitchen during the holidays. She tells me she feels
energized by helping others.

An important facet of connection is connecting with Higher
Power (if that is your path). In teaching Comparative Religion
for years, I have noted how people find connection through
prayer, reading spiritual texts, meditation, walking in nature,

attending spiritual workshops and events, and practicing belly breathing (as discussed in this book).

> *It ain't what you don't know that gets you into trouble.*
> *It's what you know for sure that just ain't so.*
>
> MARK TWAIN

Over the years, I have noticed that some of my clients think they do not have any sources for connection. After talking the situation through, they learn that they do have resources. including certain friends.

Possible solutions: Many universities offer counseling with graduate students working under the direction of a licensed therapist. The fee can be as low as $10 a session (as of this writing). Other counseling organizations offer a sliding scale. One could also get pastoral counseling from a minister.

> *What is without periods of rest will not endure.*
>
> OVID

Each person and each relationship needs restful, nourishing times. For example, one of my clients was concerned that his low income would prevent him from taking his wife out on a date night. I suggested that he and his wife develop a list of Dates With No Money Necessary. Their list included: a) go to the park and have a picnic, b) check the paper for free concerts around the city, and c) sit outside and take turns reading aloud from a novel.

As I have mentioned, I teach Comparative Religion. I notice that a number of people find solace in the process of "I rest in

God." The God-Box is a process in which a person writes up her greatest needs or problems and then places the list in the God-Box. She will never see the list again. She says a prayer like, "God, I am handing these problems to You. Please guide me on how I should take the next action. Please bless the situation for the good of all involved. I trust in You. Thank You."

Sometimes we feel so hurt that we withdraw and emotionally shut down, which prevents connection. Dr. Fred Luskin shares insights about forgiveness and healing.

Nine Steps of Forgiveness

Dr. Fred Luskin

My book *Forgive for Good: A Proven Prescription for Health and Happiness* is a primer on how to make peace when things you choose or things chosen for you do not work out well. When painful things happen you have a choice. I teach people to make more forgiving choices. I do this because I understand that as a function of life everyone will have painful experiences as well as pleasant ones. It is a singular power to be able to handle what comes your way without getting lost in blame and suffering. We do not know what the game of life has in store but we do know that forgiveness is one way that provides strength to get back into the game.

As Director of the Stanford Forgiveness Projects my forgiveness methodology has been tested and shown to be successful through a number of research projects. We have demonstrated that forgiveness can reduce stress, blood pressure, anger, depression, hurt, and increase optimism, hope, compassion, physical vitality, and forgiveness. We have worked with people who have been lied to, cheated, abandoned, physically injured, beaten, abused or had their children murdered. Forgiveness training made a significant difference in many of their lives. What follows is our nine step method of teaching and becoming forgiving.

Nine steps to forgiveness

1. Know exactly how you feel about what happened and be able to articulate what about the situation is not OK. Then, tell a couple of trusted people about your experience.

2. Make a commitment to yourself to do what you have to do to feel better. Forgiveness is for you and not for anyone else.

3. Forgiveness does not necessarily mean reconciliation with the person that upset you, or condoning of their action. What you are after is to find peace. Forgiveness can be defined as the "peace and understanding that come from blaming that which has hurt you less, taking the life experience less personally, and amending your grievance story."

4. Get the right perspective on what is happening. Recognize that your primary distress is coming from the hurt feelings, thoughts, and physical upset you are suffering now, not what offended you or hurt you two minutes – or ten years – ago.

5. At the moment you feel upset practice stress management to soothe your body's flight or fight response.

6. Give up expecting things from other people, or your life, that they do not choose to give you. Recognize the "unenforceable rules" you have for your health or how you or other people must behave. Remind yourself that you can hope for health, love, friendship, and prosperity, and work hard to get them. However, you will suffer when you demand these things occur when you do not have the power to make them happen.

7. Put your energy into looking for another way to get your positive goals met than through the experience that has hurt you. I call this step finding your positive intention. Instead of mentally replaying your hurt seek out new ways to get what you want.

8. Remember that a life well lived is your best revenge. Instead of focusing on your wounded feelings, and thereby giving the person who caused you pain power over you, learn to look for the love, beauty, and kindness around you. Appreciate what you have more than attending to what you do not have.

9. Amend your grievance story to remind you of the heroic choice to forgive.

Dr. Fred Luskin is the author of *Forgive for Good* and *Forgive for Love*. Dr. Luskin serves as the Director of the Stanford Forgiveness Projects and is a Senior Consultant in Health Promotion at Stanford University.

www.LearningToForgive.com

Dr. Fred Luskin urges us to devote energy to the forgiveness process so that we are free to enhance connections with other people.

Now, Syndi Seid guides us to make connecting easier and more fulfilling for everyone involved.

New Year, New Habits

Syndi Seid

Whenever the New Year arrives, it says to me … "Yippie! I'm leaving behind all the terrible stuff I did last year and beginning a new year with a clean slate."

For me, a clean slate means New Year's Resolutions. Do you make them? Perhaps you did at one time, but stopped when you couldn't stick with them. The key is to make a list according to the SMART method … being Specific, Measurable, Achievable, Reasonable, and Timely.

I used to list things such as "lose weight" and "make more money," yet know I will be contending with these forever … so I don't bother to list them. Instead, I work on goals and resolutions, some challenging and some mundane, to develop better habits and make me a better person.

Here are my eight New Year resolutions I listed in 2008. Yet, your list can start any month you choose to be your first month. The important things is to stick with it for twelve consecutive months thereafter.

1. Say "please" and "thank you" with every request. This means not only with co-workers, but my spouse, family,

and close friends, as well. I should treat the people most important to me as well as strangers.

2.　Be on time for appointments and parties. The primary reason I am ever late is because I do not take enough time to think through and plan for traffic and other situations. When I leave enough time, I am never late.

3.　Wait for the green light at all crosswalks. It amazes me how calm I become when I wait instead of crossing, even when I'm in a hurry. The extra few seconds don't amount to a hill of beans, compared to losing life or limb, causing traffic jams, or other disasters.

4.　Twice a week, send someone a card and note by regular mail. Thanks to new technology through a service called Send Out Cards, it's easy to build this habit. To all those I have said, "I'll be in touch" or thought, "I wonder what's new with so-and-so," I am now taking action. The responses are well worth the effort – tenfold, at least!

5.　Keep all shared items and areas at home and in the office clean and neat. I admit, I have been known to take a pair of scissors from a drawer and not put them back for my husband or others to use. I am also picking up after myself and cleaning all areas I've messed up before leaving the room.

6.　Invite someone to lunch or coffee once a month. There are certain friends, co-workers, distant family members, and other acquaintances I'd like to know better. I will now do it by having lunch or coffee with these individuals, once a month. For folks far away, a telephone call will surely be a welcome surprise.

7. Make a habit of turning off my cell phone and other electronic devices the moment I enter a meeting, restaurant, theater, museum, or other public place. Need I say more about this?

8. Not to talk over or interrupt someone while they are speaking. This, I admit, is my worst offense. I get so eager to share information or ask a question, I forget to remain silent until it is my turn to speak.

How about you? Do some of these goals sound familiar and are you willing to make SMART resolutions for this year? Here are some suggestions on how to achieve results and receive a reward for doing so.

Make a list of six to twelve items, based on displaying better manners, adhering to good etiquette, and generally transforming yourself into being a better person for life. Display this list in a visible place on your desk, on the refrigerator, or wherever you are likely to see it daily.

Send your list to me at Info@AdvancedEtiquette.com as a witness of your firm commitment. We'll check back in, by the end of a year, and if you feel you've achieved your goals, I'll send you a special complimentary gift of congratulations!

Do not tackle your entire list at once. It will be unrealistic and impossible to manage, and you will become discouraged. Choose one or two items each month. As the year progresses, you will make these a habit each month, then add more in subsequent months. By the twelfth month, you will have six to twelve new habits ingrained that will enhance your life forever.

Syndi Seid is a professional trainer, speaker, and founder of Advanced Etiquette, based in San Francisco. Advanced Etiquette was established in 1992 to be a leading training and consulting resource center, in the areas of international business and social etiquette and protocol. Syndi is the etiquette expert of choice to companies, organizations, and individuals seeking comprehensive training and consulting in international business and social etiquette and protocol. In Seid's own words, "Advanced Etiquette provides the missing link to a complete professional education, helping individuals overcome all their fears and insecurities, to gain self-confidence and authority in any business and social situation, anywhere in the world." As a graduate of the prestigious Protocol School of Washington, Syndi holds the highest certifications available as an Independent Certified Corporate, International, Protocol Officer, Children's and Teen, Tea Etiquette Trainer, and Consultant. In addition, she is also a Certified, Protocol Officer, Level I. Her clients include: Hewlett-Packard Worldwide; Sprint International; National Semiconductor, Marriott Hotels, and the Miss Universe Pageant. Her television appearances include *Good Morning America* on ABC; *Party At Home* on HGTV; *Picture This* on Discovery Home Channel; *Eye on America* on *CBS National Evening News*, and *Trading Spouses* on Fox.

advancedetiquette.com

Syndi's comments coach us to demonstrate good manners and kind actions toward others. When we nurture our connections, surprise opportunities arrive for us.

Principles:

We need to notice if we are distracted. At that time, identify how your heart truly wants connection. The solution to feel better is to shift from a self-focus to an us-focus.

Power Questions:

Who in your life gives you unconditional support? How can you get the support you need through another person, like a counselor, a mentor or a friend? What can you do to support yourself? For instance, can you: Take a bike ride, talk to friends, spend time in nature, play with your pets, or take a yoga class?

How can you shift from a self-focus to an us-focus? How can you create connection with people who are important to you? Do you want to look into support groups? Are you interested in joining a social group? (Groups are available for bicycling, hiking, writing, personal issues and almost any other topics.)

7

Unleash a Plan

*There is no scarcity of opportunity to make a living at
what you love; there's only scarcity of resolve to make
it happen.*

DR. WAYNE DYER

Do you want to strengthen your resolve? If so, create a plan
and work that plan. At one point, I was talking with a colleague
at the graduate school where I teach. She mentioned that some
spiritual advice is like "skipping the emergency room and going
straight to spiritual bliss." However, she noted that people need
to do some healing before they can rise to a higher level.

When I first thought of the Recession-Proof Cupcake, I
imagined a child going to Grandma for a hug and a cupcake
after falling and scraping her knee. Like the child, we need
nurturing when we are hit by a crisis. Hence, the cupcake idea.

Once you have a good idea, how do you communicate it? Now C.J. Hayden invites us to energize our marketing efforts and revise our current marketing plan.

Is This a Bad Time to Market?

C.J. Hayden

All economic indicators say we are in a recession. Consumer and business spending is down; unemployment is up. It's natural to wonder whether perhaps this is a bad time to be marketing your business.

Since I've been self-employed for almost two decades now, I've seen several economic cycles come and go. What I notice about these "down" periods is that people who frequently struggle to get clients typically think these are bad times to market. On the other hand, people who have been consistently successful at landing clients seem to believe that there is never a bad time to market. Personally, I'd vote to follow the lead of those who are succeeding.

Professionals who have built successful long-term businesses have learned that continuing to market pays off in both the best of times and the worst of times. But you may not be able to produce new results by marketing in the same old way. Here are six suggestions for how to keep your marketing up when the overall business climate is down.

1. **Turn up the volume**. When people are distracted by bad news and economic concerns, you may need to communicate more often or more visibly. Where an email might have done the job before,

now you may need to pick up the phone or send a postcard. Instead of just one follow-up call, you may need to make two or three. If your business is slowing down, make use of the extra time you have available to ramp up all your marketing efforts.

2. **Become a necessity**. When clients are cutting back on discretionary spending, they need to perceive your services as essential. Look for ways to "dollarize" the value of your services. How can you help your clients save money, cut expenses, or work more efficiently? Will your services help them gain more customers, increase their income, or experience less stress in tough times? Tell your prospects exactly why they need you, and why they shouldn't wait to get started.

3. **Make use of your existing network**. It's always easier to get your foot in the door when someone is holding it open. In a slow market, referrals and introductions can be the key to getting new business. Seek out opportunities to propose repeat business with former clients, too. Uncertain times encourage more reliance on trusted sources and known quantities, so warm approaches and existing contacts will pay off better than cold calls or mass mailings.

4. **Explore partnerships**. Working with a partner can create more opportunities for both of you. By sharing contacts, you each increase the size of your network. Together, you can multiply your marketing efforts and share expenses. A partner with a complementary business can allow you to offer a more complete solution than your competitors can. A photographer could team up with a graphic designer, for example. And you can help keep each other's spirits up, too.

5. **Meet people where they are**. In a down economy, prospects are even more price sensitive than usual. Instead of slashing your rates to get their business, propose a get-acquainted offer. A professional

organizer or image consultant could offer a reduced price half-day package for new clients. A management consultant or executive coach could propose a staff seminar instead of consulting/coaching work. Once clients see you in action, they'll be more willing to spend.

6. **Find the silver linings**. When companies cut back on staff, opportunities are created. With fewer people on the payroll to handle essential tasks, downsized organizations present possibilities for project work, interim assignments, and outsourced functions. Economic changes beget other needs. People who are out of work need résumé writers and career coaches. Folks concerned about their finances need investment advisors and financial planners.

Landing clients during a down period requires not just more marketing, but more strategic marketing. So instead of getting depressed by the news, get inspired by it. When you hear about coming layoffs, consider how your services could benefit those companies. When you read about negative consumer attitudes, use those words to better target your marketing copy. When prospects say, "not this year," craft a proposal that ensures your place in next year's budget.

For the successful independent professional, there's no such thing as a bad time to market.

C.J. Hayden is the author of *Get Clients Now!*™ Thousands of business owners and independent professionals have used her simple sales and marketing system to double or triple their income.

Get a copy of "Five Secrets to Finding All the Clients You'll Ever Need" at
   www.getclientsnow

C.J.'s comments invite us to step forward, shake off fears and do something proactive.

> *Just remember, you can do anything you set your mind to, but it takes action, perseverance, and facing your fears.*

GILLIAN ANDERSON

Facing your fears often involves gaining the insight and support of others. Sometimes we cannot get support from others at the time we need it. So, a good plan has three levels:

Level I – Support that takes little or no energy. (Example: devoting time with a pet.)

Level II – Support you can provide for yourself. (Example: taking a walk.)

Level III – Support that arrives when you ask for help. (Example: phoning a kind friend.)

Create a Value Plan in 20 Seconds

Every night, in order to empty my mind of concerns of the next day, I list my *Top Six Targets* on a 3x5 index card. I list two targets for me, two for work and two for family. For those people who already feel overwhelmed, this quick process of noting your Top Six Targets makes planning and prioritizing a breeze. The Top Six Targets process helps us feel that we're making progress and taking care of what is most important.

Now, Mike Robbins helps us create a plan for lightening our mood.

This Too Shall Pass

Mike Robbins

Do you ever find yourself stuck in a negative place, worrying that things won't get any better (or even that they will get worse)? Or, have you ever had things going so well in your life that you just knew it wouldn't last? If you're anything like me and most of the people I know and work with, your answer to both of these questions is, of course, "yes."

Many of us seem to forget that there is a natural ebb and flow to life, especially when things get challenging, stressful, or scary. Right now, there is a lot of agreement in our world about how "bad" things are – particularly in relation to the economy. And while I do believe it is essential for us to confront things in life directly and not put our heads in the sand, it seems that many of us (myself included at times) tend to forget an important truth about life ... this too shall pass.

Ironically, this same phenomenon is also true when things are "good." Life constantly evolves and changes ... nothing stays constant. We waste so much of our precious time and energy worrying about things, instead of appreciating and embracing them in the moment. Worrying that bad times won't pass (which they almost always do) or that good times won't last (which they almost never do) takes us out of the present moment and causes us to suffer, miss out, or both.

You or some of the people around you may be experiencing significant pain or challenge right now – based on the economic situation or other factors. Or, you may currently be experiencing a great deal of success, opportunity, and joy in your life. At some level, most of us experience a certain amount of real joy and real pain all the time, simultaneously.

Whatever our current experience of life may be, it always serves us to remember that things are in a constant state of flux and that whatever is going on in our lives right now, will pass. As difficult as this is for each of us to remember, especially when we're scared, it can be a powerful reminder and an important mantra that we hold onto and share with others as a way to keep things in perspective.

Here are a few things you can do to enhance your ability to stay present, grounded, and grateful – regardless of the external circumstances in your life.

1. **Count your blessings** – Whatever is going on in your life - no matter how "good" or "bad" things may seem, there are always many things for us to be grateful for. Take some time right now to think about or write down some of the many blessings in your life. And, as a bonus – share them with others today and this week.

2. **Support others** – Reminding others that things can and will get better (if they're tough) and that it's important to appreciate and enjoy what is happening (if things are going well), is a great way to remind ourselves, get out of our own head, and be in service. When we support others, we also support ourselves in a healthy and generous way. And, our authentic support of other people helps make sure we don't spend and waste time feeling sorry for ourselves or getting too caught up in our own narcissism.

3. **Reflect on your past in a positive way** – Think back to times in your own life when you've overcome challenges and/or created great success and fulfillment. Remembering that we've had tough times and risen above them and that we've been able to appreciate ourselves, our lives, and our success – can help us remember how strong and capable we are in the present moment. Allow your past to empower you!

What can you do to embrace life as it is and remember, in a healthy and empowering way, that whatever you are experiencing right now will pass?

> Mike Robbins, CSP, is a best-selling author of *Focus On the Good Stuff*, sought-after motivational keynote speaker, and personal growth expert who works with Fortune 500 companies, non-profits, schools, and groups and people of all kinds. He and his work have been featured on ABC News, the Oprah radio network, in *Forbes*, and many others. His books have been translated into eight different languages.
>
> To learn more about his work, check out: www.Mike-Robbins.com

---

Mike Robbins reminds us that embracing the good in the present moment is empowering.

> *Happiness is something to do, someone*
> *to love and something to hope for.*
>
> **CHINESE PROVERB**

This proverb provides the essence of a good plan. When we focus on something to do, someone to love and something to hope for, fulfillment is possible.

A good plan may also include spiritual practices.

> *In our increasingly materialistic world ... [and] despite our pleasant material surroundings, many people today experience dissatisfaction, fear, anxiety, and a sense of insecurity. There seems to be something lacking within our hearts. What we seem to be missing is a proper sense of human spirituality.*

THE DALAI LAMA

Because you are a human being, you have a built-in spiritual dimension. You must claim your spiritual gifts.

Some authors emphasize, "You must name them to claim them."

I enjoy working with people to help them uncover their natural brilliance. *We don't need you to be a copy of someone else; we need you to express your natural brilliance.*

Your true self is made up of your natural courage, brilliance and connection with all that is good in the universe. Through working with a coach or on your own, you can name the positive attributes you already have and that you want to accentuate.

> *Maturity is the capacity to endure uncertainty.*

JOHN HUSTON FINLEY

One way to endure uncertainty is to focus on something in your life that is certain. What could that be? For many of us, having a spiritual path gives us the foundation, or springboard, that we need to move forward.

*The most important question a person can
ask is, "Is the Universe a friendly place?"*

ALBERT EINSTEIN

A spiritual path that holds to a benevolent Higher Power can provide the comfort and foundation we need. With this connection, the Universe is a friendly place, a place where we learn what we need to learn.

Here is something that I start with: I am a wholesome person and I do my best.

I also feel that Higher Power is guiding me to lead a life of service, contribution and joy. My actions align with this foundation.

Align with your design.

TOM MARCOUX

We can't be certain of many things, including whether someone will acknowledge our good intentions, be kind to us, or even love us. But you can be certain of your own efforts to be loving toward a loved one. Similarly, some of my friends find that doing volunteer work also enhances their self-esteem.

Real learning is surrendering.

GUY FINLEY

Guy's comment reminds us to keep learning. Part of the process is surrendering assumptions that do not serve you. An assumption may be: "If he really loved me, he would agree with me." This can only cause disruption in a relationship.

Parents often do not agree with adult children because parents are from another era and may come from a different culture. For example, my client Sam's father cannot understand Sam's life as an entrepreneur. His father was a blue-collar worker who was fortunate to retire from the company he had worked for his entire career. On the other hand, as the leader of his own company, every day Sam is bombarded with tough decisions and disappointments that his father never faced. This leads Sam to seek others for the emotional support he needs for his work.

As Guy mentioned, Sam needs to surrender, that is, let go of his preference that his father be other than he is. Sam's father never learned how to listen without interrupting, and his father has no interest in learning how to do that now.

When we let go and give ourselves to the moment, we can experience closeness with loved ones. To give ourselves to the moment means to engage with what is available and to be grateful for what we have. And we need to avoid obsessing over what we don't have. Sam could get caught up in "I wish my father would … " Instead, he stays alert and listens to his father talk. Sam gives himself to the moment. That is a good plan.

Burt Dubin identifies essential rules for a business plan that will help you live well.

Rules of the Game

Burt Dubin

We're talkin' about the game of being an expert at living your life. These rules are unforgiving. Break them and a remorseless force simply sweeps you off the board, clicks you off the screen—and you're not even history. You're nuthin', baby.

Abide by these rules and you smile all the way to the bank. I started out not even knowing there were rules. Within 4 years I'd lost my little all. $235,000 eaten up, gone —beyond recovery. Money talks, right? Well, mine went without saying!

I learned these rules the hard way. You can too. You can learn the hard way. Do you really choose to do that? Nobody cares. Nobody will care. It's your life. Now that I've had a chance to think about it, I prefer the easy way. I'd rather learn from other people's goof-ups. So, let's get started.

Rule 1: Have something of durable value to offer the lives you touch. Something you're passionate about. If you speak or consult, address a topic or issue that comes from your bones. From your core. From your essence. From your soul. And when you say it, be it. Be your message. Allow it out of your pores, out of your heart, out of your deepest feelings and beliefs. Let it shine from your eyes, be reflected in your stance and your glance, radiate from all your fingertips. Yes, from your eyelashes. Be on fire! Be so enraptured by your feelings and desires that you magnetize your audiences before you even open your mouth. If you are an expert at something else, be it painting or sculpture, music or a craft, whatever may be your unique competence, lavish passion and energy on giving the market you serve your passionate best.

Rule 2:   Be a marketer first, an expert next, a deliverer of your expertise last. (Marketing, defined: Marketing is creating conditions by which others decide on their own that they want what you've got.) Many fine specialists do not survive because they think the world is going to welcome them with open arms. Sorry, no cigar. This is a painful lesson. You either gotta be so dazzling, charming, entertaining, gorgeous, brilliant that those to whom you market all but lose control, are beside themselves, go ape at the thought of engaging you. Frank Sinatra and Elvis had that rare quality. Most specialists don't. How to market is beyond the scope of this short piece. By whatever means, you just gotta magnetize those in your universe to desire what you offer.

Rule 3:   Have integrity. Integrity that is absolute. Would you go driving in a car with a tire that wouldn't hold air? Would you go sailing in a leaking boat? When the skin of a fruit is broken open, the fruit begins to rot right there. Nature insists on integrity. Is integrity any less important in your commitments to others who can hire you? As specialists we commit to show up, to deliver as promised and on time. We commit to be ready to go on. And to be as represented, even better if possible. Space precludes my going on and on. You've got the idea.

Rule 4:   Be exclusive. Be one-of-a-kind. Be a specialist. Create your unique market position. And a unique expertise. Be special in your corner of your world. Be the only game in town. Know more about your specialty than anyone else on earth. And don't tell me you can't do it. You can. I know you can. Your creator endowed you with a unique talent. A talent nobody else has. It is latent, quivering with potential, bursting with possibilities, eager to be engaged. Engage it!

Rule 5: Associate with brilliant achievers. People who are reaching for lofty outcomes and dedicating themselves to worthy attainments. To outcomes that make a vital difference for others as well as themselves. People who are super-positive. People who build you up by their presence. Shun ordinary work-a-day types who lack a sense of their latent magnificence.

Rule 6: Invest in Brand You. In this, my 32nd year in my specialty (the speaking business), I continue to invest tens of thousands of dollars in research each year. Not just dollars. Time. Probably 20 to 30 hours each week in pure research. Why? So I can stay on the cutting edge. And, not just time. Focus. Energy. Asking why. Contemplation. Meditation. Looking inside. Looking outside. Looking away. Here's the idea … Make yourself such a unique resource for the market you serve that there simply isn't a #2. Be so far out in front that others who would compete with you can't even shine your shoes. This is what I want you to do. You do it by using the brains your God gave you.

Rule 7: Find your North Star. Set your compass by your North Star. Your North Star is your personal mission. The North Star allows mariners to set their course and stay on course. That's what your personal mission does for you. Have a personal mission. Put it in writing. Be sure it is transcendent. You know your mission is transcendent when you awaken one morning and you discover your mission has you. You're caught up in the rapture, the energy, and the power of your mission. You're a mission samurai. A warrior. Now you're hooked. Hooked to the magnificent destiny you've created for yourself. From this moment on you have a new and vibrant energy. It's always been there. Waiting inside you. Waiting for you to release it.

Measure your every decision against your mission. Whatever action serves your mission is good. Actions that do not advance your mission are to be avoided. Create a mission. And a Mission Statement. Put it on your office wall, your refrigerator door, your bathroom mirror. Live it. Live it vividly. Let it govern your every action.

Rule 8: Set specific goals. Measurable goals. Goals with deadlines. Goals that advance your mission. Then take the bit in your teeth. Go after those goals ferociously. Relentlessly. With bulldog blood. Let setbacks strengthen your resolve.

Rule 9: Get debt-free as fast as you can. The wisest experts agree on this. Get out of the plastic trap. Then, invest your profits for the long-term.

Rule 10: Make yourself one of the best anywhere: "Be more of what you are. Be all of what you are. Do what you love; do it with your whole heart. Do it with passion and a clear vision of where you are going. And a commitment to become excellent and the courage to face your fears and to be realistic and honest with yourself and to take complete responsibility for your future. And if you do that and if every morning you wake up and hit the ground running you will be outstanding in your field!" (Brian Tracy)

Rule 11: Raise your fees. Be worth more than your fees. Most specialists lack the courage to set fees that reflect their value. This insight shows you why: Most specialists are the K-marts of their business. 17% of specialists are the Tiffany's of their business. Which are you to be?

Rule 12: Get yourself a coach, a mentor. Get the very best you can find. Then trust this person. If you can't trust this person, get somebody else. Open up. Tell your mentor where you've been, where you are, where you want to be. Get an expert in the field you've set your heart on. Someone who understands. Someone who has been around the track a few more times than you.

Someone like … someone like … well … me.

Burt Dubin is an international specialist in the speaking and consulting business. burtdubin.com

Burt is GMT -7. Reach Burt from North America at
    800-321-1225. From all other areas, at +928-793-3303

Burt Dubin encourages us to look to the basics and take care of the elements of our personal foundation.

Principle:

To keep up your spirits, you need a plan.

Power Questions:

What is your plan to get to the three levels of support?

Level I – Support that takes little or no energy.

Level II – Support you can provide for yourself.

Level III – Support that arrives when you ask for help.

How can you devote time to your spiritual path? Would writing in your personal journal about your spiritual gifts be comforting to you?

8

Linger for Joy

Where is real joy? Is it with friends and loved ones? Is it with a team united for a cause?

We remember old phrases like "my heart was touched" and "that was touching."

> *Weeping may endure for a night, but joy cometh in the morning.*
>
> PSALMS 30:5

How does joy arrive? When you have loved ones and friends to share the lows and highs of life. Researchers note that 80% of the joy in life comes from connecting with other people.

So get in touch with loved ones.

Hug more.

Get a neck message, or trade one with a friend.

When I say, *linger for joy*, I mean that you need to pause to truly connect with friends and loved ones.

There is more to life than increasing its speed.

MAHATMA GANDHI

Pull out your day planner and schedule in times with loved ones and friends. These are life-enhancing appointments! My friends and I talk about doing spontaneous little gestures like sending a card to a parent, giving flowers, and making phone calls to catch up with loved ones.

Breathe in God

As a Comparative Religion instructor to college students, I have noticed that a number of individuals gain comfort and strength from their spiritual paths. A number of paths emphasize meditation and belly breathing.

I teach my clients and students belly-breathing techniques to help them calm down and eliminate nervousness when speaking before a group. A novice speaker can easily get nervous and sprinkle sounds like "uh" and "um" throughout their speech. This can be annoying to the listeners. The solution is to replace nervousness with a breath.

For those who want nondenominational spiritual practices, I introduce the Breathe in God™ process. When you're feeling exhausted, remind yourself to say, silently, "breathe in God." Take in a deep breath, let your belly expand, and silently say "God" as you breathe in. Then say, silently, "Thank You" as you exhale. You'll find that you will start to relax.

*If the only prayer you ever say in your entire life is
thank you, it will be enough.*

MEISTER ECKHART

Some readers may prefer to silently say "Higher Power" or
"peace" as they practice the belly-breathing exercise. I realize
that people have different thoughts on Higher Power and the
universe. I guide my students to create a good space for different
ideas.

The Breathe in God process gives many of us a feeling of
strength and safety. Often, when we feel overwhelmed, we feel
small and vulnerable. When you "breathe in God" you find that
you connect with that which is bigger than yourself. During
a quiet time, I realized that Breathe in God begins with the
letters B.I.G. Learn to connect with the benevolent power of the
universe.

In my workshops, I guide audience members to move and
breathe in refreshing ways. The suggestions I give are based
on experiences I have had in martial arts (including tai chi),
yoga, comparative religion and psychology. I teach them to
raise their hands over their heads while breathing deeply, and
then gracefully bring down their hands into a tai chi move. The
lesson: When you feel overwhelmed, it helps to move your body
in a way that brings good, calming feelings.

A special benefit of Breathe in God

A client, Jeremy, finds that he has difficulty calming down
after reading troubling e-mail messages. He gets an acid feeling
in his stomach and his shoulders tense up. In such a state, he

finds that he can't calm down and be present when his wife stops by to give him a hug.

I taught him the Breathe in God process and now he can relax and hug his wife … and be present in the moment. This brought warmth and good feelings to both of them.

~~~~~~~~~~~~~~~~~~

Another powerful way to create warmth is to make room in your life for humor. Allen Klein shows us how to add humor when times are tough.

Humor-Eyes Your Stress

Allen Klein, MA, CSP (aka Mr. Jollytologist®)

> *In order to keep a true perspective of one's importance,*
> *everyone should have a dog that will worship him and*
> *a cat that will ignore him.*
>
> ANONYMOUS

There is a funny thing about humor. You never knew where or when it will happen. In fact, it is often the surprise element of a situation that makes it so laughable. Two of my professional-speaker colleagues recently told me a story that illustrates this point extremely well.

One of them said that she was glowing after giving a very successful humor presentation at a luncheon. As she was heading home, her car
~~~~~~~~~~~~~~~~~~

started to billow smoke. She pulled over and stood at the back of the car. Shortly after the smoke died down, a policeman pulled up and demanded that she move the car and get out of the line of backed up traffic. She started to head around the car to the driver's door but she couldn't move. Her high heels were stuck in the hot roadside tar.

The next thing she knew, she has a cop on one side and a traffic control officer on the other trying to pull her feet out of the tar.

"Just then, and I swear to God this is true," she says, "a van tries to pull around her car and it is loaded with women who just heard her humorous presentation at the luncheon. They roll down the window and shout, 'What's so funny about this?' And, Lyon shares, 'I'm laughing so hard, I just about wet my pants!'"

Another colleague said that she was giving a presentation in an unusually dark room. The walls were black, the carpeting was black, the stage curtain behind her was black.

At one point in her talk, she stepped forward, missed the edge of the stage, and found herself flat on the floor. Although she was a little startled, she realized that she wasn't hurt. Just slightly embarrassed. She also realized that the microphone had fallen right nearby. So, still lying on the floor, she picked it up and announced to the audience, "And now I will take questions from the floor."

How you can find more humor in daily life

Can you remember five letters? If you can, then you are well on your way to finding more humor, laughter and mirth in your daily Maalox moments. Those letters … are you ready? - are …

L – A – U – G – H

Each of the letters stands for one thing you can do immediately to keep your humor up when you are down. The acronym is:

L – Let Go

A – Attitude

U – You (OK, I cheated a little bit here.)

G – Go Do It

H – Humor eyes & ears

Let go

If you are upset, angry or frustrated with anything, you cannot laugh about it. So the first way to get more laughter in your life is to start to let go. And the quickest way that I know of letting go of anything is through play. Play changes your energy.

For example:

Think about some small stress you are having. Then, say out loud the thing that causes that stress.

Now repeat what you just said but this time, after it, say: "Ho, ho. Ha, ha. Or, hee, hee." O.K., what happened?

You are probably laughing, or at least smiling, about that stressor. Another thing you can do to let go of your stress is to get a balloon. Then think about some small stress you are having and blow that stress into a balloon. Get it as big as you can, then let go of the balloon and the stress you just blew into it.

Attitude

The world is the way it is. What makes it otherwise, is your attitude. Change your attitude and you change your world.

My mom, who just turned 94 years-old, has a great attitude. When an entire stack of dishes fell and broke, she declared, "Well now I have less to wash!"

You

You need to do it. Everyone's sense of humor is different so you need to find out what makes you laugh and seek that out - rent your favorite comedy, call a humor buddy, giggle with your grandkids.

Go do it

In my *Healing Power of Humor* book, I have 14 techniques of how the reader can increase their sense of humor. One of my favorites is to have a prop or toy around - perhaps a red-sponge-rubber clown nose.

Next time you get upset, put one of these on and look in the mirror. I bet you will be hard-pressed to stay angry.

Humor eyes and ears

There is humor all around. Open your humor eyes and ears and find some. For example, A sign I once saw on the wall of a Laundromat read, "When the machine stops remove all your clothing."

Which I did!

Allen Klein, aka "Mr. Jollytologist," is a best-selling author whose books include *The Healing Power of Humor, The Courage to Laugh,* and *WorkLaughs: A Jollytologist Book: Quips, Quotes, and Anecdotes about Making a Buck.* Klein is an award-winning professional speaker who shows audiences worldwide how to find and use humor to deal with changes, challenges, and not-so-funny stuff. He is a recipient of a Toastmaster's Communication and Leadership Award, a Certified Speaking Professional designation from the National Speakers Association, and a Lifetime

Achievement Award from the Association for Applied and Therapeutic Humor.

www.allenklein.com.

Allen Klein invites to shift to a space of openness so that humor may flow. Humor has been called inner jogging. The flow of endorphins can enhance your immune system and energize your soul.

In addition to humor helping enhance your immune system, positive friends and family can strengthen you during extremely stressful times. Tina Macuha now shares with us the importance of health checkups and how she coped with a life-changing situation.

Take Care of Yourself

An Interview with Tina Macuha

Tom: Tina, thanks so much for joining us. A close friend told me about the powerful newscast when you told your "Good Day Sacramento" television viewers that you had been diagnosed with breast cancer.

Tina: I wanted to share my story so that people take care of themselves and get mammograms. You're your own best advocate.

Tom: I'm glad you did. I can relate: My mother endured three breast cancer related operations – during one of them, I wore a surgical mask and held her hand.

Tina: It's good you were there for her. I'm sure she felt very loved.

Tom: I'm just glad that my mother has been cancer-free for many years.

Tina: Excellent!

Tom: Thanks. I remember that your mother also endured breast cancer.

Tina: Yes – she died of breast cancer in 1983. It was a time that people didn't want to talk about the disease, a time people didn't want to say the word "breast," and a time my mother felt like an outcast. I remember how hurt she was after she had chemo and her hair fell out. She said people acted differently towards her - as though she was contagious. Times are different now. We've come a long way in our society. I'm so thankful I have supportive people around me. I appreciate the kind support of our viewers in their comments on my blog. Many of them have touched me with letters and emails and their personal stories. I wish my mom had that back then. I wish she had the medical opportunities that I have … maybe she'd be around today.

Tom: Yes. How did you take care of yourself as you went through the journey of the diagnosis, the double mastectomy, and recovery?

Tina: I was fortunate to have supportive friends and loved ones. Even watching *Oprah* was helpful. I watched Oprah's repeat show on breast cancer. Her guests included actress Christina Applegate and Nancy Brinker (founder of Susan G. Komen

Foundation). Christina talked about her radical decision to have a mastectomy at age 36. The whole show was moving as well as informative. Okay, I cried a lot watching it. There were so many thoughts and feelings that went through my mind. It was so hard to keep track of everything that crossed my mind. It was just nice to know there are so many women out there that know how I feel. There's a grieving process that we go through when we decide to let go of a very important part of our bodies. There's the fear of the unknown - no matter what decisions we make for our health.

Tom: During your recovery, how did you cope?

Tina: It was difficult to do simple things – getting a bowl high up in the cupboard or putting a shirt on. I did stretching exercises everyday but got a little frustrated and impatient. It made me think about how lucky I am to be able to enjoy the simple things many of us take for granted … our arms, our legs, running water. My life is different now. It's forever changed. I look at everything in a new light. Writing my blog helped, too. I was able to express my truth and to express what I was grateful for. I asked on my blog: "Have you (or someone you know) scheduled a mammogram recently? Do you normally get them yearly?" I have received a lot of kind letters and comments to my blog entries in which people say they've scheduled a mammogram because I shared my story. I finally feel I have accomplished something big – that I have given to people – and that makes me feel good. There's still a lot I want to do on this Earth. Most importantly, I want to be around for my family.

> Tina Macuha has been an Anchor/Reporter on CW 31's *Good Day Sacramento* since August 1995. She can be seen every morning reporting the Sacramento, Central Valley, and Bay Area commute. Tina shares her Thought of the Day by placing it next to her on the set. She awards a free lunch, called Grub Run, to a lucky office usually once per week. Tina also comes up with Question of the Day in order to get to know her co-workers better and enjoys stumping their music knowledge during Teen's Tune. In March 2000, she received the Women of Color Day 2000 Award for Caring and Responsive Journalism and as An Outstanding Woman of Color. Tina served as the on-court emcee for the Sacramento Monarchs WNBA team during the 1999, 2000, and 2001 seasons. She is a frequent speaker at local events and enjoys speaking at schools to encourage youth to follow their dreams. Tina is also a certified facilitator with Motivating the Teen Spirit and does teen empowerment workshops.
>
> pod08.prospero.com/n/blogs/blog.aspx?webtag=KOVR_TinaJullis

I appreciate Tina's candor about her journey through a health crisis. Her comments remind us that we need to take care of our health and the health of our relationships before difficult times.

Love is another way to access joy. But researchers identify that not everyone finds the same actions to be loving. We have differences.

Dr. Gary Chapman, author of *The Five Love Languages*, lists the love languages as:

1. Words of affirmation

2. Gifts

3. Quality time

4. Acts of service

5. Physical touch

It helps to ask your loved one: When do you feel really loved by me? Listen carefully. Sometimes a loved one will give you hints like, "I was looking at my ring this morning and I really felt good."

Also, check in with yourself. When do you feel loved? I know that I feel loved when a friend or loved one helps me improve a project that will benefit my readers or audiences. In my case, acts of service touch my heart. Learn to gently ask for those things that mean a lot to you. Make sure that your heart is touched and that you touch the hearts of other people.

Consider giving:

- **Words of affirmation** – Thank you for listening to me. That means so much. I feel really loved by you.

- **Gifts** – Flowers, chocolate, a poem, a gift certificate to a favorite restaurant

- **Quality time** – Dinner with the television turned off, time together in nature, a daily stroll in your neighborhood

- **Acts of service** – Proofreading someone's work, volunteering at the local homeless shelter

- **Physical touch** – A hug, backrub, foot massage, neck massage, holding hands

It's important to pay close attention to your loved one's hobbies and interests. Take notes whenever you hear something that may be of interest to them. This is a good way to express your love.

Principles:

Be sure to linger for joy. Gently ask for what you need in a way that matches your preferred "love language."

Power Questions:

How can you touch the hearts of those who are important to you? How would you like to be supported? How can you gently ask for what you need?

Conclusion to Chapter Eight

We have explored the S.O.U.L. process:

> S – Support yourself
>
> O – Open connection
>
> U – Unleash a plan
>
> L – Linger to joy

To endure and thrive, we must feed our soul. No one will take the action for us. To be kind and helpful to important people in our lives, we must make sure to replenish our energy so that we can truly be there for our loved ones. Get the support you need.

Part III

9

Recession-Proof Strategies

How to Save a Business

What could you do if your business was spiraling downward due to the economic recession?

Powerful methods came to my mind in response to viewing a distraught woman as she was interviewed on the Oprah Winfrey television show. With tears in her eyes, she told how her family's 401(k) funds and savings had been sunk into her failing bakery. She was concerned that her family would become homeless.

The way the television show was edited, not much was said about how the woman could nurture herself during the pain and grief she was experiencing. I realized that her first step would be to feed her soul (the subject of the previous section).

Let's discuss how she can take action to save her business.

In the middle of difficulty lies opportunity.

ALBERT EINSTEIN

Opportunity? That, at first glance, seems unrealistic. The truth no one will tell you: During a recession, someone is making money. And it could be you.

Who's making money? Some successful business people help others survive and thrive during the recession.

The idea behind The Recession-Proof Cupcake begins with a magic *what if*:

- What if her bakery made a Recession-Proof Cupcake?

- What if she gathered local speakers and authors to write fortune cookie-sized nuggets of wisdom she included with each cupcake?

- What if she helped with charity events? Charities are in tough times during a recession. People would appreciate her efforts, which could lead to work providing baked goods for local businesses.

- What if she downsized her business, researched local zoning laws, and moved her bakery into her own kitchen?

- What if she provided "care packages" of cupcakes for students at local colleges? Parents and grandparents are the target market because they would purchase the care packages as gifts for their college students. (By the way, there is an Internet-based company that does this using cookies.)

- What if her Recession-Proof Cupcake gained media attention on radio, television, blogs and other outlets?

- What if she could work out something with the landlord where her business is located? Sometimes smaller payments are accepted in order to keep buildings occupied.

And most of all:

- What if she positioned her bakery as The Little Bakery that Could! Remember the little engine that could who said, "I think I can, I think I can," while trudging up that mountain. The idea is to create a new label that customers, the media and employees can keep firmly in their minds.

- What if she networked with a group of people who wanted her to succeed? For example, she could brainstorm with other business owners at her local Chamber of Commerce.

The Big Secret to Save Your Business:

Create a community that wants you to succeed.

Of course, it takes energy and insight to make this happen. If you feel depleted of energy, please return to the feed your soul section in this book. The idea is to keep up your self-nurturing efforts while you go into action with the following methods.

We will use the C.A.K.E. process:

> C – Create community
>
> A – Adapt
>
> K – Keep learning
>
> E – Encourage help

Let's step forward together …

10

Create Community

How do you build a community that wants you to succeed? It starts with passion.

Passion is energy. Feel the power that comes from focusing on what excites you.

OPRAH WINFREY

Here are the 5 Rs of creating a community that wants you to succeed:

1. Reconnect Enthusiasm

2. Reward Them

3. Receive Praise

4. Repeat Updates

5. Realize Mutual Benefits

Reconnect Enthusiasm

Business, just like public speaking, is often a transfer of enthusiasm.

> *The more powerful question than "What do you want?" is "What excites you?"*
>
> TIMOTHY FERRIS

Write in your personal journal the answers to these questions:

- Who do you want to help?
- Who do you want to serve?
- What makes your business different?
- How can you be a hero to a specific set of customers?

An interviewer asked me: "Is there a difference between help and serve?" I replied: "Yes. There can be. If you're helping someone, you might start with a preconception. You might feel that you're good at helping with a certain detail, and you offer that. On the other hand, to serve is to approach the situation with no preconception. You ask the person how he or she wants to be helped. You serve the person in the way he or she prefers to be supported."

Now, the first step is to reconnect with your passion so that you experience enthusiasm for the work that needs to be done.

Reward Them

The second step in creating a community is to make sure people get rewarded for helping you.

What gets rewarded, gets repeated.

MICHAEL LEBEOUF

In today's economic downturn, it's helpful to get creative and seek rewards that will benefit you and the customer. For instance, make it easy for someone to give your business a referral. One idea: Provide a special coupon. I find that the Borders Bookstore is a master at this process. As a Borders Rewards member, almost every week I get an e-mail message with a coupon for 25% or 30% off the purchase of a book.

You can make this process automatic on your Web site. Some authors provide a free downloadable e-book for giving referrals or for just joining their e-newsletter subscriber list.

The owner of a bakery could provide a cupcake-decorating contest for children, which might gain her media attention. She could also offer pastry-decorating classes, the first class free for previous customers.

Receive Praise

People like to be appreciated. They're hungry for it. Too often people are taken for granted by family members and co-workers. Be the exception and offer praise.

Pretend that every single person you meet has a sign around his or her neck that says, Make Me Feel Important. Not only will you succeed in sales, you will succeed in life.

MARY KAY ASH

If appropriate, set up a wall at your business that has framed photos. Call it the Wall of Fame for Top Customers We Appreciate. You can also have a virtual Wall of Fame on your Web site.

Repeat Updates

Praise people who helped your business by announcing the good news in your e-newsletter. One example is a friend who worked to set up a bicycling highway. Through his e-newsletter, he kept everyone informed about each step of progress and gave praise to each person who had helped in his effort. Everyone receiving the e-newsletter could feel the forward momentum of the project.

Find ways to keep your customers informed, and repeat good news.

Now, Danek Kaus demonstrates how we can keep the media updated and spread good news to thousands of people.

Free Publicity to Help Your Business Prosper in Hard Times

Danek Kaus

In a down economy, marketing budgets tend to shrink so business owners cut back on advertising. Getting free publicity in the media and online can help you to keep your name in front of the public.

In addition to being free, or nearly so, publicity offers more credibility than a paid ad. With that in mind, here are some of the types of story ideas the media are most receptive to. Some of these will apply to you, others won't; but you can use them as a springboard for your own ideas.

Do well by doing good. Sponsor a charitable event or volunteer for a charity. If you're a business owner or a manager, you might encourage your entire staff to participate. Doing good works offers two chances for publicity. You can send out a news release to announce the commitment you've made before the event and another one after the event detailing some of your accomplishments.

Celebrate an anniversary or a milestone. Has your business reached its 10th, 25th or 50th anniversary? Just sold your 10,000th car? Let the media know.

Write a how-to article. If you own a pastry shop, offer an article on how to get a flakier piecrust. If you own an auto repair shop, offer tips on trouble-shooting or basic maintenance.

Tie in to current events. There are many possibilities for tie-ins. Let's say a big Hollywood couple announces that they're getting a divorce. If you're a psychologist or a marriage counselor, you could offer tips on how to have a better marriage. If you're a divorce attorney or an accountant, you might issue a press release on the financial consequences of divorce.

Conduct a survey. If you sell or service computers, do a survey about the most common customer complaints and announce your results to the media. If you own a health spa, you might do a survey to determine whether jogging or walking is more popular.

Malcolm Kushner, humor consultant to Fortune 500 companies and author of such books as *Public Speaking for Dummies* and *Presentations for Dummies*, has gotten national publicity for his annual "Cost of Humor Index." Each year he surveys the cost of such humor-related items as rubber chickens and whoopee cushions, then sends out a press release announcing his findings. He's been featured on several top TV talk shows and other national venues.

Hold an event. Do you own a bakery? How about having a pie-eating contest, with the proceeds going to a local charity? Or a bake-off or a recipe contest? Again, with the proceeds going to charity. As a health club owner, you can recruit all those pie-eaters to come in and lose weight. Each one of them could get sponsors who will contribute a specific amount to local charities for every pound a contestant loses.

Teach a class. Translate your expertise into publicity by offering free classes on the subject. You can send a press release to the appropriate section of the paper and to the calendar of events. If any of your local TV and radio stations announce events over the air or have calendars on their websites, be sure to notify them, as well. If you offer a really interesting class, it might be worth pitching as a story. You'll usually need to notify calendars at least a couple of weeks before the event, in some cases longer.

Promote with PSAs (Public Service Announcements). Most, if not all, radio and TV stations donate airtime to non-profits to promote their organization or events through PSAs. The free time can be anywhere from 10 seconds to a minute or more. Contact each station to find out what their time requirements are, as well as the lead-time, if you are holding an event. Some will want you to produce the PSA yourself while others will want you to send them the completed copy (text) of the PSA. Some will prefer to have you send them the basic facts so they can write their own copy.

Coordinate with editorial calendars. Not to be confused with calendars of events, newspapers and magazines usually have themed editions throughout the year. One month they might feature stories on automobiles. The next month, they may focus on health, and so on. Contact the newsroom (the place where all the reporters live) and ask for an editorial calendar. If they don't help you, try the advertising department. They have copies of the editorial calendars that they use to sell ads around. Armed with this information, you can time your story pitches to the times when journalists will be most receptive. Keep in mind, newspapers will usually want such stories from a couple to several weeks ahead of time and magazines will probably want them several months in advance. Once you have an idea for a pitch, contact the appropriate editor to find out what their lead-time is.

Be unusual. Do you do business in a unique way or have an unusual lifestyle? The media love these kinds of stories. Be careful when pitching the story and being interviewed that you don't come off as strange or odd; that can work against you, especially in business.

Receive an award. Have you or your organization received special recognition for something? Let the world know about it.

Create a list. As a stockbroker, you might offer seven tips to be better at picking stocks. If you own an auto repair shop, you might create a list of 10 things to do to prepare your vehicle for summer or winter. These lists are often published or read on air in their entirety.

Now you have an idea of what journalists are looking for. There are other types of stories you can pitch, but these offer the greatest chances for getting free press. Go down the list and think about how you might use each type of approach and how you can benefit. Then write your press release.

Adapted from the book, *You Can Be Famous! Insider Secrets to Getting Free Publicity*, by Danek S. Kaus.

Danek S. Kaus is a veteran journalist and publicist. He has published hundreds of articles in about 75 newspapers and magazines. His publicity clients have been featured in such media outlets as CNN, USA, *The New York Times,* and hundreds of newspapers, magazines, and TV and radio shows. He is also a produced screenwriter.

To contact him, or get more publicity tips, visit getfreepublicitynow.com or write dkaus@sbcglobal.net

---

Realize Mutual Benefits

You can team up with other business owners to launch mutually beneficial publicity campaigns. For example, some professional speakers team up to offer free events. Splitting the room rental fees between each speaker is a great way to save on costs. In addition, offering a free promotional event is helpful because the two main ways speakers get hired are: (1) someone heard the speaker or (2) her trusted colleague heard the speaker.

With this setup, the speakers are seen and heard by more people. Each speaker can also send out invitations to their own e-mail lists. The benefit is multiplied for each speaker and each audience member. The speakers are introduced to new potential clients, and audiences are introduced to new speakers they had never heard before.

We see a similar process for the launch of a new book. For example, Miranda, an author, invites other authors to provide a free e-book or MP3 download to be included on her promotional Web site. In this way Miranda's new book is promoted to the combined e-subscribers lists belonging to the participating authors. Just imagine the benefit when 20 authors team up.

If each author has an list of 10,000 subscribers, then 200,000 people will be alerted about Miranda's new book. Readers are not only enticed to buy Miranda's book, but they are rewarded with 19 free items provided by the other authors.

Authors love this method because of the huge number of potential readers who are introduced to their name and their work. This technique also drives the sales number high at Amazon.com.

Another example of setting up mutual benefits is when a single mother teams up with other mothers in her neighborhood. They babysit each other's children on different nights, which opens up the possibility of having more time to devote to work – when necessary.

A final example: a local day care center teams up with a local children's clothing store for cross-promotion.

Each business does better when people form alliances that provide mutual benefits.

~~~~~~~~~~~~~~~~~~~~~~~~

Set up your business so that the 5 Rs are automatically in place to build a community that wants you to succeed. It is worth the effort to automate how you reward people for helping you. The old principle: is: Set and forget. For example, having a technical person set up your Web site to provide free downloadable materials alleviates extra work for you. That's a relief. And you multiply your effectiveness. Good for you!
~~~~~~~~~~~~~~~~~~~~~~~~

Principle:

Surround yourself with a group of people who want you to succeed.

Power Questions:

How can you bring attention to your business? How can you create a community that wants you to do well? Can you volunteer for a community project?

11

Adapt

Do you remember a time when you adapted to a new situation? Were you able to change directions?

When you can adapt, you're like a flexible dancer – poised to go in any direction.

The ability to adapt to changing situations is one of the true freedoms of a small business. A small business owner can try new things when appropriate.

Adapting also means making hard decisions to save a dying business. My colleagues mention these tough decisions:

- Having to fire two people to save ten

- Selling an expensive delivery van and using the family SUV

- Canceling the family vacation to pay back-rent on one's business

- Working overtime to stay valuable to the company one works for

An important part of adapting is holding faith. You have faith that you can flow with changing situations.

Faith is to believe what you do not see; the reward of this faith is to see what you believe.

SAINT AUGUSTINE

In order to save your business, you need to hold to a vision that things can get better. You create things twice: first in your mind and then by your actions. If someone makes ten extra marketing calls a day, it is nearly inevitable that some positive results will occur. Only the person with a vision of success will actually make those extra calls.

To one who has faith, no explanation is necessary. To one without faith, no explanation is possible.

ST. THOMAS AQUINAS

For many of us, somewhere along the line a key person has reassured us with: "You can do this. I know you can." Be sure to find people who truly believe in you and devote time to those relationships.

A number of us can recall a teacher who believed in us. I'm fortunate to have had three high school teachers who believed in me. The subjects they taught were psychology, advanced English literature and theology. The result – I earned a degree in psychology, write screenplays and other fiction, and teach Comparative Religion at the college level.

To maintain the strength you need to adapt to changes, hold close the memories of those who believed in you. If you also listen to empowering, educational audio programs (even while doing household chores), you have the support of a human voice encouraging you to apply helpful methods.

Now it's your turn. In your personal journal, write down a list of people who have supported you in the past. Then write a list of people who can support you right now. If you find that your current list is short, look into joining a support group for entrepreneurs or business people in your line of work. If there isn't one, consider starting your own support group.

> *Hold faithfulness and sincerity as first principles.*
>
> CONFUCIUS

When you help other people, the universe backs you up.

> *The moment one definitely commits*
> *oneself, then Providence moves too.*
>
> W.H. MURRAY

Adapting means that we move with poise into a new direction when necessary. When we really pay attention, we realize that adapting takes practice. Richard Carlson, author of *Don't Sweat the Small Stuff*, told me something important about adapting. He said that he learned how to change his thoughts and to spend much less time being upset when things went wrong.

Richard Carlson wrote, "Make allowances for incompetence." That is, he would take extra measures so that someone's possible mistake would not cause a devastating effect. It can be as simple as making a copy of a check before mailing it out, in case your check gets lost in the mail.

Another way to adapt is to practice deep breathing and a quieter response. In this way, you'll find yourself losing less time to being upset.

On the other hand we may be misguided and attempt to resist change.

> *Sometimes we stare so long at a door that is closing*
> *that we see too late the one that is open.*
>
> ALEXANDER GRAHAM BELL

The truth is, in order to be able to adapt, you need the basics: sleep, good nutrition, exercise, and time with loved ones. Then you'll see new doors opening.

Here are examples of new doors:

1. My client Allen does not get a new job as a financial planner. His new door opens when he rents a conference room at a small hotel to give free public seminars that will gain him new clients.

2. My client Naomi is told by an agent that her book is not suitable. Her new door opens when she contacts BookSurge.com to print and distribute her book. She also places it on Amazon.com.

3. Someone I know loses her corporate job, goes back to school and becomes a nurse.

We need to be flexible in order to adapt to the surprise challenges life brings us.

Dr. JoAnn Dahlkoetter guides us in methods to strengthen our bodies and minds.

Building Motivation & Maximizing Your Potential

Dr. JoAnn Dahlkoetter

The people who develop these following qualities and practice these skills regularly have the best chance of excelling in athletics as well as personally and professionally. Each of us begins at a different starting point physically and mentally. We all have strengths that we can build upon. How do you begin to build the traits of truly successful people into your life? How do you turn these qualities into useful behaviors that will make a difference in the way you train and race or perform at work? Numerous researchers in the sports psychology field have reported on the critical skills and behaviors of successful athletes. Below I have offered suggestions that have helped many of my own clients tremendously toward excelling in their sport or in business.

Generate a positive outlook

Direct your focus to what is possible, to what can happen, toward success. Rather than complaining about the weather or criticizing the competition, the mentally trained athlete attends to only those things that he or she can control. You have control over your thoughts, your emotions, your training form, and how you perceive each situation. You have a choice in what you believe about yourself. Positive energy makes peak performances possible.

Visualize your goals daily

Put yourself in a relaxed state through deep abdominal breathing. Then, as vividly as possible, create an image in your mind, of what you want to achieve in your sport. You can produce a replay of one of your best performances in the past. Then use all those positive feelings of self-confidence, energy, and strength in your mental rehearsal of an upcoming event. See yourself doing it right. Then use your imagery during the event itself. Practice being focused and yet relaxed: Develop the ability to maintain concentration for longer periods of time. You can tune in what's critical to your performance and tune out what's not. You can easily let go of distractions and take control of your attention. As you focus more on the task at hand (e.g. your training form, how you're feeling) there will be less room for the negative thoughts to enter your mind.

Build a balanced lifestyle

Create a broad-based lifestyle with a variety of interests; strive for a balance between work and fun, social time, personal quiet time, and time to be creative. Develop patterns of healthy behavior. Eat regularly, get a consistent amount of sleep each night, reduce your workload at times if possible, and allow time to relax and reflect between activities. Develop a social support network of close friends and family, some who are sports oriented, and some with other interests. Learn to communicate openly; resolve personal conflicts as they occur, so they don't build to a crisis on the night before an important race.

Vary your workouts

Train at a new, scenic place at least once a week. Change your normal training schedule, even if only for two days. Try "active rest" by doing a different sport for a few days (e.g. hiking, swimming, inline skating, cycling, or cross-country skiing). You'll get a tremendous psychological boost and probably not lose any of your fitness level. Put new spark in your training schedule by doing interval work, tempo work (fast 20-30 minute training), varying your speed and doing endurance work, rather than slogging along at the same old pace.

Enjoy and take the pressure off

Make a deliberate effort each day to create enjoyment in your sport (or exercise routine), renewing your enthusiasm and excitement for training. Don't try to force your physical improvement. Lighten up on your rigid training schedule and exercise according to your feelings each day. Remove the strict deadlines and race dates which have been cast in stone. Let your next breakthrough occur naturally, at its own pace, when the internal conditions are right. Use setbacks as learning opportunities. Do the best that you can do, draw out the constructive lessons from every workout and race (or other situation), and then move on. Look for advantages in every situation, even if the conditions are less than ideal. Sport offers a wonderful chance to free ourselves for short periods and experience intensity and excitement not readily available elsewhere in our lives. In endurance sports we can live out our quest for personal control by seeking out and continuously meeting challenges that are within our capability. To develop an inner desire and maximize your true potential, make the most of the talents you have, and stretch the limits of your abilities, both physically and psychologically. Athletics can become a means to personal growth and enjoyment of the pursuit of your goals. Try incorporating the profile above into your mental preparation, and you can learn to live more fully, train more healthfully, and feel exactly the way you want to feel.

Excerpt from the book, *Your Performing Edge*

Dr. JoAnn Dahlkoetter, best-selling author of *Your Performing Edge*, has been a Medical Staff Member at Stanford University Medical Center for 10 years. As a sports psychologist and performance coach, she is one of America's most in-demand Keynote speakers, performance consultants, and a world-class athlete with several Olympic gold medalist clients. Winner of the San Francisco Marathon and 2nd in the Hawaii Ironman Triathlon, Dr. JoAnn has been on *Oprah and Friends*, and is an expert commentator on ABC, NBC, *FOX News*, and BBC-TV. She has appeared on ABC's Wide World of Sports, and is featured in *USA Today, Time Magazine*, the *Wall Street Journal*, the *New York Times*, and *Sports Illustrated*. Dr. JoAnn contributes to *Triathlete* and *Running Times Magazine*. She was a credentialed sports psychologist in Greece working with her Olympic gold medalist clients at the Olympic Training Center during the Summer Games. Her consultations and interviews with elite athletes, including Lance Armstrong, and top CEOs give her special insight into using the mind-body connection to achieve the best in personal performance. Her best-selling book is endorsed by Jack Canfield, Mark Victor Hansen, Brian Tracy, Zig Zigler, Dr. Denis Waitley and her Olympic gold medalist clients. You can go to www.sports-psych.com/pressroom.html to view her professional speaking-coaching video.

joann@sports-psych.com or www.YourPerformingEdge.com

Dr. JoAnn Dahlkoetter coaches us to use a virtual menu of methods to maintain personal balance.

Principle:

Be flexible like a dancer – poised to go in any direction.

Power Questions:

How can you nurture yourself so that you have the strength to adapt to tough situations? What do you need to adapt to now? Name five things you can do to adapt to a tough situation you are currently facing. Who can help you brainstorm about ideas to help you adapt better? (For example, one of my editors recommends The Brain Exchange in Albany, California. She explains that this is a group of women from all ages and backgrounds who meet monthly to brainstorm on how to help each other get through life's transitions. The group was written up in *O Magazine.* Similar groups are forming around the country.)

12

Keep Learning

*The greatest and most important problems
of life are all fundamentally insoluble. They
can never be solved but only outgrown.*

CARL JUNG

Building on Carl Jung's comment, we must take action so that we are growing as people. Learning is a vital part of the process.

Learning never exhausts the mind.

LEONARDO DA VINCI

I have found that learning actually energizes me and gets me excited about new and hopeful possibilities. At one point I counted the books I read in a two-year span of time: 108 books in the first year and 109 books in the second year. I found it invaluable to have all of those ideas in my mind as I faced the challenges of leading three companies.

People who believe they have the power to exercise some measure of control over their lives are healthier, more effective and more successful than those who lack faith in their ability to effect changes in their lives.

ALBERT BANDURA

Effective people are life-long learners. Learning provides us with hope. If we study and learn from the methods of people who have overcome adversity, we become empowered to improve our own situation. We can persist.

I do not think there is any other quality so essential to success of any kind as the quality of perseverance. It overcomes almost everything, even nature.

JOHN D. ROCKEFELLER

Olympic athletes persist to an extraordinary degree. They get injured, often perform injured, heal up, and then return to the field. We notice that they all have coaches. The athletes who reach new heights are coachable.

If you see a slowdown in sales, take a survey or ask people if they want something different from what you offer. See if you can make appropriate changes to reflect your customers' changing preferences. Learn how your customers feel. Remember, to learn is to endure.

Now we'll learn about cultural differences from Michael Soon Lee.

Overcoming Fear

Michael Soon Lee

Where do you encounter fear in business? The answer is ... everywhere. It could keep you from growing or even saving your business during tough economic times.

When does fear occur? One of the most common instances is when salespeople are afraid to call or visit strangers because the chances of rejection have increased exponentially over the last couple of years. This could literally be the death of a salesman as well as a company because without clients there is no one to sell your product or service to.

Recognize that fear is natural. It starts from the moment we are born. We know who our mom and dad are but anyone else is a potential danger to us so we have an innate suspicion about strangers. While this fear protects us from harm when we're young, as we grow older it can also keeps us from making friends and building a bigger client base.

I teach salespeople how to sell to customers whose culture may be different from their own. While professional salespeople may be used to talking to strangers, approaching people who may be different from themselves can be a daunting task. In the United States we have a great deal of trepidation around asking others about their culture. We are afraid to offend a potential customer. In reality, there's nothing to be afraid of because most people in the U.S. who are not European American are happy to educate others about their culture.

On the other hand, if you don't ask people about their culture you are forced to make assumptions that can be very often wrong. So go ahead and ask. Minorities in America know that they look different from Caucasian Americans and they also know that there is a lot of myth and misunderstanding about minorities so they look forward to the opportunity to educate others.

By being open to discuss culture you can also learn about peoples' preferences and needs and thereby increase sales as well as levels of customer service. Different cultures may want different benefits from your product or service. For instance, when buying a home Hispanics often want room to expand to accommodate friends and family who may come and stay for extended periods of time. For African Americans a home is sometimes a place in which they can take pride and exhibit art or other objects. On the other hand, Asians commonly buy homes for their future resale value in addition to being a place where they can raise a family. Obviously, these are generalities and the only way you can know what a particular customer wants from you is to get to know them on a personal basis.

Being willing to ask people about their culture not only increase rapport with multicultural customers much more quickly but will feed your soul at the same time. You'll gain a great appreciation for different languages, foods, religions and more. In addition, you're likely to discover how fascinating other cultures can be and how similar you are after all.

To get started on your journey to increasing your multicultural clientele, first find out who your potential customers are. Check the U.S. Census Bureau website which can give you broad data about Hispanics, Blacks, Asians and others. Then ask around and find out exactly where these customers come from. For instance, Hispanics are not one group but instead there are six major countries that are categorized this way: Mexico, Puerto Rico, South America, Central America, Cuba, and Spain. Blacks are not one group but could be African Americans or from Africa, Jamaica, Haiti or other countries. At least seventeen groups fall under the category of Asians including Chinese, Filipinos, Japanese, Koreans, Asian Indians, Vietnamese and others. Many of these subgroups have different foods, religions and even languages from others in the same category. If you'll ask, people will be more than happy to tell you exactly where their ancestors are from.

Then survey your customers and find out what products and services you could carry that would meet their needs. Sometimes there is absolutely no difference and sometimes there is a vast difference. You may be very surprised.

Finally, ask your new customers for referrals to their friends and family. In many countries outside the United States the best way to find a trusted vendor of a product or service is strictly by word-of-mouth. Anytime a customer says, "Thank you" it's an invitation to ask for a referral.

Getting to know your customers, regardless of culture, will help your business. Many people are afraid to "sell" because they think it means high-pressuring customers to buy something they don't want. Nothing could be further from the truth. High-pressure doesn't work very effectively unless you threaten people with a gun and then you can forget about referrals!

Professional selling is nothing more than building a relationship with a customer, getting to know their needs, demonstrating how your product or service meets those needs and then asking for the order. That's it. People buy what they need from people they like and if you treat them the way you'd want to be treated they will love you.

So don't be afraid to reach out to new customers and get to know them, especially with multicultural customers. You will find it a very rewarding experience because it will be like getting to take an around-the-world cruise without losing one piece of luggage or becoming seasick.

> Michael Soon Lee, MBA, is an expert on marketing and selling to people from diverse cultures. He is the coauthor of the book, *Cross-Cultural Selling for Dummies*. Michael's clients include: Coca-Cola, Chevron, State Farm Insurance, Virginia Tech University, and over a thousand others.
>
> Contact him at (800) 417-7325 and visit him at www.EthnoConnect.com.

Michael's comments urge us to stay vigilant and adapt so we can connect with various customers.

Now, Mike Gospe introduces us to marketing strategies and changes we need to learn and implement.

Marketing into the Storm

How the financial crisis will turn you into a better marketer

Mike Gospe

The financial crisis will have a detrimental impact on our marketing and sales budgets in 2009 and beyond. In this crisis, marketing leaders need to re-invent marketing not just as a functional discipline, but as the business fiber that connects prospects to companies like never before.

For the last 10 years, if not longer, the marketing function has been trapped within a confining connotation of "tactical, logistics execution." In fact, many CMOs I know continue to struggle against internal perception regarding the unappreciated strategic versus the taken-for-granted tactical natures of their role. To further compound this perception, product marketers everywhere still believe they are entitled to produce the traditional marketing materials created for their products whether they are appropriate or not – the press release, direct mail piece, website article and landing pages, etc. It's the marcom obligatory checklist where each marketing activity and offer is produced in a silo without any connection in message or time with other deliverables being produced by other team members. Survival of the marketing function depends on our ability to change this reality and break down these silos. Now.

Crisis creates opportunity

Rather than falling victim to the "deer in the headlights" stance, a time of crisis is an opportunity for re-evaluation and change. It's time to look anew at our marketing assumptions and reprioritize our choices. Against the hard edge of this crisis, we must hone our marketing skills and refocus on what are truly the only important things: the prospect and the customer.

Gone are the days of flamboyant marketing budgets that include Donna Summer as the headliner for a customer event. Tossed aside is the mantra that "more (products, datasheets, webinars, marketing programs and campaigns) is better". Marketing silos can no longer be accepted. Truly integrated marketing campaigns must replace yesterday's isolated and random "marketing popcorn" activities.

"Marketing as usual" must change. Those companies that succeed and excel in the next few years will be the ones that embrace three marketing truths and proactively act upon them with vigor:

"It's about the prospect and customer, stupid. Not the product." Successfully selling to business people means that marketers effectively understand the business problem the customer is trying to solve. Only then can you really know how your products and services will be relevant and meaningful to this audience. If you don't know, conduct a Customer Advisory Board Meeting and find out.

It's not enough to target "CFOs of the global 3000". Tighten your market segmentation criteria using adjectives and descriptors to clearly identify the demographics, psychographics, and behaviors of the target audience. Success requires being even more draconian in your target audience selection and prioritization.

To better understand your target audience(s), take time to build and refine a persona to challenge your assumptions. On a scale of 1 – 10, how well do you really understand the person you are marketing to? Anything lower than an 8 is not good enough. Whoever understands the target audience the best, wins.

Hold a marketing sales summit to talk about customers and align priorities. Talk to sales reps to find out who they are talking to and what conversations they are having. Too many marketers spend their whole career never talking to an actual customer. Team up with sales to bridge the gap.

"Plans are nothing. Planning is everything." This quote by Dwight Eisenhower, U.S. General and President, tells it like it is. Pursuing an annual business or marketing plan is only as relevant as the cross-functional dialog it inspires. Plans are static documents that gather dust, but planning is the ongoing, effective interchange that challenges our perceptions and priorities in order to focus our marketing efforts.

Approach marketing like you are playing a game of chess. Take the time to look two or three moves ahead. What happens after you launch a new product? How will the competition likely respond? What messages will you communicate during the launch as well as post-launch? How can you nurture a meaningful dialog with prospects throughout the year so you can guide them quickly through (or out of) the sales funnel?

Take 30 minutes to craft a Marketing Blueprint that visually links your activities and offers together in a meaningful, logical way. Marketing blueprints are the newest tool in a marketer's arsenal. Learn what they are and how to use them.

Hire a marketing operations expert if you aren't sure where to start. Seasoned marketing operations experts can help you quickly assess the quality of your team and their skills, the caliber of any current planning templates and documents, and the effectiveness of any existing (formal or informal) processes. Their focused recommendations can help you establish an effective planning process with confidence so you can get ahead of your annual planning curve.

"Marketing is not an event. It's a process." I like this quote from Jay Conrad Levinson, father of "guerilla marketing," because it challenges the notion that if we suspend marketing activities and assume a "wait it out" strategy until economic times improve, we'll somehow survive. Avoid this temptation! While marketing budgets will be tighter and our ability to execute will be curtailed, prospects and customers will still have needs. If they forget who we are, how can we ever hope to sell to them? The real issue is to separate the wasteful ineffective marketing tactics from the high-ROI engagement tactics that are worth continued investment. The good news is that it is possible to determine which half of your marketing investment is the half you need to keep.

Instead of starting the year with a pre-defined list of marketing projects, use the persona exercise and the marketing blueprint exercises described above. The most effective marketing activities and offers will become immediately apparent and will flow out of these exercises. And because the activities and offers will now be directly linked to a marketing blueprint, they will be easier to prioritize and defend internally.

The act of marketing is a cross-functional team sport. Although we have the word "marketing" on our business cards, the fact is that everyone from sales to customer support plays a role in the successful marketing of a company. The most effective marketing blueprints are developed by cross-functional team players working together. Use these exercises to build camaraderie, gain buy-in, and energize the team.

Stick to the marketing blueprint, but be willing to make changes. Life never proceeds according to plan. As you monitor the success of any marketing campaign or program, be ready to change messages and offers in order to optimize your campaigns and programs.

Reshaping marketing

The truth is that this financial crisis will cause many enterprises and consumers to delay spending. It's already happening. As such, many of us will see our marketing budgets and staff shrink. Ironically, the critical importance of the marketing role will only increase as companies strive to maximize lead conversion rates while demanding higher ROI for their decreasing marketing investment. This will put marketers in the hot seat, but we'll have a new opportunity to show leadership to guide our companies through the financial storm.

The companies left standing at the end of 2009 and 2010 will be the ones that have invested in their marketing teams to teach them how to become better marketers.

For more information on awareness and lead generation programs, please visit my blog, *Marketing Campaign Development*, or follow me on Twitter.

Mike Gospe leads KickStart Alliance's marketing operations practice where he conducts team-based "practical application working sessions" to improve the effectiveness of lead generation campaigns and product launches. His fun, practical approach and roll-up-his-sleeves attitude energizes teams, helping them to get "real work done" while guiding them to the next level of excellence. Mike is the author of the book, *Marketing Campaign Development* (available on Amazon.com), and his methodology is being used by San Francisco State University's College of Extended Learning course: "Essentials of Integrated Marketing"

www.kickstartall.com

Mike reminds us to keep marketing and to market with better strategies.

Keep learning and you'll expand your capabilities – and matching opportunities arise.

Principle:

Be coachable and you'll rise to heights you've never dreamed.

Are you really coachable? Where might you need some flexibility? What good outcomes would you gain if you showed some flexibility?

13

Encourage Help

To save your business, it is crucial to create a community that wants you to succeed.

First, a quick review of the 5 Rs:

1. Reconnect Enthusiasm (your passion is the starting point)

2. Reward Them (be sure people are rewarded for giving you referrals)

3. Receive Praise (praise any customer who gives you a helpful idea or referral)

4. Repeat Updates (show your progress through an e-newsletter or other sources)

5. Realize Mutual Benefits (team up with other business people to enhance your publicity efforts)

Make it easy and fun for others to help you.

TOM MARCOUX

It's fun to help someone who has already helped you. This is in line with the Law of Reciprocity. If you help someone, then that person wants to return the favor and act in a reciprocal manner. So help others and start the flow of cooperation and giving.

Make sure also that anyone who has offered you an idea feels appreciated. Do not dismiss an idea because it seems unusual. Thank the person offering the idea. I often say, "Thanks. I'll ponder that." Frequently, I have found that a slight adjustment can make an unusual idea work well.

For example, I felt frustrated when I wasn't able to quickly schedule a recording session for a new audio program. But the next day, a team member suggested that we change the subtitle from "How to Raise Your Spirits" to "How to Feed Your Soul." This revision tied in well with the main title, and the program turned out even better than I had imagined. That's an example of a slight adjustment which arrives when we're open to receiving help.

No matter how hard it gets, you make it easier when you keep an upbeat attitude around the people who are supporting you. It's best to pour out your heartfelt pain with a counselor and not with customers or co-workers. Memorize empowering phases to help keep your chin up.

> *Hope is the companion of power, and mother of success;*
> *for who so hopes strongly has within him the gift of*
> *miracles.*

SAMUEL SMILES

Without hope, we cannot take one step forward to making dreams come true. If you don't hope that someone will eventually answer your voicemail, you may not even place the call.

Instead, devise a plan that includes hope. Consider this idea: A saleswoman starts with a plan to contact 20 people. She writes out the word No 20 times and the word Yes once. Each time she hears No, she crosses off one No on her list. She knows that she is one step closer to hearing the golden Yes.

If contacting 20 people on her sales call list doesn't work, she then needs to change something. The saleswoman must change her list or change the people she aims to target. It is reported that it took 141 rejections before authors Jack Canfield and Mark Victor Hansen found a receptive publisher for their book *Chicken Soup for the Soul*. Their success turned into a series of more than 160 books with over 100 million copies in print in 54 languages.

By the way, Jack and Mark asked for help. They consulted with successful authors like M. Scott Peck, who wrote *The Road Not Traveled*. They asked how to make their book a bestseller. Scott Peck said to give radio and other media interviews every day for several years.

Now Paul Gillin will introduce us to the process of "friending" so that we can use social networks to build a circle of friends and business colleagues for mutual benefit.

The Magic of Social Networks

Paul Gillin

Social networks are relationship managers for the 21st-century. They're free, easy to use and enormously effective at coordinating far-flung networks of friends and contacts. In my work, I frequently educate business people on how to make the most of social networks. Here's a condensed version of the advice I give.

Tried and true concept

Social networks are really an updated version of the oldest form of human interaction: the campfire. Online communities have been around since the earliest days of the Internet in newsgroups and private groups like Compuserve and The Well. What's different today is the concept of "profiles" and "friends." These are powerful tools to create and sustain relationships.

The profile is your home base. It not only contains personal information about you, but it also keeps track of your activity within the community. This is important, because as you accumulate friends, join groups and help other members, all of those activities and relationships are captured in your profile. The more you contribute, the more valuable you are to the community and the more your personal status grows.

"Friending" is the process of sharing personal information with others. When you friend someone, you exchange glimpses into each other's lives, much as we create and nurture real-life friendships. Friend relationships are very strong, whether real or electronic. The chance to build and solidify relationships with our friends is one of the greatest appeals of social networks.

There's also great utility in these relationships. Social networks are great contact managers. Instead of maintaining our own address books, it's easy to let the network keep track of where people are, what companies they work for, who they're dating, etc. They also make it easy for us to capture fleeting relationships. Once we friend someone we've met at a conference or football game, we never need to lose touch with that person again.

Groups are a natural outgrowth of profiles and friends. Social networks keep track of information that can be used to find other people with whom we share common interests. The advantage of starting a group on Facebook, for example, is that Facebook already has information about a vast community of people. As a group organizer, you can take advantage of this information to quickly grow their membership without starting from the ground up.

Getting LinkedIn

Facebook is the number one social network for after-hours fun. In contrast, LinkedIn is for business professionals. It's a buttoned-down, no-nonsense business destination with a two-color, text-heavy design that almost screams "Boring!"

LinkedIn is anything but boring, however. Its value as a way to establish and further business relationships is unparalleled, thanks to the unique services it offers. If you signed up long ago and forgot about it, I recommend you take another look.

Like any social network, LinkedIn has personal profiles, groups, and the concept of "friends," which it calls "connections." Its most distinctive feature is based on these connections: a six-degrees-of-separation structure that enables members to connect to people they don't necessarily know through intermediaries within their trusted circle. It's the online equivalent of arranging an introduction.

Even if you don't use connections to reach out to others, there are some cool LinkedIn features that take advantage of this unique concept.

One is Answers, a section where members can post their questions about nearly anything to a select group of connections or to the entire membership. Answers is a great way to get questions resolved quickly, but it's also a means to expose your skills. Believe it or not, some people answer more than 200 questions a week on LinkedIn. One reason for their generosity: the site enables members to rate the quality of responses and showcases the most prolific contributors in a Hall of Fame section (the all-time leader has answered an incredible 14,000 questions).

LinkedIn is also unparalleled in its database of company information, but it takes a bottoms-up approach, focusing not on corporate leadership but rather on individual employees. If you need to find a specific person within a company or just check out a potential partner or employer, you can go in through the back door by consulting current employees. LinkedIn will tell you if you have a direct or second-degree connection to the people you seek.

Job listings go beyond the standard titles and description to provide contact information for people within the companies that advertise opportunities. If a job interests you, you can click through to find out who you know at the company and then contact that person for insight or a referral.

LinkedIn also excels at search engine performance. Its public profiles do so well on Google that they frequently outrank personal websites in search results. This alone is enough reason to set up your personal profile. It's a great way to get visibility for your skills and show off your expertise.

Given all this career-boosting utility, it's not surprising that traffic to LinkedIn reportedly doubled in the weeks following the 2008 stock market meltdown. Members can brush up their personal profiles by swapping recommendations with others, updating their qualifications and showcasing their expertise through integrated applications. Unlike Facebook, LinkedIn keeps a tight rein on the applications it chooses to support, limiting the current selection to just 10 business-focused services.

While LinkedIn doesn't have nearly the membership numbers of Facebook, its business focus is an advantage. The CEO was recently quoted saying that the demographics of LinkedIn members are better than those of *Wall Street Journal* subscribers. In troubled times, that's a very good place to be.

Tips for success

Here are a few tips for making the most of your LinkedIn profile:

- Pay careful attention to creating a thorough and professional history of your job experiences. Watch your spelling and grammar. This is your public face to the world and you want to look your best.

- Speaking of looking your best, choose a professional photograph to go with your profile.

- Be sure your description accurately reflects your skills and interests. This is the snapshot that people will see most often.

- Choose connections carefully. When people ask to connect to you, check their profiles to be sure you know them. Others will try to reach you through your connections and you want to be sure you can rely on those people to pass along the request.

- Ask for recommendations. When someone is nice enough to write a recommendation for you, offer the same in return.

- Join a few groups, but not too many. Your selection of groups provides insight on your interests. Be sure to choose groups that match interests you've expressed.

- List honors and awards. Take advantage of every opportunity LinkedIn offers you to show off your achievements.

- Add your blog to your profile. It's easy to automatically include entries. Just be sure the topics are professional in nature.

- Take advantage of LinkedIn applications, such as SlideShare Amazon reading lists and TripIt travel. These present further opportunities to connect with like-minded people.

- Include your LinkedIn profile in your e-mail signature.

Paul Gillin is the author of *The New Influencers* and *Secrets of Social Media Marketing*.

Paul Gillin Communications
Content Strategies for Social Media
4 Thurber St., Framingham, MA 01702
508-202-9807 office, 781-929-6754 mobile
email: paul@gillin.com, web: gillin.com
Twitter: pgillin, LinkedIn: paulgillin

Paul coaches us to devote appropriate time to our LinkedIn profile which can serve as a springboard to more opportunities. Begin relationships by finding ways to be helpful – perhaps with a link to an appropriate article.

Don't rush the friendship. Stay in contact and make phone calls "Just to catch up" and ask, "How can I be supportive of what you're doing." Finally, when you ask for a *small* favor like the answer to "where would I find information about how to get into a new industry?" be sure to make it simple and easy for someone to help you.

Principle:

Make it easy and fun for others to help you.

Power Questions:

Who can help you? How can you make it fun and easy for someone to help you? How can you report on the actions you take with every suggestion?

Part IV

14

How to Get a Job in an Economic Crisis

What if you knew how to respond to the toughest questions in a job interview?

In recent years, it has been be my honor to train graduate students and clients in powerful interviewing skills. I get calls and e-mails that exclaim, "I got the job!" That's music to my ears.

The truth no one will tell you – You must have an extraordinary personal brand to get a job during an economic crisis. Your personal brand is your answer to the question: What are you best known for?

Your answer is a shortcut to trust.

How do you relay this information in an interview?

- You show that you provide value.

- You say something memorable.

- You demonstrate confidence.

- You provide the words that the interviewer will use to describe you to other people in the company.

To develop your extraordinary personal brand, learn to use the B.R.A.N.D. process:

B – Bring your best stories

R – Reveal overcoming a weakness

A – Announce your strengths

N – Notice your interviewer

D – Devote yourself to the job

Let's take our best step forward …

15

Bring Your Best Stories

*Opportunity dances with those
already on the dance floor.*

H. JACKSON BROWN, JR.

What's the best way to be offered the job you're interviewing for? You bring out your best stories. An old sales refrain is "Stories sell; facts just tell."

The problem is that many people feel they merely need to express the facts or just refer to the details on their résumé.

It's not real until you tell a story.

TOM MARCOUX

The interviewer must actually see the value you provide. The way to do that is with a story.

How do you tell a story in a powerful way? When I trained people at Experience Unlimited (connected to the California

Employment Development Department), I noticed that other trainers emphasized the P.S.R. pattern, which stands for Problem, Solution, Result. This is a good start, but an important element is missing: E for emotion!

Here is an example of telling a story that uses P.S.R.E:

> *I was hired to be a unit production manager for a feature film. The screenplay called for a bus. But the budget was strained. We needed a public place so that the romantic leads could meet by happenstance. A bus would require rental fees, hiring an off-duty police officer, hiring a bunch of extras, feeding everyone, and getting costly permits. I suggested the solution of having the two people meet in an elevator. Then I suggested that we could build an inexpensive elevator set in a living room using two by fours. The face of the producer lit up with relief. She told me, "Joe, I can always count on you to solve a problem with creativity and to guard the budget. Good work."*

The E for emotion comes from the comment from the happy producer. The story presents the problem, some suspense, and the triumphant and happy ending. It also inspires good feelings in the interviewer because she has experienced the value the storyteller brought to a situation.

Here is another example of P.S.R.E:

> *A client came to our advertising firm and said that she needed a project done in three days. Usually, such a full campaign takes two weeks. I asked her careful questions, and I worked like a detective to see if any parts of the campaign could be dropped to get her*

project done in time. I helped her make the hard decisions. Our team pulled together and we got the work done in three days. The client told me, "Mary, I can always count on you to make me look good!"

Authors David Barron and Danek Kaus share some startling ideas and methods that may make you truly stand out in a job interview.

Use Hypnosis to Get that Job

David R. Barron & Danek S. Kaus

What if there were a way to hypnotize HR people into hiring you? Although it sounds like the stuff of movies, you really can influence the job interviewers' subconscious mind to hire you, or at least move your résumé to the top of the stack. How do you do this? There are three steps. You begin by creating instant rapport with the HR person. Then you learn what is important to them on a deep emotional level. Finally, you use this information to help them decide who the best candidate is. That's you, of course. So let's begin.

Rapport

With rapport, everything is possible. Without it, nothing is possible. So what is rapport? It is a feeling of being in sync with another person. Usually people try to create rapport by throwing spaghetti on the wall to see what sticks. They talk about sports, a hit TV show or the weather, hoping to find something in common.

This is hit or miss. Although we all seek some form of kinship, many HR people feel they should not have rapport with the people they interview. That doesn't matter. You will create rapport without them knowing it. You can reliably create rapport by physically acting like the HR person. If she leans to the left side of her chair and crosses her arms, you lean to the right side of your chair and cross you arms. This is called mirroring. You can also lean to the left side of your chair and cross your arms. This called matching. Either way, mirroring and matching are quick ways to create rapport, because on a subconscious level, she's thinking: he's just like me. And people respond positively to others who are like them.

You can also create rapport by matching someone's way of speaking. If he machine guns words like a fast-talking New Yorker, you do the same. If he speaks more slowly and softly, slow down and soften your voice. A word of warning: when someone shifts their body position or changes they way they speak, wait four to five seconds and then gradually change. If you mirror and match too quickly, you will appear to be mocking the other person, which could be offensive.

Values

Despite what we like to tell ourselves, we do things for emotional reasons, not logical ones. Our values move us through the world. In a work context, one HR person may value the sense of doing a good job while another simply wants to get the boss off his back. Uncovering and reflecting back someone's deepest values (in a work context) will make them want to hire you. For them to do otherwise would be to go against the very fiber of their being.

Info Quest

Once the formal part of the interview is concluded, the HR person will usually ask you if you have any questions. This is the point at which you mine for information. Will she make the decision herself or pass on a recommendation? Does she have to interview a specific number of applicants or can she stop when she feels she has found the right person? This information is critical because you are going to feed it back to her later on.

The next step will only work if you have established rapport. You can test rapport by purposely breaking it. Shift your body to another position, if she does the same, you've established rapport. If she doesn't shift to match you, go back to the former position and try to mirror and match her more exactly. You can refine the process by matching such things as accents or the rhythm of someone's speech, the highs and lows.

One of the most powerful ways to create rapport is to breath at the same rate as the other person. Once you have tweaked your techniques, test rapport again. Remember, make these changes gradually. Once you know you have rapport, you can take the conversation to a higher, and more intimate level. You want to learn the HR person's values. You might say something to the effect of: "I'm curious. I'm sure you have interviewed a lot of very qualified people and had times when you knew this person was right for the job. You may have been sitting in this very chair. When you find this person and think this person, not that person, what is important to you about that?"

It is critical to ask what is important, not why is that important. If you ask someone why they can get defensive and then decide to come up with lots of reasons why. You don't want that. So back to your question. A very typical response will probably have to do with the company line. He may say they want the most experienced candidate or the one who fits their culture. Whatever he says, your job is to listen very attentively and agree with him. You might say, I absolutely agree that (company line) is important and what I'm wondering is, when you are able to pick this person who is right for the job, what does that give you? You have started to take the HR person away from the company line and are moving toward communication on a more personal level.

At this point, the interviewer might say something such as, finding the right person gives me a sense of satisfaction. Or, it gets the boss off my back. Regardless of what he says, you agree with him and acknowledge it and in some way try to repeat and reemphasize what he just said. You might say, "I understand how important it is to have a sense of satisfaction (or boss off your back, etc.) What would that give you that's even more important?"

You are now probably going to a much higher value of the HR person. He might respond that he will have a feeling of personal satisfaction or a sense of relief. Once again, feed back the response, and ask at least one or two more such questions, learning what each (deeper value) will give the HR person. Somewhere between the third and fifth level of values, you will see a physical change in their demeanor. He may sit back and smile. His face may light up. You have discovered his highest value in hiring someone. You have just struck gold. It's time to demonstrate how you, and you alone, will fulfill that value.

Closing the Deal

Let's say that an HR exec has revealed that her highest value is a sense of contributing to the organization. This would be a great time to hand her your résumé as you say something such as, "What I'd like you to think about is contributing to the organization and how much I can contribute to it also." Another step you can take to seal the deal is to inoculate the exec from thinking that anyone else could possibly qualify for the position. You might say: "I was taking to a friend of mine who hires people for jobs that are similar to the openings you have and he was telling me that when you find someone that really does demonstrate an ability to contribute, he really does stick in your mind and everyone else's. Other applicants may seem to say the right things. They may try in vain to impress you, but I know that you are not going to be impressed by that. You know who the right person for the job is."

You can also add your understanding of the process and reaffirm it. "I realize that you have to interview 25 applicants before you make your decision. But I think you already know that it is now just a formality that you must go through." Or, "I realize that you are required to choose five candidates to pass on to your boss. I think we both know which résumé will go on top. Don't we? It's someone who will contribute in a meaningful way." It will be almost impossible for the HR exec to seriously recommend anyone else.

These techniques are not a substitute for being genuinely qualified for the job. And you must polish your other interview skills. Those you can find in any good job search book. But if you add in rapport, learning someone's values and then feeding those values back to them, you can have a powerful impact on the HR exec.

Finally, you must practice these skills before attempting to use them during an interview. Try them out on people you know. Try them out on people you don't know. Once you feel that you have mastered these techniques, you can walk into the interview knowing who's really in charge. You can get that job, or have your résumé magically move to the top.

Danek S. Kaus, author of *You Can Be Famous: Insider Secrets to Getting Free Publicity.* This extract was adapted from the book, *Power Persuasion: Using Hypnotic Influence to Win in Life, Love and Business,* by David R. Barron and Danek S. Kaus

yourpowerpublicity.com, smallbusinessbucks.com, jointventure4you.com

The hypnotic techniques described by Danek Kaus and David Barron can be effective when you make sure to accomplish two crucial elements: (1) fully believe in yourself, and (2) rehearse thoroughly. If you wish to pursue hypnotic job interviewing techniques, please realize that they are as volatile as fire. You could really cook with these techniques or, without proper caution, you could be burned. I invite you to move forward carefully. Start from a solid base of personal competence that relays your confidence.

In this section, I talked about bringing your best stories to the interview. Realize that rehearsal is crucial. It is truly how you tell your story that makes you influential.

Principle:

It's not real until you tell a story.

Power Questions:

Using P.S.R.E., what are three stories you can tell to help you in a job interview? Which three friends or family members would be a good match to help you rehearse and choose your stories?

16

Reveal Overcoming a Weakness

What is the toughest question to answer in a job interview? Most people would choose, "What is one of your weaknesses?"

For many people, this feels like a no-win question. If you tell a significant weakness, no one will want to hire you. By the way, don't mention your tendency to be late or procrastinate. These weaknesses kill your prospects for being hired.

Any interviewer can also see through a clever attempt to present a weakness as a hidden strength.

> *Failure is simply the opportunity to begin again, this time more intelligently.*
>
> HENRY FORD

We find the solution to the "weakness" question in Henry Ford's comment. Show the interviewer how you overcame the weakness and how you began again more intelligently.

Here's an example of how to reply to that difficult question:

> "I've given this a lot of thought. Some time ago I had trouble prioritizing my work. So I went to a time management workshop. I learned about the 80/20 rule, which says that 20% of what I do in a day leads to 80% of the best results. So now, as a reminder to plan my day more effectively, I have a Post-It note in my day planner and also a message on my cell phone screen that reads 80/20."

Your answer to the weakness question needs to explain how you made significant progress to overcome a failing, and how you make diligent effort every day to stay on top of the problem.

Next, share details of what you love about your work. Add a closing sentence like: "Now that I use the 80/20 rule, I'm confident that I'm doing the most important tasks each day. That feels great."

Principle:

Trustworthy people reveal to job interviewers how they are learning and getting better.

Power Questions:

What are three stories you use to answer the "what is your weakness" question? How can you effectively show that you overcame a failing? Which friends do you trust to give you good feedback when you rehearse?

17

Announce Your Strengths

When I say announce, I mean carefully blow your own horn. That is, you need to effectively express your strengths as a team member and skilled professional. You announce or express the value you bring to a company during a job interview.

A job interview is no time to be overly modest. The interviewer, particularly if she is the hiring manager, wants someone to solve her problems. You need to confidently express your expertise and experience. I emphasize with audiences: No one will hear your music if you don't blow your own horn.

As mentioned previously, you can tell a story. This is a gentle way to announce your virtues. A story gets under the radar and can avoid creating resistance. Tell a story about how you helped clients, a supervisor or a work-team.

The best stories end with a quote from a happy client, supervisor or co-worker that praises your performance.

How you announce or express your story is truly important. Craig Harrison shows us how to rev up our positive energy so that we make a terrific impression.

Get Psyched for Success!

Psych up … cool down … chill out & ace your interviews – "self-talk" can prop you up prior to your job interview

Craig Harrison

Coaches psych up their teams before a big game.

Army bands traditionally played march music to incite their troops before battle.

Pilots use an extensive pre-flight checklist to prepare for each flight.

What do you do before your big job interview?

How are you preparing and motivating yourself?

How are you fortifying yourself for success?

Since interviewing is all about confidence, you should build yours before your interview begins. Whether you psych yourself up, cool yourself down or otherwise optimize yourself, think peak performance before you walk into your next interview.

PSYCH UP

The pep talk

Why not give yourself a pep talk to remind yourself how talented, experienced and ready you are for your next job?

Psychologists have long known the importance of self-talk in motivating star athletes, actors and musicians to excel. Why not apply these same techniques that high performers use to your own activities?

Whether you are in need of a psych up, a cool down or a rev-up before your interview, you can use this pep talk approach to better handle your job interview. Here are some tips for doing so.

Just say "Now!"

Before your next interview, give yourself a pep talk to remind yourself of all you have to offer. Look into the mirror, praise yourself for past successes and buoy yourself with confidence for having reached this point in the interview process. Remind yourself how lucky they will be to get a talent such as yourself. After all, there is nobody else quite like you: your blend of experience, skill, personality and background. You know you can do it. Tell yourself! Then it's easier to tell others.

Cool Down

Just say Om

If you are the type of person who gets too excited before an interview, try this approach to stay calm and focused. Find a quiet place, free of clutter and distractions. Take a few deep breaths. Breathe in deeply through your nose as if you are smelling a rose. Now exhale slowly through your pursed lips as if blowing out a candle. Try to focus just on your breathing. If thoughts enter your mind, recognize them and then let them go, refocusing on your breathing pattern.

A meditative state can help you clear your mind of noise and distractions. By lowering your heart rate through deep breathing, you can quell any nervousness that might normally arise before a stressful event such as a job interview. Just as great athletes adopt tunnel vision to see only their goals prior to a big game, so too can you concentrate on the task at hand: acing your interview!

By sitting quietly for ten minutes before your next interview, you can become more single-minded as you approach your interview. Once you've slowed your breathing down, mentally let go of the various nagging matters that clutter the mind and bring us all down. You are on the precipice of a new job. Your whole life can benefit from successfully handling this interview. Build your confidence from within. Know in your heart that you are ready, willing and able to accept this next challenge. Now seize the moment!

RALLY TIME

Start me up!

Some people's pep talk more resembles a spirit rally. Yours can too. You may wish to "rev your engines" to prepare for your interview. In that case, pump yourself up like a prizefighter before the next bout. Play some inspirational music to pump up your heartbeat. Anthems abound. Pick yours: For a first interview: "Start Me Up" by the Rolling Stones gets some candidates in gear. For a second interview, McFadden and Whitehead's "Ain't No Stoppin' Us Now" is a winner. Others prefer Queen's "We are the Champions." And for that final interview and its salary negotiations, it's time for Aretha Franklin's "Respect!" Create the soundtrack for your Oscar worthy performance.

WARM ME UP

Let's get physical

Don't presume the interview preparation is primarily a cerebral exercise. There's a physical aspect to successful interviewing too. Schedule some physical activity the day of your interview to stimulate your mind, ameliorate pent up nervousness, and speed up your metabolism. You actually sharpen your mind through physical activity. The exertion will help your brain fire in more creative ways once you've exercised. Don't forget to hydrate before and after exercising. Water, the forgotten nutrient, is an important component in your success program.

Visualizing success

Whether you psych up through music, jogging, power lifting or use meditation to prepare for your interview, visualize success. What does it look like? What does it feel like? See yourself answering questions confidently, showcasing your skill set and experience, and exuding a confident demeanor. And project a clear focus. "If you don't know what you have going for yourself, don't expect your prospective employer to figure it out. Do your homework first. Know what you are bringing to the table before you expect something in return." So says Dr. Alan Zimmerman of Prior Lake, MN. Dr. Zimmerman works with a variety of clients on performance improvement and positive work relationships. (1-800-621-7881)

ZONE ALONE

Get into the success zone

"The zone is that state of mind that puts us into performance mode – where everything flows effortlessly, we have laser focus, we are relaxed, confident and our performance seems to just happen, with no thinking or direction on our part. Anything you can do to help you shift focus into the zone should be part of your psych-up rituals." These words of wisdom come from Bill Cole, MS, MA, founder and CEO of ProCoach Systems, a Silicon Valley firm dedicated to helping organizations reach peak performance solutions through their people.

Cole recommends the creation of a routine for optimal success: "Psyching up is all about having a ritual or routine. It's about making the transition from normal focus to laser focus for your performance during the interview." Cole feels the ritual serves as a funnel to get you into the zone: "Your ritual is really a series of tasks you complete in a short time frame that helps you relax, tune-out unwanted thoughts, feelings and images and instead replaces them with the internal mental climate that is most conducive to a great performance." Thus the ritual is a precursor to success.

Fly right

You know best what you need before an interview. Whether your charge is to get fired up, chill out, or otherwise focus your energy, create a pre-interview program to position you for success. Just as pilots have a pre-flight routine, so too should you strive for a consistent preparation before your next big interview. Not only will you be cleared for takeoff, you'll soar to new heights. Up, Up and Away!

> Speaker, trainer and frequent flier Craig Harrison's routine includes receiving a pep talk from his number one fan, his Mom, before each big engagement.

> Craig can be reached at www.ExpressionsOfExcellence.com, or Craig@ExpressionsOfExcellence.com, or (510) 547-0664.

Craig Harrison's comments remind us to use a whole menu of methods to "get ready for the game." You need lots of positive energy to perform at your best in a job interview.

If opportunity doesn't knock, build a door.

MILTON BERLE

When you confidently express your skills, it's like you're building a new door. This is important because researchers report that hiring managers will often create a new job when an exceptional interviewee demonstrates multiple talents and skills. In essence, this interviewee has built a new door for opportunity.

Part of building that new door is to express your enthusiasm for the job. Whoever wants the job more usually gets it. That's because everyone who is interviewed is qualified. So your enthusiasm is that extra spark that makes you stand out.

Principle:

No one will hear your music if you don't blow your own horn.

Power Question:

How can you add a quote from a happy client, supervisor or co-worker to the end of the stories you tell to the job interviewer?

18

Notice Your Interviewer

What one technique can help you stand out from other job applicants?

The truth no one will tell you: Ask questions of the job interviewer and then take notice of how the person answers. You can then figure out how to cement the new relationship with the interviewer.

Ask something like: In order for you to feel that someone is an ideal candidate for this position, what has to happen?

Here are specific reasons for this question to be phrased in this manner. You ask "what has to happen" so that you can get the interviewer to reveal the next steps. Perhaps, she responds: "I'll need to hear from your happy clients" or "I'd need to see further items of your past work." Now you and the interviewer have a metaphorical road map.

You have also received special information. Each person takes in information in a preferred way. When someone says "I'll need to hear," that indicates she likes to hear information to make a decision. She has an auditory preferred mode of taking in information. Other people say, "I need to see" and that is a visual preference. Finally, when someone says, "You'll need to interview with the team to see if we're comfortable about …," that indicates a kinesthetic preference. In summary, there are three preferred modes: auditory, visual and kinesthetic.

If you're talking with a hiring manager, respond to her requirements in a supportive way. That is, pay close attention and notice if you can start working with the manager as if you were already hired.

Offer ideas. In order to do that, do research on the company and its key employees before your interview. Do a Google search to find relevant articles on the Internet.

When you offer ideas, you are helping the manager to see other possibilities. Get over any fear that you're giving away your special thoughts. Trust yourself to come up with more and more valuable ideas. It is essential that you stand out in such a competitive marketplace.

You'll need to tread lightly. Some interviewers may take offense at someone with too many suggestions for their company.

A person in one of my audiences said, "Doesn't that take guts?" While replying, I remembered a number of ideas Dr. Tony Alessandra conveys about getting into a positive frame of mind before the interview. Here are Dr. Tony's comments:

Skills for Job Interviews

Dr. Tony Alessandra

1. **How to make friends in five seconds:**

We accomplish much more when we learn to focus on others. There's an old story of a young lady who was taken to dinner one evening by William Gladstone, and the following evening by Benjamin Disraeli, both eminent British statesmen in the late nineteenth century. "When I left the dining room after sitting next to Mr. Gladstone, I thought he was the cleverest man in England," she said. "But after sitting next to Mr. Disraeli, I thought I was the cleverest woman in England."

Disraeli obviously had a knack for making the other person the center of his universe, if only for the evening. If you practice attentiveness to others, you'll find it does wonders for both of you. They'll enjoy it; you'll enjoy it. And together you'll accomplish much more.

Make a conscious effort to think of others' wants and needs before your own. Start training your mind not to focus automatically on what separates you from the other person. Rather, figure out what unites you, and how you can build upon that base. Soon such empathy will become a habit - a very good habit that will improve all your relationships immeasurably!

2. How to achieve a positive state of mind

You are what you think! Occasionally we hear stories of people who struggle against great odds, prove the naysayers wrong, and achieve the nearly impossible. They turn around a defunct company; they stop a highway from going through virgin land; they beat the odds on terminal cancer.

In order to do extraordinary things, these people - and you! - don't need to be superhuman; you just need some positive tools to get you through rough times. You need a positive philosophy to give yourself direction and an understanding of what you can do yourself and when you need help from others. Dr. Norman Vincent Peale's book, *The Power of Positive Thinking*, was published over 50 years ago and it continues to sell well because it contains such a universal truth: the attitudes we hold help shape the reality we experience.

Having a positive attitude isn't something you just tack on to your old personality. It comes from deep within you; it has to or it would get wiped out with the first sign of a countervailing negative force. But you also have to have some other source of positive energy outside yourself that keeps you going. Most probably it is other people you can rely on for support, who are also positive about your ability to succeed. Perhaps you are also motivated by the example of some historical or spiritual figure. (Martin Luther King was inspired by Gandhi … who in turn was inspired by Thoreau.)

The point is, you don't do it alone - a positive state of mind comes from within and without. It requires that you embed yourself in a context of positiveness - to tap sources beyond yourself. If this trait isn't already in your repertoire, then begin here. The trait of positiveness is so attractive, other people will be drawn to you.

3. Confidence comes from a series of small victories

Confidence in yourself gets built up gradually, one success at a time. You can fake confidence, and you may need to at first, but real self-confidence comes from a history of small victories and accomplishments that add up to a sense that you can handle yourself well in most every situation. In his many books on self-esteem, Dr. Nathaniel Branden agrees as much. For him, self-confidence is knowing that you have the wherewithal to function reasonably well in the world. In other words, you can't be confident if you're fearful or easily intimidated.

Here's an exercise: I suggest you take an inventory of the major accomplishments you've achieved over the past few years. Then remind yourself of the minor ones too. What about the computer course you completed? Have you built anything that's still standing? What about those kids you're raising? That's an accomplishment! Don't be modest. Tell the truth about how hard you worked, what sacrifices you've made. If you can't think of any, then begin by congratulating yourself for living as long as you have. Sheer survival is an accomplishment these days! What's unique about you? What skills do you bring to an organization or project that you can count on?

Seriously, it pays to take the time to know your strengths and appreciate them. That's the only path to developing self-confidence.

4. How to make powerful first impressions

People are way more critical than you think - don't give them fuel for the fire! Back in the early 70's, recently accredited with my MBA and happily engaged in my first college teaching position, a friend asked me what my long-term career goal was. When I answered that I would like to eventually become the president of a large university, my friend chuckled and replied, "Tony, there's no way!" I took offense at this and demanded to know why he would react that way. He said, "Don't misunderstand me, Tony. You're certainly intelligent and ambitious enough. But can you imagine yourself addressing the student body with your Brooklyn accent?" I realized that he was right. My accent was so heavy (lots of 'dees' and 'dose') that it would have had a negative impact on my credibility and my career. I resolved to change that aspect of myself and eventually became a professional speaker.

The old adage is true: "First impressions are lasting impressions." But if you're like most people, you probably can't see the first impressions you're making. In that case, here's some simple advice you can take from the story above: Take the risk of asking one or more of your close friends if you are guilty of any of the following image deficiencies below. If so, first thank your friends for their honesty, and then immediately do something to correct them! Try creating an impression you want to last.

Common first-impression killers & solutions

A heavy accent: The Brooklyn accent is just one of many ... Bostonians and Southerners beware!!! Some people read this as a sign of intellectual inferiority; others just won't understand what you're saying. Consult a speech coach if you must, but don't let this habit get in your way!

A limp handshake: For a man, a sign of weakness ... for a woman, a sign that she lacks confidence! Don't squeeze the hand or hold it like a dead mouse, just give it a firm grip, a couple of pumps, and let go. Along with making consistent eye contact, this is one of the easiest first-impression blunders to correct!

Sloppy grooming (*long hair, sideburns, three-day stubble, bad makeup job, un-tucked shirt or blouse, unpolished shoes*):   Says to hiring manager: "Can't be left alone for a second with prospective clients" - also a sign of intellectual sloppiness!

Poor hygiene (*foul body odor, dirty fingernails, chronic bad breath*):   One of those things you want to ask your most trusted best friend about because (1) chances are, you can't notice it, and (2) some people won't want to hurt your feelings.

Weak vocabulary: Beside "like" "ah," and "um" try to avoid weak words ("awesome," "cool," and "super") that make you sound like you just graduated from Sweet Valley High.

Poor posture: People notice the way you enter a room, the way you carry yourself. Take a few deep breaths to collect yourself. Stand tall and hold your head up high. Walk with purpose and direction.

Ill-fitting clothing: Even if your body is in perfect shape, the clothes you wear can make you look ridiculous if they are too big and bulky, or one size too small and reveal too much (stomach, hairy shins). Nothing screams "success" like well-tailored suits … do yourself a favor and make a serious investment in clothes that fit!

5. **How to keep up your self-motivation**

While at times success is sufficient to serve as an incentive; often, additional incentives may be required to create self-motivation. Set up a reward system that is directly linked to goals and accomplishments. Take time to recognize the progress you have made and to identify the next steps that you should take. Remain on task and avoid procrastination; momentum builds motivation.

Inform friends, family, and associates of your plans and ask them to hold you accountable. Train yourself to be positive in your thoughts and actions.

> Dr. Tony Alessandra has a street-wise, college-smart perspective on business, having been raised in the housing projects of NYC and eventually realizing success as a graduate professor of marketing, entrepreneur, business author, and hall-of-fame keynote speaker. He earned a BBA from the Univ. of Notre Dame, an MBA from the Univ. of Connecticut and his PhD in marketing from Georgia State University. In addition to being president of Assessment Business Center, a company that offers online 360° assessments, Tony is chairman of BrainX.com a company that created the first Online Learning Mastery System™. He is also a founding partner in The Cyrano Group and Platinum Rule Group – companies which have successfully combined cutting-edge technology and proven psychology to give salespeople the ability to build and maintain positive relationships with hundreds of clients and prospects. Dr. Alessandra is a prolific author with 18 books translated into 49 foreign language editions, including the newly revised, best-selling *The New Art of Managing People*. He is featured in over 50 audio/video programs and films, including *Relationship Strategies*. He is also the originator of the internationally recognized behavioral style assessment tool - The Platinum Rule. Dr. Alessandra was inducted into the Speakers Hall of Fame in 1985 and is a member of the Speakers Roundtable, a group of 20 of the world's top professional speakers. Tony's polished style, powerful message, and proven ability as a consummate business strategist consistently earn rave reviews and loyal clients.

> Dr. Tony's Products:
>   www.PlatinumRule.com

> Keynote speeches:
>   Holli Catchpole, (760) 603-8110, Holli@SpeakersOffice.com

---

Dr. Tony Alessandra emphasizes that first impressions count, and that we have many options to improve how we come across.

Don't hesitate. Make a list of things to improve about yourself and get to work. You'll certainly be glad that you took action.

Remember to notice how the interviewer responds to your questions and how he or she emphasizes certain points. When you listen closely and observe with your full attention, you'll discover what the interviewer's priorities are. Then you can align your replies to his or her preferences and values. You'll step closer to the job you desire.

Principle:

Ask questions, listen and reply in a way that's aligned with the interviewer's priorities and values.

Power Question:

Which questions do you feel comfortable asking so that you can discover what the interviewer is truly looking for?

19

Devote Yourself to the Job

The job interviewer asks, "Why do you want this particular job?"

Are you ready for this question to be posed?

> *Your work is to discover your world and then*
> *with all your heart give yourself to it.*
>
> BUDDHA

If you only want the job for the money, then the interviewer will probably pick up on that. Unfortunately, in today's economic climate, the reality is that you may need the job for survival – to pay your mortgage and feed your family. Job interviewers understand this, and may not take points away if you show you're worth it.

The truth no one will tell you: You must find something in the job to which you can devote yourself.

Like so many others, at the beginning of my work life I had a number of survival jobs. I sold pants and Teflon-coated cookware, cleaned toilets and windows, and so much more. I also built Web sites and served as an executive assistant to a vice president and five managers simultaneously. Ugh.

But I always found something to which I could devote myself. I always looked for opportunities to help my supervisor, co-workers, clients or customers.

Wherever you work, find ways to get involved. Perhaps you'll find a project (that won't step on others' toes), and you can volunteer for it. This will later serve you when you recount your success – during a job interview.

> *To write a successful book … Come from your heart,*
> *tell the truth, and write for yourself.*
>
> ALAN COHEN

Work for yourself, too. Work can be fun when you know that you're doing it well. I have observed people who looked bored because they approached their job as "just doing time," like a prisoner. Break out of that! Find a way to serve and be friendly and kind with your co-workers. Be pleasant and your day goes pleasantly – most of the time.

Now it's your turn. In your personal journal, write down ten possible things you could find fulfilling or even fun in the job you're applying for.

> *Drop the idea of making a hit record,*
> *and call in the energy of truth.*
>
> KENNY LOGGINS

As mentioned earlier, the big question is: Why do you want to work here?

Here's a sample answer:

> *Earlier this week, I went into one of your cell phone stores and looked around like a typical shopper. Martin Smith came up to me and greeted me like I was the most important person of his day. I felt welcomed. He helped me learn about the options to upgrade my cell phone. I realized: This store is different. I even asked Martin what he likes best about working here. Part of what he said was, in his store, employees go out of their way to help people have at least one good thing happen in their day. And I thought, I want to be a part of that. I want to be part of a team that's really alive and truly helping people. And that's why I want to work here.*

One of the most important things we can do in life is to devote ourselves to enhancing our relationships. Like anyone, I have made a number of errors in my relationships. I now seek to continuously get better. My thoughts on the matter led to my developing The Empathy Switch, a process that helps us shift into a mode of connection. The Empathy Switch can even help during a job interview. We must remember that the interviewer is another human being who's only doing the best that he or she can.

The Empathy Switch

1. Pause

2. Move your body to connect

3. Ask a question

4. Give a Reflective Reply

Pause

Often we move or think too fast to truly connect with the level of feelings that the other person is expressing. So let the word "pause" chime and flash across the inner screen of your mind. Stop in your tracks.

The truth no one will tell you: Everyone has a metaphorical song playing in their mind – make me feel important. If you do not pause to really listen, then your message is that the person is not really important to you. Be sure to pause.

Move your body to connect

Do something helpful to connect with the other person on her level of energy. If appropriate, sit down. Move your body to mirror hers. That means, without being obvious, cross your legs when the other person crosses her legs. Confucius said, "I do and I understand." Along those lines, researchers have discovered that when we move and mirror another person's body position we begin to understand his or her state of mind.

Make sure also that your heart faces the other person's heart. People feel slighted if we allow our body to be facing away from them. You can remind yourself by silently repeating in your mind, "heart faces heart."

Be sure to move your body to create connection. I have found it valuable to sit down. Sometimes, at home with a family member, I'll sit on the floor while the family member sits on a chair. Then she will feel stronger in the situation and know that I am paying close attention.

Ask a question

Effective listening is not merely keeping your mouth shut. It helps when you demonstrate true interest by asking a gentle question like:

- How did you feel when … ?

- If things would be better, how would you like them to go?

Give a reflective reply

Sometimes I have felt I'm not heard when talking with a family member. My solution was to ask: "What did you hear me say?" I ask that question because of my understanding of communication. You can give the support a speaker craves and may not even know that she is missing.

Provide a Reflective Reply. Be like a pool of clear water and reflect the person's feelings back to them. Say something like:

- That sounds frustrating.

- That's intense. How did you feel when he said that?

- That sounds overwhelming.

Practice the elements of the Empathy Switch and you, like me, will experience more loving relationships. I also notice that my business relationships get stronger as I practice this method.

Rich Fettke's article shows us how to gain the energy we need to use methods like the Empathy Switch. He explains how to create a foundation for a new year of achievement, devotion and fulfillment. We'll feel better and have the energy to do better in our relationships – both business and personal.

What Will This Next Year Be For You?

Rich Fettke

Let's look at how you want the new year to be.

Below are a few questions that I ask my clients (and myself) each year. They help clarify how you want to learn, grow and succeed over the next twelve months. Give yourself permission to take some time over the next week to reflect and record your thoughts. Here we go …

Looking forward at the new year, what do you want the overall theme to be for you? (Here's another way to look at this: One year from today, if they were to make a movie about your life in this new year, what would you want the title to be?)

- What are your top three personal goals for this new year?

- What are your top three professional goals for this new year?

- What one personal quality do you most want to develop in this new year? (For example: patience, boldness, courage, calmness, integrity, humor, etc.)

I recommend that you keep you answers in a place you can read them on a daily basis. That will help you stay aware of the opportunities that can help you move toward your intentions. I wish you the best as you move into this new year with clarity, action and focus.

Keep reaching high!

Rich Fettke has helped thousands of executives, entrepreneurs, and salespeople push their limits and expand their success. He is the author of *Extreme Success* (Simon & Schuster) and the audio programs *FOCUS* and *Momentum*. Rich has been featured in *USA Today*, the *Wall Street Journal*, *Self*, and *Entrepreneur Magazine*. He has also been a guest on every major TV network and on dozens of radio shows including *NPR*, *SPN* and the *Dr. Laura Show*. Rich is past-president of the Professional & Personal Coaches Association and is a former vice president of the International Coach Federation (ICF). He also holds one of the ICF's first Master Certified Coach credentials. Rich has over 20 years experience in business start-ups, management, and training and holds a bachelor's degree in Business Management from Merrimack College in Andover, Massachusetts. He is also a graduate and former instructor of The Coaches Training Institute, the world's largest, non-profit and accredited coach training organization. Rich has competed in the ESPN X-Games and is a record-holding bungee jumper, licensed skydiver, and an experienced rock climber.

www.fettke.com

Rich Fettke's process helps us create a foundation for our new year.

At a recent book signing, a man buying a set of my books asked, "You mentioned meditation. How can I get the most from the process?" For years I have taught Comparative Religion and traveled and participated in spiritual processes. I answered the man with words from my heart and intuition: "Before you meditate, focus on these words, 'Higher Power – or God if you prefer – please guide me with the next expansive action that I will take. May this be for my good and everyone involved.'"

The man asked me to slowly repeat the phrase, and he wrote down each word. To be guided for the good of all involved is a devoted stance toward life. I saw a smile come to his face. Then, he handed me a book to sign.

Principle:

Devotion brings good feelings to you and your listener.

Power Questions:

What can you devote yourself to? What would make you excited about working at a particular company?

20

Part IV: Conclusion

This section has been devoted to guiding you with Recession-Proof Strategies that will help you feed your soul, save a business, or get a job in an economic crisis.

To feed your soul, continue to use the S.O.U.L. process:

> S – Support yourself
>
> O – Open connection
>
> U – Unleash a plan
>
> L – Linger for joy

For saving a business, remember the C.A.K.E. process:

> C – Create community
>
> A – Adapt
>
> K – Keep learning
>
> E – Encourage help

Finally, to get a job in a competitive marketplace, use the B.R.A.N.D. process:

> B – Bring your best stories
>
> R – Reveal overcoming a weakness
>
> A – Announce your strengths
>
> N – Notice your interviewer
>
> D – Devote yourself to the job

In Part V, "Get Out of Debt and Back on Your Feet," you will learn how to effectively work with creditors. When you put these methods to work, you will feel much less stress. It's worth it!

Let's move forward …

Part V

21

Get Out of Debt & Back on Your Feet

Effectively work with creditors

What causes major breakups of romantic couples? Money troubles. What creates anxiety for many people? Intimidating calls from creditors and collection agencies.

If you are upset in relation to money troubles, it is hard to have the energy to remain patient when dealing with a creditor*

* At the time of this writing, people are dealing with doctor/hospital bills, disabilities, long-term unemployment, family member addiction, and legal fees. Top financial advisors, including Suze Orman, suggest contacting resources including the National Foundation for Credit Counseling (nfcc. org). Some people find it necessary to seek local resources like a food bank or a shelter or signing up for reduced utility bills when income is low. Suze Orman discusses the true last resort of bankruptcy, and she recommends the overview at www.credit.com/slp/chapter8/Bankruptcy.jsp. On the Fair Debt Collection Practices Act (FDCPA), which limits the actions creditors can take, she recommends the discussion at www.credit.com/credit_information/credit_law/Understanding-Your-Debt-Collection-Rights.jsp#2

who is pushing you. So this section will help you improve tough situations.

When I looked up "debt quotes" with Google.com, I noticed an interesting label: "Debt quotes/Financial Responsibility." Empower yourself by seeing responsibility as the ability to respond. In this section, we will arm you with methods so that you can respond. You'll learn how to talk with creditors in ways to set up reasonable repayment schedules.

Sometimes a profound idea appears very simple:

> *If you want to be rich, solve problems.*
>
> ROBERT KIYOSAKI

If you solve important problems at work, you are likely to gain raises and promotions.

If you create a product and it solves problems, you are likely to gain a significant number of customers.

In fact, I was inspired to write this section because I recalled the idea *solve problems.* This led me to the question: What problem dominates people's thoughts? Money troubles.

When it comes to debt, the target is to learn how to turn things around. We will use the T.U.R.N. process:*

> T – Talk
>
> U – Understand
>
> R – Right-size
>
> N – Nurture

• •

* The T.U.R.N. Process was first revealed in my book *Secret Influence to Get You Out of Trouble.* Visible at www.TomSuperCoach.com.

Let's step forward …

22

Talk

W hat's one of the most important things a person needs to do if he or she can't pay bills?

Talk to the creditors. You heard that right.

> *You must call credit card collectors, tell them the truth and deal with your situation head-on.*
>
> SUZE ORMAN

In this section we will cover:

1. How to ask for lower payments

2. How to create a positive atmosphere during the call so that the person is more likely to cooperate

3. How to ask to talk with a supervisor and how to flow with the conversation once the supervisor arrives

The Benefit of Making Arrangements with Your Creditors

Once you make arrangements to make small payments toward your debts, you'll feel better in some important ways.

> *Keeping what you have and creating what you deserve is not only about money. It is about the absence of fear, which is an even greater blessing than the absence of want; and fear tends to disappear when you tell the truth.*
>
> SUZE ORMAN

You make the call to the creditor; don't wait for the creditor to harass you.

How to Ask for Lower Payments

First, rehearse with a friend so that you feel you're ready. Also have your notes in front of you. The clerk on the phone will not see that you have your notes and a "script" in front of you.

> *Courage is easier when I'm prepared.*
>
> TOM MARCOUX

Second, before you dial the phone number be sure to sit down and make sure you have calmed down. My client Marina found that she felt better after she chose an affirmation and repeated it before calling a creditor. Her choice was: "God holds me safe." An affirmation can work when it is personal and means something to your heart.

Once you dial and have a creditor's team member on the line, you can say something like: "Hello, I want to set up a payment arrangement … "

Please know that even a small payment of $5 is a demonstration of good faith. It is truly a good start. At this point, the person on the other side is feeling good – at least a little bit. The creditor has someone calling her and seeking to make the situation better. Good for you!

An interviewer asked, "Won't some creditors say, 'That's not enough,' and then say something intimidating and require at least $50.00?"

Yes. That can happen. However, if you start making payments, you'll see that creditors will usually cash the checks. You are also creating a good history of taking positive action.

You can say, "I can only send $5.00 at this time. I'm certainly looking to make this better. And I am aiming to make a good start now."

Create a Positive Atmosphere to Encourage Cooperation

The idea is to turn the creditor into a friendly associate. You do this by expressing appreciation.

> *If properly appreciated, we feel better … We become*
> *more open to listening and more motivated to*
> *cooperate … You are more likely to reach a wise*
> *agreement than if each side feels unappreciated.*
>
> ROGER FISHER & DANIEL SHAPIRO

So as soon as possible in your conversation with the creditor, say sincerely, "I appreciate how you're making this as pleasant as possible."

As a side note, years ago, I found that I often gained cooperation quickly (even when getting a vendor to correct his mistake) by starting my conversation with: "I'm hoping you'll have good news for me."

How to Escalate Your Request to a Supervisor

Sometimes the first person you talk with truly cannot help you. They are probably bound by policies that hold no flexibility. The person often starts merely repeating himself, and says that he cannot do what you're asking for. But the supervisor often has more leeway.

You can say, "Well, it looks like it's time to talk with your supervisor."

Sometimes, you need to maintain a firm voice and keep repeating your request. You may need to ask, "Are you saying I cannot talk with the supervisor?" Your conversation is being recorded, and it is likely that the clerk on the phone does not want to be caught telling something that is not true. So he may pass you to the supervisor at that point.

There are times when you need to say, "Oh, something is happening here. I'm going to have to hang up now." And then you end the call. The reason for this strategy is that when you call back, you may be fortunate to get a different clerk. In any case, be prepared to repeatedly, firmly and politely ask to speak with a supervisor. (I have found it helpful to even call another time and get a different supervisor.)

When you talk with the supervisor, gently ask for his or her name with: "Hello, I'm [your name]. And you are … ?" A few times during the conversation add appreciative comments while using the person's name. You can say, "Trina, I appreciate your helping me with this." You may need to ask the supervisor to repeat an explanation or detail, and you can say, "Oh. I appreciate you giving me that information. Would you please repeat the part about XYZ, I'm putting that into my notes."

When you say the above you are expressing appreciation and you are giving a quiet alert that you are taking notes.

A Place for Truth-Telling … Your Friends & Family

A number of people get into significant credit card debt by charging vacations and consumer goods. To get out of debt, it will be necessary to change habits.

One time, my sweetheart and I wanted to take a vacation with friends. But then a project did not yield the funds that we had expected. So I had to call our friends and tell the truth: my sweetheart and I could not attend because a project had not worked out as planned. Over the years, I have made it a practice to save up in advance before taking a vacation.

In fact, I know a couple who saved for five years so that they could go on a cruise.

Never spend your money before you have it.

THOMAS JEFFERSON

Good Debt versus Bad Debt

It is true that there are some expenses that are valuable enough for using "good debt." For many people, getting a college education leads to a higher paying, more satisfying job – so student loans would be "good debt." But going into debt to buy the latest consumer goods, such as a top-flight home entertainment system, may be not be a match for building a life of financial abundance.

Good debt could be an appropriate business loan. For example, once I obtained a loan for a project that contributed immensely to my credibility. This credibility led to my later making $223,760. That established the original debt as good debt. Basically, good debt involves creating an asset. A college education can be an asset. My business project was an asset. You get the picture.

As this is being written, many Americans have been hit by a foreclosure crisis involving variable interest rates on their mortgages. Be sure to get advice from someone who is on your side – that is, a person who does not have an agenda in conflict with your well-being. (For example, be aware that mortgage brokers truly want to close the deal with you – too many for no other reason than the commission.)

Make informed choices and you can improve your financial situation.

Principle:

Rehearse before you talk to creditors.

Power Question:

Which friends or family members can help you through good rehearsals before you talk to creditors?

23

Understand

Understand this: if the creditor gets any kind of payment from you, the creditor feels as if he or she is winning. Making a $5 payment is a good start. Financial advisors such as David Bach and Suze Orman emphasize that it is often advisable to pay the highest interest loan or credit card first.

You can influence a creditor to improve a situation. For example, financial advisors note that you can search out the lowest interest rate credit cards, and armed with this information you can return to your own credit card vendor and encourage them to lower your rate. The credit card vendor would rather retain you as customer than lose you to another credit card company. It is important for you to study reputable sources of financial information so that you have the tools and information you need to improve your situation. Remember that creditors value on-time payments. Make sure your payments are on-time for a period before you search for better rates.

If you feed your mind as often as you feed your stomach, then you'll never have to worry about feeding your stomach or a roof over your head or clothes on your back.

ALBERT EINSTEIN

Often, we notice that many people who truly succeed had to work two jobs simultaneously – for years. For example, Albert Einstein worked as a clerk in a patent office while he pondered light, space, and time. In 1905, while working in that patent office, Einstein had four papers published in the *Annalen der Physik*, the leading German language physics journal. Physicists to this day look on these papers as significant achievements. And Albert Einstein did two things simultaneously: he worked to make a living and he pursued the area of his natural brilliance to make a life.

Principle:

Understand that you'll need to do extraordinary things: study financial information and perhaps work more than one job.

Power Questions:

Where do your talents and skills actually reside? Could you invest in yourself by taking a class or getting coaching to help you turn a hobby into a side source of income? (Today's economy often requires people to develop multiple sources of income.)

24

Right-Size

What do many chronic debtors have in common? Their lives are out of balance; in other words, their lives are "wrong-sized." For our discussion, a definition of wrong-sized includes these elements noted by experts who assist people to recover from financial mistakes.

"Wrong-sized" means:

1. A person's expenditures have exceeded his or her income

2. A person uses the act of buying stuff to feel some pleasure and to numb some hidden pain

3. The person is out of balance and uses stuff to distract him or her from pain or a sense of emptiness

> *If you borrow $10,000 on your credit cards and pay only the minimum payment with an interest rate of $19.98%, it will take you more than 37 years to get out of debt ... [and] you will have forked over nearly $19,000 in interest charges.*

DAVID BACH

Early in my working life, I learned two things. Have two nice pairs of pants and avoid using a clothes dryer on your dress shirts. By not using a dryer on my dress shirts I avoided shrinkage of my shirts—and I avoided having to buy new shirts! At that time in my life, that was an example of taking action to "right-size" my life and purchases.

Reduce the amount of your purchases. Put in safety measures so that you do not overspend. Financial advisors talk about: a) only bringing cash to the grocery store; b) batching (grouping) your errands so that you save gas money; and c) writing down a spending plan. A number of people avoid the word "budget." Instead, they use the name "spending plan" as something that can empower one to make effective choices. My clients often use the title: Financial Abundance Plan.

Remember to include some enjoyable experiences. Otherwise, you may find an unhealthy pattern occurring. For example, someone who does not eat breakfast may find herself eating a huge dinner. Deprivation can cause binge behavior. This is the reason that I am emphasizing putting a plan in place so that you have some enjoyment (on a modest scale) each month.

To set a plan and follow through does take effort.

*I will do what others will not do, so in the
future I can do what others cannot do.*

RANDY GAGE

*Success is having good relationships, fulfilling
employment, and being as healthy as you can be.*

LARRY WINGET

Our definition of success and our beliefs about "the good life" impact our daily actions. If a person says, "I deserve this," every time he is near the display of DVDs in a store, it is likely that he will purchase another DVD (that will eventually sit on a shelf, gathering dust).

Let's go back to Larry Winget's definition of success: Success is having good relationships, fulfilling employment, and being as healthy as you can be.

We notice that this list does not include: a car as good or better than the Jones'; the best-looking house in the neighborhood; 27 pairs of shoes …

Oh-oh! Perhaps, I have gone too far. It's true that many of us tend to have a soft spot for something (like shoes). I admit it: my soft spot is books. Early in my work life, I was strategic in how I gained books. A debuting hardcover book is most expensive. If I would demonstrate patience, I could wait for the paperback book to appear one year later. Less cost. And today, you can purchase the paperback book as a serviceable used book through Amazon.com, used book stores, or garage sales.

An interviewer asked, "So how do we avoid making impulse purchases?"

I replied, "It's a multi-layered process. You need a plan and then to work your plan."

Avoid Impulse Purchases & Handle Your "Soft Spot"

1. Carefully choose your definition of success.

2. Have safety measures; for example, go shopping with a friend who tends to save money and is careful with purchases.

3. Replace troublesome behavior with helpful behavior; for example, take a walk in a park instead of a shopping mall.

4. Use a Self-Nurture Chart and make sure that you experience enjoyment (without spending money) on a daily basis.

My client Kevin came to me about concerns that he might make some spending mistakes while his wife was away visiting family. Kevin wisely understood that with his wife temporarily absent, he would be experiencing loneliness and some pain. From our conversation, Kevin created this Self-Nurture Chart:

Self-Nurture Chart™							
Nurturing Action	*Mon*	*Tues*	*Wed*	*Thu*	*Fri*	*Sat*	*Sun*
Reading in hot bath	√			√			√
Hot bath listening to music and resting his eyes			√		√		
Comment in a journal to Becky (wife)		√				√	
Prayer for Becky to be safe and have a good trip	√			√			
Tai chi (outside?)	√		√			√	√
Yoga (outside?)					√		
3 minutes of silence			√				
Have a list of friends—and call one		√				√	
Watch episode of a funny TV show				√			
Ride bicycle outside			√				
Walk outside, even for 10 minutes	√					√	

Kevin did at least two of these actions on each day and found that he felt better and he avoided impulse-spending.

It's all about making choices that empower you.

You may decide to increase your value to the company where you work. Or you may decide to start a company of your own on the side. Author Michael Masterson writes:

> *"Every successful start-up business is one that has quickly and correctly answered [these] questions: 1) What is the most cost-effective way of attracting customers? And 2) What is the best way to keep those customers buying?"*

Michael Masterson emphasizes that each business needs to focus on "1) Lowering the cost of acquiring new customers and 2) Increasing the lifetime value of each existing customer."

Rather go to bed supperless than rise in debt.

BENJAMIN FRANKLIN

Now that is an extreme idea. How about we change the idea to something like: go without some lattes and fancy restaurant dinners*. I have a bachelor friend who spends (not invests) thousands of dollars on eating out. Then, at one point he came across the idea: "$1,200 saved with compound interest of 8% would yield $12,000 in 30 years." At that point, he realized that he wasn't only losing $1,200 in that year, he was also losing $12,000, too!

And yet, I remember my own bachelor days in which I lived for a time on spinach, brown rice, some vegetables and tuna fish. I was saving my funds for my projects. That is, I was devoting money to building assets: projects that would gain me professional credibility.

We're talking about right-sizing your life and your expenses. And this is really about focusing on your true values and priorities.

Low overhead equals freedom.

RAYMOND TELLER
of the team Penn + Teller

Principle:

"Right-size" your life and purchases so that you can build a future of financial abundance.

Power Question:

What is your soft spot? (Shoes? DVDs? books?) How can you make a spending budget so that you can occasionally reward yourself with your "soft spot," but have ways to restrain yourself from going overboard?

25

Nurture

Getting out of debt is hard work. You absolutely need to nurture yourself. You must keep your strength up.

But the big question is: what are you working for as you stretch yourself to get out of debt? What is your big benefit?

> *Financial Independence is [when] you have the resources to live a satisfying, comfortable life, accomplish your dreams and goals, and have more fun doing what you do.*
>
> BARBARA STANNY

Here is a secret: You can feel financial independence now. How? This quote gives us a good direction:

> *We do not remember days, we remember moments.*
>
> CESARE PAVESE

The idea is to focus on times when you felt good and had what you needed to enjoy the moment. For example, years ago I was in Disneyland with a friend. At the time, I did not have much money. But as I looked around the theme park I felt rich—as if the whole park was there for me. Certainly, Disneyland was there for the thousands of people present in the park. But I could stroll through the theme park with a big, joyful smile on my face.

On the other hand, my friend, who also was on a limited budget, had a completely different mindset. She was upset because she could not buy everything that she had a passing fancy for in the stores. She did not enjoy the abundance of just being in Disneyland!

My point is when I looked around Disneyland and smiled, I was, in that moment, feeling financial independence. I wasn't thinking about payments to the dentist, health insurance or anything else. I was in the moment. Again, let's remember the above quote: "We do not remember days, we remember moments."

It is crucial that we nurture ourselves. This is especially true for those of us who have entrepreneurial pursuits. For example, there was a time that I was feeling overwhelmed. I mentioned to my sweetheart, "I feel like a racehorse." She replied, "Run in better races."

What would "better races" be? I decided to pull back from certain activities that were not yielding the best results in both serving people and bringing in financial abundance. For example, there was a time that I chose to stop leading acting workshops. I found that my location was home to wannabe actors who had no money. So the workshops were not a lucrative way to gain income. Instead, I started to speak to people in corporate settings.

A second insight arose from the "run in better races" conversation. I thought, "If I am a racehorse, I do not want to be a stableperson, too." What that meant was that I needed to work smart and focus on doing what I was uniquely capable of doing. So I started to hire interns and contractors to work by the hour. I made a promise to myself that I would write my books but not typeset them.

We notice a difficulty for a number of people who run their own businesses: they burn out because they're wearing too many hats. It is better to hire independent contractors to relieve you of the burdens of bookkeeping and other tasks.

Business owners with a small budget can engage interns. For example, one of my friends recently went to a high school computer club and engaged an exceptional high school student to work on Web site-related projects.

The truth is that business owners truly need to focus on caring for current customers and gaining new customers. Once a business owner begins to work *on* the business instead of just in the business, her business starts to run better.

If you're a business owner and you feel overwhelmed, here is an important question: What can you do to guard your energy? Perhaps you might visit score.org or a local office of SCORE,

"Counselors to America's Small Business." Without working smart, you may be running a deficit in energy.

Pull out your personal journal and note how you might get help. Or at least how you can nurture yourself by scheduling in breaks.

The Central Idea About Nurturing Yourself

As I mentioned, getting out of debt is hard work, and you need to nurture yourself.

Here is what is important: Find ways that do not cost money to soothe yourself, comfort yourself and put salve on your wounds.

My clients have identified these healing actions:

1. An evening walk with my spouse

2. A hot bath

3. Listening to relaxing music

4. Playing with my children

5. Going for a run

6. Reading a book I borrowed from the library

7. Bringing a brown bag lunch and enjoying time with a friend

Watch out for this phenomenon: more pain equals more susceptibility to fall for bigger toys. Have you noticed that after working extremely hard, you want more expensive vacations, more DVDs, more chocolate, more lattes? And have you heard yourself telling a friend, "Hey, I deserve to have … "

You can't get enough of what you don't really want. Let's face it together. It is not really stuff that we truly want, it's feelings. What do we really want? To feel good—plain and simple. How? Here are the feelings we want:

- To feel comfortable

- To enjoy new sights and sounds

- To feel proud of ourselves

- To play

- To be heard (this is so valuable that I wrote a book entitled *Be Heard and Be Trusted*)

- To be admired

- To feel loved

- To feel relief from fears and concerns

My own coach suggested that I talk with my sweetheart for us to train each other in how to soothe each other. For example, my sweetheart likes when I massage her feet. That's important for me to know.

And, I like when my sweetheart massages my neck with a plastic massage tool while I'm typing this sentence.

Be careful to take care of yourself so you avoid feeling deprived as much as possible. For example, years ago, I only had two suits. But they were good suits. So when I wore them I felt good.

One important way to nurture yourself is to direct your attention to all the blessings already in your life. It helps to write down five details you're grateful for—just before you go to sleep each night.

> *I live in the space of thankfulness … the more thankful I became, the more my bounty increased. That's because what you focus on expands, and when you focus on the goodness in your life, you create more of it. Opportunities, relationships, even money flowed my way when I learned to be grateful no matter what happened in my life. I keep a gratitude journal … listing at least five things that I'm grateful for. My list includes small pleasures: the feel of Kentucky bluegrass under my feet (like damp silk); a walk in the woods … My thank-you list also includes things too important to take for granted: an "okay" mammogram, friends who love me …*
>
> OPRAH WINFREY

Principle:

Nurture yourself and unleash the flow of positive energy to you and through you.

Power Questions:

How can you nurture yourself on a daily basis? What brings relief and peace? (A hot bath, music, quiet time, calling a dear friend or something else?)

Conclusion to Part V

In Part V, we have covered the T.U.R.N process to help you improve your situation with creditors:

> T – Talk
>
> U – Understand
>
> R – Right-size
>
> N – Nurture

Remember to rehearse with friends or family members before you make a call to a creditor. Creditors want to be paid, and if you take action and start making small payments you are on the road to less stress.

In Part VI, we cover what I have learned from really successful people – that has made all the difference. Inspiration and wisdom can save you time, money and heartache. It also helps you feel better on your journey. Let's move forward …

Part VI

26

What I Learned from Really Successful People

That has made all the difference

Introduction

What if you learned the strategies that truly successful people lived by? How would your life improve?

Since 1981, I have been on a quest to learn from really effective people so that I might move forward faster.

The truth no one will tell you: Successful people streamline their process of accomplishment by learning from people who have already blazed the trails.

Here is a distillation of much wisdom that has helped me accomplish so many of my dreams. We use the S.U.C.C.E.S.S.-N.O.W. process:

> S – Start with a castle
>
> U – Unwrap fulfillment
>
> C – Change habits
>
> C – Conquer fear
>
> E – Enhance relationships

S – Show a personal brand

S – Stimulate productivity

N – Nurture yourself

O – Open the Trigger-Sequence

W – Win

Your best days are ahead when you apply wisdom from top professionals and spiritual leaders. This is the truth that will set you free from past limitations and propel you into a world of positive possibilities.

27

Start With a Castle

One interviewer asked me, "Tom, you lead people to fulfill big dreams. What is a guiding principle of your leadership?" I answered with this quote:

> *Build the castle first.*
>
> WALT DISNEY

When Walt Disney built Disneyland, he had the workers construct the castle first. Then all the workers knew what they were building: a place of magic and joy.

Start with a castle means begin with a vision – and communicate that vision.

When I start a motion picture project I go beyond the screenplay. I have versions of the poster created. I often have music composed. In this way, I give people a preview of the feelings that the movie will inspire. This is how I build the castle first, and get investors, actors and production people all on the same page. For example, at this moment, my team is preparing a trilogy of science fiction motion pictures entitled "TimePulse." To create clarity for the team and another profit center, we are also producing a graphic novel. The images of the graphic novel form the pre-production storyboards. You can view images at www.TimePulse.com.

Gain Clarity

To build your castle first is to have a vision of what you want to achieve. How is your life going to improve once you get the job, complete a project, or improve a relationship? You need a target. What has helped me for years is to focus on principles like: Build your castle first.

The second part is to identify your role models. And the third part is to answer the question: Where is the joy?

My client, Marina wrote down: "My business has grown so that I now have two subcontractors doing graphic designs. My role models are Gina and Emily. The joy is in: a) playing with ideas, b) seeing the finished projects, and c) seeing the smiling faces of happy clients."

The part about "where is the joy" is very important. At one time, I found myself feeling fatigued and without energy to move forward on a project. I had to ask myself, "Where is the joy?" The question served to jumpstart my energy.

> *So many of our dreams at first seem impossible,*
> *then they seem improbable, and then, when we*
> *summon the will, they soon become inevitable.*

CHRISTOPHER REEVE

We need the kind of focus that Chris Reeve emphasized. Although paralyzed and confined to a wheelchair, he was able to accomplish so much with just his spoken words.

> *The love and support of my family [keeps me*
> *going], and the fact that I'm needed. I'm working.*
> *I focus on the opportunities that come my way*
> *rather than on the things that haven't arrived yet.*

CHRISTOPHER REEVE

Chris Reeve's comment reminds me that, to feel fulfillment in life, we need to answer for ourselves: Where is the joy?

Your own applause

Recently, I attended a live performance of the musical *Wicked*. That night while driving home with my family, I realized why a musical is more fun than watching a DVD. It's because we applaud! And in my case, I express joyful and appreciative sounds, sort of like Wahoo!

Later, as I studied the behind-the-scenes descriptions of the making of *Wicked*, I learned how a particular scene's lighting was redesigned to help the audience feel the closure of a particular song. "The audience more readily understood the closure of the piece and then acknowledged it with their applause," said Stephen Schwartz, composer and lyricist. That's what we need! Closure and the acknowledgment of what we're doing right. Give yourself some type of applause, even if it's just dancing around and exclaiming, "Yes! Yes!"

To keep up our spirits, we must experience our own applause. It helps to have rituals that put your body into motion. I remember the TV sitcom "Perfect Strangers" in which the best buddies would do "the dance of joy."

In your personal journal, write down what your vision is for a project or particular area of your life. Remember to build the castle first. Remember to identify your role models and answer the question, Where is the joy?

28

Unwrap Fulfillment

To me, fulfillment is a gift that keeps giving. People who feel fulfilled have more energy and they are a joy to be near.

The challenge is that you need to take unusual steps to uncover or "unwrap" fulfillment. It is a truly individual experience, and it takes significant effort.

> *Let no one come to you without leaving better.*
>
> MOTHER TERESA

You will find great joy when you focus on making a meaningful contribution. For example, I make sure that I encourage each online student with each e-mail I send to them.

> *Nothing liberates our greatness like the*
> *desire to help, the desire to serve.*
>
> MARIANNE WILLIAMSON

> *Everybody can be great because anybody can serve.*
> *You don't have to have a college degree to serve.*
> *You don't have to make your subject and verb agree*
> *to serve. You only need a heart full of grace. A soul*
> *generated by love.*

MARTIN LUTHER KING, JR.

Focusing on how you can serve helps to add fulfillment to your success.

> *I no longer have to prove anything to*
> *anyone. I no longer have to prove anything*
> *to myself. I just need to stay interested.*

STEVEN SPIELBERG

That sounds good for Steven, you may respond. But Steven's comment also serves as a goal as bright as the lamp of a lighthouse. We can choose to move on a path that includes what we love doing and what we're interested in. We can also learn to focus on the doing as opposed to trying to gain social approval.

This also reminds me that I connect with my true self when I help others and express my creativity. My true self is that part of me that realizes I am a human being and not just a "human doing."

Focusing on yourself as a human being (feeling connected and whole) is a constructive mode of living. On the other hand, a destructive fixation would be making one's self-esteem solely dependent on external praise.

Oprah Winfrey has a number of ideas about significance:

> *The key to realizing a dream is to focus not on success but on significance – and then even the small steps and little victories along your path will take on greater meaning ... For every one of us that succeeds, it's because there's somebody there to show you the way out. The light doesn't always necessarily have to be in your family; for me it was teachers and school ... My philosophy is that not only are you responsible for your life, but doing the best at this moment puts you in the best place for the next moment ... You get in life what you have the courage to ask for.*

OPRAH WINFREY

Along the lines of connecting with the true self, I find it helpful to hold in mind the thought, How may I serve?

I say this prayer just before I step on stage to give a speech. This helps me have an enriching perspective on my place in the universe. For example, as I write these words, I hold this thought: *It's Higher Power's book. I am participating.**

I'm inspired by this quote:

> *I am neither a man of letters nor of science,*
> *but I humbly claim to be a man of prayer.*

MAHATMA GANDHI

In your personal journal, write down two of your favorite spiritual or philosophical quotes. This will help add significance to your success.

• •

* I feel guided as I write drafts of material. I also engage the efforts of professional editors and consultants to ensure excellence.

How do you serve (or can you serve) as you do your work?

29

Change Habits

How can you permanently change your behavior?

This powerful question is at the center of my Science of Emotional Leverage™. First, we observe the problem with traditional training is that people try to graft new methods onto their old behavior patterns. It doesn't work. Many people know this trap: You read a book, get inspired by it, try the new process, and then fall back into your old bad habits. I nod empathetically as I remember how that pattern once bothered me several years ago.

Using my Science of Emotional Leverage, I work with clients to merge with their true self. The true self is the part of you that is strong, focused and glad to be alive. The truth that no one will tell you: Your true self is always nearby, but it may be obscured from view. Some people refer to their true self as their Higher Self or Sacred Self. The true self is the opposite of the false self. The false self is the fearful part of you that feels small and vulnerable. I'll give you an example that makes this clear.

My client Trina wants to make her new small business successful. But she hates selling. Actually, her false self is full of fear about selling. She pictures a salesperson as a used car salesman. That holds her back. Trina doesn't make the necessary phone calls and she doesn't go to networking events.

To help Trina with her new start, I helped her connect with her true self – what she really wants.

Trina wants to serve and help people. With my guidance, she dropped her image of "salesperson" in favor of taking on the empowering role of *coach to action.*

What does a coach do? Trina replies that a coach helps a person do what she wants. I agreed, and asked: "Whose agenda is it?"

"The agenda of the person getting the coaching," Trina said, smiling.

A coach or mentor helps the person being coached see what she desires to achieve. And a coach shows that person how to get what she wants. A good coach acts quickly and with full integrity. If what the coach offers is not a match for what his client needs, then he guides the client to other resources. That person may then become a source of future referrals.

This is part of a system I call The Leverage Triangle™.

> *The Leverage Triangle is the process by which you literally free yourself for success. It enables you to overcome fear, release yourself from the confines of your false self, and escape limiting beliefs.*

Free yourself from hesitation and get in touch with your truest values and goals.

The title, The Leverage Triangle, explains why this process works. The word leverage signifies using a lever to get something done. If you've ever seen a picture of a lone person moving a huge boulder with a long pole, you understand that the leverage of the pole enables her to achieve an outcome she could never accomplish with just her own hands. A lever allows you to come up with tremendous results with the least amount of effort.

To create lasting change in your life, the kind that leads to fulfillment and success, you must use a stable process, one that can withstand resistance, doubt, despair, stress, obstacles and bad hair days. The beauty of The Leverage Triangle is that it allows you to change from a position of power, not weakness. This three-element process provides you with the steps you need, each of which builds on the other and is dependent on the other.

The three steps of this triangle are:

- Merge with your true self.

- Strategize how to proceed.

- Act according to your real goals.

Why these three? The first aligns you with what's real inside of you. Merging with your true self leads to real success. Otherwise you're just feeding false needs, and that is an endless process that never leads to fulfillment. The second is important because a strategy will help you stick with a course of action in spite of paralyzing fear. As a coach, I have often seen that many people are stopped by fear, paralysis and the need to be perfect. Strategizing also teaches you to save time and energy, and it keeps you from falling into potholes along the way. The final step is to act. Action is required for lasting change.

Merge

The key to success is changing your behavior. You can have all the lofty thoughts and sophisticated concepts in the world, but if you don't initiate a change in the way in which you operate, your life will continue on in the direction it is going. Let's face it together, if you had total satisfaction by doing what you are doing right now, you wouldn't be reading this book. But you are reading this book, which tells me you are attracted to bringing about change in your life. We need to identify the kind of change that brings the success and fulfillment you long for.

Many people are locked into a set of limiting behavior patterns put into motion by the false self.

The false self was formed to protect you during childhood. As parents socialize their child, the child's developing mind ultimately makes unhelpful associations. For example, a child might think, "Mommy and Daddy fight about money, so it must be bad." Along these lines, author Brent Kessel wrote, "A four-year-old runs your financial life."

Your false self is formed long ago and it has a hidden strategy to fill its own needs. Any move the person now makes that threatens those patterns is met with constriction and resistance.

For most, an alarm bell goes off inside of them, warning against stepping into the unknown. The false self pushes you to avoid trying anything risky and to avoid rocking the boat. It is difficult to ignore this alarm and to make a shift to explore a new path.

The voice of fear coming from inside a person makes her stop in her tracks, and usually she thinks she has to obey it. "Don't change the way you've always done things. How do you know what will happen? It may ruin everything!"

This reminds me of a bumper sticker: "Don't believe everything you think." Sometimes your oldest voice, the one that comes from deep inside you, is lying to you. Now what? How do you make decisions if you can't trust what your own mind is telling you?

The answer begins with the first element of The Leverage Triangle – *Merge with your true self.* You have to start listening to something besides fear. This voice of fear that's been commanding you all of your life is not the real you. It is a false construct, a rigid structure that organizes how you think about yourself under the umbrella of an identity that was manufactured in early childhood. "I've never been very smart." "I'm not an adventurous person." "I'm not lovable." All these identifying statements influence you as you try to move forward to improve your life. This voice of fear or false self is what many call the ego.

If you truly believe you aren't lovable, for instance, how will you ever convince yourself to seek a loving relationship? If you believe you're not adventurous, how will you take risks? If you're convinced that you're not intelligent, how will you forge ahead and learn new things that could improve your life?

> *In this first step: You have to see beyond the limited identity of your false self in order to discover your true self, which has virtually no limitations.*

The true self is not identified with past experiences the way the false self is. The false self is often traumatized by the disappointments and failures that occurred early in life, and it forms an identity around them.

For example, I know a woman who gave a speech when she was in high school and was booed by her classmates. It had a profound effect on her. She believed that she would be humiliated if she ever spoke in public again. This identity statement, "I'm terrible at public speaking," sabotaged her career as a toy company executive who was expected to speak at board meetings. She continually failed to speak up and make her opinion known, and consequently, her peers did not look on her as a team player. Her false self kept her from acting in her own best interests.

The true self is not hampered by bad experiences because it is not a pattern in the mind. It is the real you, unconditioned, pure, basic and authentic.

> *If you try to change your life without connecting with your true self, the conditioning of the false self will pull you back to the same limited behavior patterns.*

Many people make noble efforts to make fundamental changes in the way they operate. It works for a little while, but then they bounce back into the same old patterns as if they're attached to a rubber band. I often hear people complain that they start out with a great plan to change their life, and then they find themselves sabotaging it and returning to their old ways. They experience an attack of fear and then turn back. Researchers note that some dieters lose weight but feel uncomfortable with getting new attention and gain it all back.

My client Nora finally found the courage to apply for and become a first-time manager. In the course of my coaching sessions with her, I uncovered an identity. "I'm a nice, sensitive person. Managers are pushy and manipulative. I don't want to be like that." As we can see, not all identities are negative, but they all are limiting. Nora was so afraid of becoming a bad person in her own eyes that she couldn't do what she had to as a manager.

Nora had to break away from her fear by trusting that if she stayed true to herself, she could guide her team without turning into an obnoxious monster. I also helped her by replacing the "pushy manager" with the term *leader*. A leader serves the team's objectives and helps team members do well, which raises their self-esteem.

As long as Nora was stuck in a false identity, she couldn't break out of her constrictive patterns. Whenever you try a new strategy without merging with your true self, you might be able to stretch temporarily, but you cannot sustain the change. What you really need is a framework to help you keep stretching. This framework is The Leverage Triangle.

Use your imagination to connect to your true self

Many people try to connect with what is hidden deep inside of them through therapy, especially therapy that has spiritual overtones. Clients talk out their thoughts and feelings. Talking is effective in some ways, and yet in others it isn't. This is because words represent concepts, which tie into the conditioned mind, not your true self.

Because images have meanings that speak directly to your true self, images tend to bypass conditioned responses and go straight to the source. Verbalizing an image forces you to filter your thought process, which distorts the meaning.

To understand this, it is useful to observe babies flowing with life – because they don't yet have language. They have to "speak" in images. When they want something, they look around and point to it, usually making some kind of sound. To an infant, there is no difference at all between what they need and what they want. The two are one and the same. On a primary level, the same is true for you. What the heart wants is what the heart needs. And sometimes words are not enough to describe it. Images will help you get in touch with what your heart truly wants, without being deflected by the world of concepts.

Connecting Imagination & Your True Self

Imagination is more important that knowledge.

ALBERT EINSTEIN

The imagination can open you up to deeper meaning and catapult you toward a search for truth – *truth no one will tell you.*

The following is an exercise that will help you find images that you connect with emotionally. Through your imaginative interpretation, you will be able to understand what your heart really wants in life and what goals will help you blossom into fulfillment.

An important element in this exercise is imagining the support of a genie or guardian angel, a being whose only purpose is to help you find what you truly want. I coach people to imagine that the genie from *Aladdin* is here to help them.

The genie or guardian angel will keep you from sabotaging your imagination, which some adults restrict from their minds. The reason for this is that many people learned from a young age not to want that which they cannot have. Wanting what you can't have just hurts too much. Instead, learn how to flow with both: appreciating what you already have and going for more.

In this exercise we will work with images in order to avoid a particular problem: Wishes are often squelched before they reach the conscious mind. Not only do some people avoid asking for what they want, they don't even let themselves feel the desire. In effect, wishing is suppressed before it ever rises to the level of expression.

To let yourself fully wish, you must imagine that you are in a world of unlimited possibilities, and that you can actually fulfill your wish, no matter how big or how crazy it is.

Complete the following

1.	Gather magazines, old throwaway books and any other printed material that has lots of pictures. Be sure to pick items you will feel comfortable cutting up into pieces. Also collect three candles, matches, scissors, glue, a pencil, tinted pens, one large sheet of paper and your personal journal.

2. Light the three candles to create the feeling of a sacred space. Place them in a circle around you.

3. Place the large sheet of paper in front of you and write across the top: If my genie (or guardian angel) grants me wishes to make my life the way I want, what would my life look like?

4. Divide the rest of the paper into three sections and give each section one of the following titles: To live, To be happy, To love – through relationships and making a contribution through work.

5. Now open the magazines and books and search for images that speak to you, the ones that stop you and make you look deeper. They might produce a sense of wonder, joy or happiness, peace, or a feeling of depth and mystery. Some might just throw you back to childhood and make you feel like playing. Tear out the images that seize your attention and glue them on your paper. If you sense that you are onto something and you cannot find a picture to match it, feel free to sketch it out.

6. Once you have filled the paper, stop for a moment. Notice the cumulative effect of creating this collage of images. They are reflections of your true self and what it desires. Notice your feelings. You may feel a rush of excitement or a tinge of sadness, or anything

in between. Whatever your feelings are, just be with them. All are trying to tell you something.

7. Ask yourself this important question: If this collection of images were talking to me, what would it be saying?

8. Once you start to hear an answer, begin writing your observations in your journal. At this stage, words won't hamper the process since the images have already affected you. Words will help you interpret what you have seen. But don't hesitate or censor what you have to say. Just let the words flow. (Some of my clients prefer to record their thoughts on an audio recorder.)

9. Now call a friend, someone who is receptive and understanding, and discuss the exercise. It is often helpful just to have a friendly ear to share your observations with. The person can allow you to verbalize what you have learned and help you grasp some new meaning.

When I conduct this exercise in class, students discuss their results in groups. I often see their faces light up as they experience fresh insights, perceptions and profoundly deep feelings.

Congratulations on completing this exercise.

A powerful source of personal energy

I have guided you in the process of merging with your true self because this is the ultimate source of personal power. I know how energizing it is to have a dream. It made this book come together. I take the following ideas to heart:

> *When you sell a [person] a book, you don't sell just twelve ounces of paper and ink and glue, you sell him a whole new life. Love and friendship and humor and ships at sea by night. There's all heaven and earth in a book.*

CHRISTOPHER MORLEY

Merge with your true self. When you discover what moves your heart, you experience a new blossoming of energy and fun in your life.

Strategize

The second part of The Leverage Triangle is to strategize. The key to strategizing for success is to set specific and practical criteria for excellence. Too many people try to set a standard of perfection, and not one for excellence. Perfection is an ideal state that cannot be achieved in real life. However, anyone can excel, which simply means that you can continually surpass your own accomplishments. To strategize, we use a process summed up in the acrostic R.E.A.C.H., which we will explore in the next section entitled "Conquer Fear."

> *A problem is simply a question that hasn't been answered yet.*

NOAH ST. JOHN

One of my friends didn't find value in Noah's comment. I replied: "To me, this comment represents a mindset that seeks to become effective with asking problem-solving questions. I've noticed that many of my best triumphs arrived first as problems of deep concern."

This perception leads to the question: How can I strategize more effectively?

I guide my clients to ask the right questions so that they come up with empowering answers.

If you can solve a problem with money, it is no longer
a problem. It is an expense.

HARVEY MACKAY

Some readers may respond to Harvey's comment with "Well, that's good for you. You probably have plenty of money." My point is: when we have a path to solve a problem, we can breathe easier. So, Harvey's comment reminds me to seek better solutions.

Your strategy should highlight your problem-solving capabilities. Study the various sections of this book so that you become an effective decision-maker.

Here are some hallmarks of a good decision

1. It's timely.

2. It's proportional (devoting too much time to trivial details can keep you from your real priorities).

3. It may be informed by the expertise of others.

4. It feels "intuitively right." (For example, Walt Disney felt his vision of Disneyland was worth overcoming the objections of his wife, brother/business partner Roy and the board of directors. Walt had to cash in his life insurance policy to fund the initial stages of Disneyland.)

Act

The final part of The Leverage Triangle is to Act. An old phrase is "knowledge is power." We can see the value in the idea: Knowledge is potential; consistent action is power.

Identify the parts of you that feel strong and on purpose. Many people find inner strength through meditation or prayer. Put your thoughts in your personal journal.

Merge with your true self. Then act from the authentic place in your being.

Action is essential for creating the life of fulfillment, success, love and joy we all crave.

> *The possibilities are numerous once*
> *we decide to act and not react.*
>
> GEORGE BERNARD SHAW

Of many quotes I uncovered in my research, I found George's comment to be powerful. To act is when we assert our individuality, our choice and our freedom. I have heard so many people complain about how something is being done to them. On the other hand, I recall the comment of Victor Frankl, renowned psychiatrist and Auschwitz survivor:

*Everything can be taken from a man or a woman but
one thing: the last of human freedoms to choose one's
attitude in any given set of circumstances, to choose
one's own way.*

VIKTOR E. FRANKL

So I invite you to choose carefully and to take action for your
benefit and that of others.

*You will get all you want in life if you help
enough other people get what they want.*

ZIG ZIGLAR

Action is the key to a happy life.

*Act as if you were already happy and
that will tend to make you happy.*

DALE CARNEGIE

Ask yourself: what would I do if I were happy? Perhaps, you
would call someone or update your résumé or take a relaxing
bath. Act! Do something that brings value into this world.

Action is also crucial related to what many of us long for:
love. One of the times I remember most feeling love was when I
was acting in a loving way. It was the Holiday Season and I was
wrapping a gift for my sweetheart.

*Love is an act of endless forgiveness, a
tender look which becomes a habit.*

PETER USTINOV

Love is a powerful springboard to get us moving and acting. However, something can stop us in our tracks. Fear. Our next section will provide you with tools so that you can act in an extraordinary and beneficial manner.

30

Conquer Fear

How do you deal with fear when it comes up? Let's focus on this statement:

*Our fears must never hold us back
from pursuing our hopes.*

JOHN F. KENNEDY

I developed a process for dealing with my fears. I don't deny my fears. I use my fears as signals for more preparation. Courage is easier when you're prepared. For example, if I feel jitters before an appearance on television or radio, I rehearse possible questions and my responses that I pose in the form of sound bites.

How Can You Get Yourself to Take Risks?

Become strategic in how you approach risks. It is important to take appropriate risks. You need to set reasonable criteria for excellence. To set reasonable criteria when strategizing on a goal, use the R.E.A.C.H. process:

> R – Reduce risk
>
> E – Expect results
>
> A – Adjust to circumstances
>
> C – Compensate for your own shortcomings
>
> H – Hook your attention

Reduce Risk

When you are working toward a goal, especially one that will change your life, huge fears are likely to loom in front of you. Many of them are unreal, although they will paralyze you if you let them. Risks that are created within your own mind cannot be overcome. But others will be quite real, and you will have to face them. Your task is to identify which risks are likely to pop up and which ones are being generated by fear gone wild.

For instance, Tara is a stay-at-home mom who wants to go back to school so she can apply for a top-level job. The problem is she must deal with childcare issues. Who can she trust with her child? What can go wrong?

The real challenge is finding responsible daycare that can accommodate her needs. But if Tara's mind races ahead, she might become fearful that putting her little darling in childcare will ruin his life and that he'll start stealing hubcaps when he's thirteen because his mother abandoned him. Tara needs to pause and consider that no daycare center can reduce that imagined risk.

Like Tara, we cannot control the distant future.

You can only face what is in front of you right now.
The best way to do that is to identify what will likely
go wrong and then create a plan to reduce the chances
that it will.

On the other hand, letting fear run out of control will not only distract you from important tasks, but, at its worst, it will shut you down. It is almost impossible to have a sense of adventure and to be creative when you're locked in fear. Thus, whenever you reduce unnecessary fear, you open yourself to creativity. And ultimately, you reduce unnecessary risks because you head trouble off at the pass.

At this first stage, think ahead to what you are likely to encounter when you execute your plan. What snafus could arise? What challenges lie ahead? Sometimes it helps to ask friends to brainstorm with you possible scenarios you might need to prepare for.

Now identify the problems you can actually prepare for and begin to form a strategy. When people do this, they immediately feel stronger because they feel more in control of their own destiny. My clients protect their jobs by maintaining a job diary; they log their successes for composing a summary page for their annual performance review. What I have just described is the core of preparation, and it will greatly improve your chances for success.

Expect Results

You have identified what can go wrong and developed some ideas for avoiding adverse consequences. Now it is time to focus on the kind of results you expect. Specific results. It's not good enough to say, "I want to be a happier person," or "I want to find love in my life," or "I want to reduce stress so I can just relax." Admirable goals, certainly, but they're too vague.

You need to identify precisely the results you hope to achieve. What do they look like? What benefits will they bring you? How will you feel better when the results occur? Asking yourself these questions will help you tailor your plan toward the right destination, which will keep you on track.

Keep in mind that you are not the only person who will be affected by this goal. Your life touches so many others. The benefits of your success may affect your mate, children, extended family, friends, co-workers or your clients or customers. I call these people your "stakeholders" because they have a stake in the outcome of your goals. Consequently, you need to also consider the expectations of others.

Others peoples' expectations are likely to be different from your own. For instance, if you are contemplating a change in careers, your only concern could be that the new career is more satisfying and interesting than your current one. Your spouse's concern, however, could be that you bring in a higher salary. It is important to communicate your plans to those who will be most affected, and to make sure you are all on the same page.

Find out your spouse's expectations and priorities. Whose satisfaction matters the most? If you are married, you have to consider your mate first. But what about customers? If you change a product or service, will you lose your client base?

Consider interviewing those who will be impacted by your plan. Conduct surveys among your stakeholders to determine what priorities and results are important to them.

Adjust to Circumstances

Now that you know your risks and expectations, you need to evaluate your life circumstances. Are you in a position to go after your goal or do you have to adjust either the goal or your life? Right now you are only in the strategy stage, so you're not making adjustments for anything that is actually happening to you. You are sitting down and playing out your future in your own mind.

What position are you in financially, domestically, socially and with your career? What constraints are on you? Now consider the demands that your goal will place on your life. What challenges will it throw your way? Try to picture the changes in your life when you're asked to devote more money, time or effort. What adjustments will you have to consider in order to make your plan work?

> *Nothing is free. If we don't pay for it with money,*
> *we pay for it with our time, energy or health.*
>
> CARMEN RENEE BERRY

Carmen's quote means that when you set a goal for yourself, you have to understand that it's going to cost you something.

Years ago I was the sole proprietor of my own company. I knew before I ever started that family members might need me during tough times, and that I would have to be there for them. I was prepared to care for my sweetheart when she fell ill. I was able to hire a friend to help out.

An important part of your strategy is to identify what aspects you can drop when necessary. These droppables are significant because the enthusiasm that comes from the planning process sometimes makes us blind to our life's inevitable limitations. We may not have the time or resources for everything. So know ahead of time what the keepers are and what can be let go.

> *A man is rich in proportion to the number of things he can afford to let alone.*
>
> HENRY DAVID THOREAU

My client Maggie wanted to be a full-time professional speaker. She researched the career and found that she had to provide speaker products: books, audio programs and so on. At first she planned on making a first-rate audio program with a music soundtrack. Once she evaluated the situation, she decided that background music was an expensive addition and was droppable. Though a year later, when Maggie was pulling in one speaking engagement after another, she made a second edition of her program and added music to it.

Sharon, a realtor, planned to create full color brochures but the recession slowed her business to a trickle. She adjusted her approach to include much more in-person networking and relied on her business card, personal warmth and sending out e-newsletters.

Nedra, the founder of a non-profit organization, shifted her plans and started blogging and linking to other blogs. Her strategy was to increase her efforts with social networking in ways that involved her energy but not using up funds.

Compensate for Your Own Shortcomings

As you pictured this project in your mind, you have imagined all the things that could possibly go wrong "out there." But what about you? What about your own personal shortcomings – the qualities or liabilities that could hold you back? It is time to look inward. You stand a much better chance of crossing the finish line if you aren't grandiose about your own capacities, and if you can realistically assess what you're capable of.

Identify your tendencies or shortcomings now in the planning stage, and then figure out how to compensate for them. For example, I am a fast-moving person. When I edit my own films, I naturally create quick cuts, which is a sequence of images of short duration. I know that I have this general tendency in whatever I do, which can work against me. This is why I always have two people with me in the editing room who will continually offer their opinion on the output. Remember this phrase:

Know your tendencies and compensate for them.

TOM MARCOUX

One tendency can prevent success: Letting fear of rejection cause a dead stop to your efforts.

Being rejected doesn't hold you back from anything. Only YOU hold yourself back. If you are told no, ask for what you'd have to do to get it, or ask again at another time when the circumstances have changed. Ask if they know someone else who might say yes. When you realize that there's no merit to rejection, you'll feel more comfortable asking for things. But you may need a bit of help learning how to ask for what you want.

JACK CANFIELD

Every top achiever I have interviewed has demonstrated the power to persist through rejection. As I mentioned earlier, the bestselling series of books, *Chicken Soup for the Soul* (over 100 million sold), was rejected by publishers 141 times. It only took one publisher to team up with the authors to make their first book a success.

To successfully deal with rejection, make your reason to do something so huge that you'll push past any hesitation. One of my secrets is to have a team of consultants assist me with my projects. This ensures that my work is of top caliber and will truly serve the intended audience.

Hook Your Attention

How can you inspire yourself? You need to find out what it is about your goal that really grabs you. Your inspiration will allow you to stick with it even when your energy sags. You are about to invest a great deal of time, energy and money in the pursuit of your goal. You might even be asking loved ones to do the same and take a stake in your future. Find the heart of your passion, the fire that will keep burning no matter what failure and heartaches might come. And you have to do this before you take a single step on the path.

In the early sixties, President John F. Kennedy said these words:

> *I believe that this nation should commit itself to achieving the goal, before this decade is out, of landing a man on the moon and returning him safely to the earth.*
>
> JOHN F. KENNEDY

Let's realize that there was no space program to speak of when Kennedy made this statement. He was envisioning something that didn't exist, and he committed to it simply because he believed in it. Those few choice words mobilized a nation and gave it hope. It was a catchphrase that had great power. You need a catchphrase or a hook that does the same for you: one that inspires a belief in yourself and in your future. A hook, by its very nature, is short and to the point. My own mission caption for my coaching/speaking work is:

> *I help people experience enthusiasm, love, and wisdom to fulfill big dreams.*

The mainstay of *hook your attention* is to zero-in on your unique essence. To create a life of fulfillment, you must be different from the average person. You need to have an extraordinary focus.

The problems of the world cannot possibly be solved by skeptics or cynics whose horizons are limited by the obvious realities. We need [people] who can dream of things that never were.

JOHN F. KENNEDY

Another example of a hook is Roy O. Disney's statement:

Decision making is easy when your values are clear.

ROY O. DISNEY

As the brother and business partner of Walt Disney, Roy knew that whatever new ventures the Disney Company went into (after Walt's death), they wouldn't go wrong if they stuck to the company's established values.

Make your hook short, simple, and articulate. Make sure it encapsulates the heart and soul of your goal. When you repeat it to yourself, make sure it brings up powerful emotions and gives you a strong sense of direction.

We create encouraging, energizing entertainment and edutainment in joy of contribution because our work enlivens us and outlives us to serve humankind's rise.

MISSION CAPTION OF TOM MARCOUX MEDIA, LLC

Your hook or catchphrase will help you connect emotionally with the essence of your goal every time you say it.

Write two versions of your personal catchphrase into your personal journal.

31

Enhance Relationships

Have you lost a job or is your business slowing down during the recession? What's the solution? Relationships.

A number of people feel cast adrift at sea, and they feel uncomfortable in networking or asking favors of people they know.

What can you do? Let's look at the essence of a healthy relationship. It's a place you go to give, create connection and later to receive.

Many details that work for a good friendship also work for a good professional relationship.

First, people want to know that you care. And they want to feel important. When you help your supervisor look good to her boss, you are building your relationship with your supervisor.

> *To improve your relationship: a) accept feelings,*
> *b) keep agreements, c) turn complaints into*
> *action or a request and d) tell the truth.*
>
> GAY HENDRICKS

When networking, the idea is make a small promise to someone when you meet the person. As you listen carefully to a new person, find some kind action you can do on her behalf. If she mentions a hobby or an interest of her son or daughter, make a promise to send a link to a web site (if possible). Follow through on such a promise that same day. This is a process of keeping your agreements.

I often say, "How can I be supportive of what you're doing?" Then I listen carefully.

To build stronger friendships, let's remember:

> *To love a person is to learn the song*
> *that's in their heart, and to sing it to*
> *them when they have forgotten.*
>
> THOMAS CHANDLER

Remember to build relationships, you need to listen well, make appropriate promises, keep agreements and truly look out for the well-being of people in your circle. A simple important process is to call up people and catch up with their lives. Pay attention. People have a deep craving to feel important. Provide your attention and you'll be a welcome part of their lives. Give your attention first and later some people in your circle will be glad to help you with job leads and other supportive activities.

32

Show a Personal Brand

Our struggles today are unprecedented, with all the layoffs, the outsourcing of American jobs to India and elsewhere, and the struggle to get enough clients to simply stay in business.

Learn to form or improve your personal brand. The personal brand is the safety net for people in the new economy.

What is a personal brand?

> *A personal brand is a promise of performance that creates expectations in its audience. Done well, it clearly communicates the values, personality, and abilities of the person behind it.*
>
> PETER MONTOYA

How is your personal brand a safety net?

An interviewer asked me these questions: "How can the average person have a personal brand? And how is your personal brand a safety net?"

I explained that a personal brand is the shortest distance between you and getting what you want. Your personal brand creates the impression of you as a trustworthy person. You need to be trusted to keep your job. That's how the personal brand is a safety net.

Want to protect your job? Use a personal brand. Want to get clients? Use a personal brand. Want to feel good about your work? Use a personal brand.

Numerous authors have been discussing the personal brand, and they mention:

- The idea is to market oneself and career as a brand.

- It's about self-packaging as opposed to the traditional self-improvement.

- Your personal brand is what makes you memorable and easily distinguishable from other people.

How can a personal brand make you feel happy?

Your personal brand blossoms from your true self. Your true self is that part of you that feels strong, on purpose and connected with what is good. When you start from this place, it is natural for you to feel happy.

For example, my client Geoffrey is a graphic design consultant. His true self is an artist. He helps his clients communicate by creating great graphics for them. At this time, Geoffrey is working with me to develop his personal brand – something that emphasizes his expertise and heartfelt focus on helping people communicate powerfully. Geoffrey tells me that he now feels better about his business and what he does.

> *Always continue the climb. It is possible for you to do whatever you choose, if you first get to know who you are and are willing to work with a power that is greater than ourselves to do it.*
>
> OPRAH WINFREY
> Attributed to Ella Wheeler Wilcox

In line with this comment, I emphasize the true self. The personal brand also helps you communicate effectively with people.

> *What you'll discover if you begin to meet clients in person, talk to them on the phone, and ask directly for their business, is that it gets easier the more you do it. It will build your confidence in yourself – and the confidence your prospective clients have in you – at the same time. If you're in the business of serving people, your best marketing tool is your own voice. So put it to work and start talking to them.*
>
> C.J. HAYDEN

When people think of a brand, they think of Nike or Mercedes, and not necessarily a feeling. How does a personal brand fit into this?

We can think of a personal brand as a communication tool. For example, the *San Francisco Examiner* dubbed me "The Personal Branding Instructor." This conveys a quick idea.

We need to realize that we now live in a sound-bite society. Our message has to be clear and in few words. My personal brand, "America's Communication Coach," clearly conveys how I help people. They can trust that I have expertise in communication skills. A brand is the shortest distance to trust.

Where does a personal brand start?

It starts inside you. With your true self. Answer these three questions:

1. What are four major ways you get satisfaction in your work?

2. What are your key strengths?

3. What are you best known for?

Here's an example. My satisfaction comes from: (a) I like playing with ideas, and (b) I enjoy helping clients in these three areas: Power Communication, Power Time Management and Personal Branding.

One of my key strengths is my ability to find the emotional key in others. I then help them inspire emotion and action in their clients or customers. I am best known for my enthusiasm, compassion and methods for encouraging people to take action to improve their lives.

Now it's your turn. Please answer the three questions in your personal journal.

33

Stimulate Productivity

What can you do if you find it hard to relax or slow down?

Nothing contributes so much to tranquilize the mind as a steady purpose – a point on which the soul may fix its intellectual eye.

MARY SHELLEY

It is focus which can bring us satisfaction and contentment. In addition, with proper focus you can drop nonessential items from your life. A friend had so many interests and magazine subscriptions that she felt overwhelmed. When she zeroed in on her most treasured interests for this year, she found that she had more energy. And her productivity soared.

There are times when replenishing energy is crucial to productivity. If one feels tired, one can do sloppy work, which ultimately requires redoing the task. That is unproductive.

The most effective person alternates periods of activity with recovery – that is an Activity-Recovery Pattern (discussed in greater detail later in this book). For example, at certain times, I step away from the computer for 20 hours.

Some people find it hard to make their business successful. They're concerned about their personal productivity.

> *No matter what you think you do for a living, you're really in four businesses at once. The first is … the one mentioned on your business card. The second is the marketing business … The third is the service business … the fourth is the people business … There's a close correlation between your interest in people and your ability to convince and motivate them.*

JAY CONRAD LEVINSON

I help clients build on the principles noted in Jay's quote. I have them write down the four business areas in their weekly schedule and then write "next action" under each category.

The truth no one will tell you: Determining your next action gives you something to focus on, which guides you to start feeling better. You can schedule your next action for the next day or even the next month. This process helps you find your bearings.

Here are some steps to improve your productivity:

- Find your values.

- Target your goals.

- Write down your projects.

- Note a "next action" by each project.

- Schedule your actions in your day planner.

Some business owners find themselves approaching burnout. What can they do?

Michael Gerber writes books that demonstrate how a small business can thrive when it is organized like a franchise. Here Michael identifies an important distinction:

> *[A business is better as] a systems-dependent business*
> *– not a people-dependent business … The purpose of*
> *a system is to free you to do the things you want to do*
> *… The purpose for going into business is to get free of*
> *a job.*
>
> MICHAEL GERBER

Michael invites business owners to put systems in place so they are free to work as they choose.

Now, the question is: How can you use these ideas to make your work life better? Here's how: My client Kerry writes down how prospective clients first hear about her business. She notes how she and her team can gain those people as paying clients. When Kerry receives a query by e-mail, she or her assistant runs down the list of possible actions that can be taken. She doesn't waste time pausing, hesitating or rethinking steps. Kerry then uses the best idea and contacts the customer to further the business relationship.

Another way to save time is to set up your Web site to effectively build your credibility. Return to your work on your personal brand. Make sure that your Web site expresses your personal brand in hard-hitting, clear and brief statements. Often you generate more credibility by having clear, brief testimonials that point out the benefits you bring to a customer. For example, this quote has helped me: "'Using one of Tom's methods, I got more done in 2 weeks than in 6 months.' – Jacqlyn Freitas."

Your Web site enhances your productivity because people will know you better and what you offer. It's the difference between a business card and an informative and compelling brochure.

A Productivity Secret for Making a Product

So much of business is about offering something of value and then communicating that value. People devote hundreds of hours and large sums of money to find that perfect product name. My productivity secret: put the benefit for the user into the title like *Online Secrets to Build Your Brand* or *Power Time Management: More Time, Less Stress and Zero Procrastination.* *

In your personal journal, write down the necessary steps to gain new clients or customers. How can you make this into a system that you practice regularly?

Or, if you're looking for a job, write down the steps you need to take advantage of a new opportunity. This might include: optimize your résumé; do research on the company you are targeting; prepare for the first interview; send a thank-you card, and more.

----

* Get empowering books and audio programs at www.TomSuperCoach.com.

34

Nurture Yourself

Do not die with your music still inside you.

DR. WAYNE DYER

Do you often feel overwhelmed? Would you like to learn how to nurture yourself and find your smile again?

Many people use my strategies based on the S.A.Y.—Y.E.S. process:*

S – Step off the stage

A – Accept better care

Y – Yield to recovery

Y – Yearn for energy

E – Encourage your best

S – Support your team

* The S.A.Y.—Y.E.S. process comes from both my presentation "Say Yes to Yourself: Secrets to Overcome Stress and Change in Your Workplace" and my book *Secret Influence to Get You Out of Trouble*. www.TomSuperCoach.com.

Step Off the Stage

It takes a lot of energy to keep up your "professional face." It's a façade. You need times during your workday when you can catch your breath and step away from other people. Just a little time will do.

Years ago, I worked for an organization in downtown San Francisco. There was no spare room at this firm. During my lunch break, I would step onto the balcony with a chair, sit down, and meditate. Find ways that you can step off the stage. If necessary, take a short walk or rest in your car. The important point is to find time to rest your mind and replenish your energy.

Ask yourself: How can I step off the stage?

Accept Better Care

Many of us get so caught up in our work that we do not take care of ourselves. Imagine if you saw your best friend working way too hard. Would you counsel him or her to take an appropriate break? It's likely that you would.

Here is the important question to ask yourself repeatedly through the workday: How can I take better care of myself right now?

Yield to Recovery

I use the word *yield* with care. When we drive a car, we must yield to oncoming traffic. And in life, we must yield to the truth researchers discovered about optimal human functioning: Humans do best when they use an Activity-Recovery Pattern. This process is when a person is active and then rests. Top tennis pros demonstrate this process. They are actually active for 20 minutes in each two-hour match. They rest in between outbursts of energy. An office worker can write a report in the morning and then later rest by doing something less taxing like using the photocopier.

How can you use the Activity-Recovery Pattern?

Yearn for Energy

One day I was feeling unusually fatigued but still had a lot of work to do to complete a report I needed for a speech. Normally I would have felt a great connection to the work and its purpose. I knew that writing this particular report would ultimately help people. The problem was, I did not feel the connection at that moment. Then I asked myself, "Where is the joy?" I realized the joy would come when I spoke before an audience and shared these ideas. That's when the fun would come. And that's where the joy would be. At that point, I had a connection to the purpose for the report I was working on, and I felt energetic.

Where is the joy?

Encourage your Best

Today's economic climate causes many people to hold great fear about losing their jobs. The solution is to become known at your workplace for being excellent at the skills you provide in your job. Ask yourself, "What I am best known for?" Then work hard to become a crucial team member.

What are you best known for?

Support your Team

In order to experience support from your supervisor and co-workers, you need first to support them. Remember that they are all individuals with different personality styles. This next set of insights is built on the discoveries of a number of researchers.

We can view personality styles in this manner:

- **The Lion**: A director-type person who is a hard-charger with little patience. This person wants to hear the brief details and to know the impact to the bottom line.

- **The Dog**: A relater-type person who values a human connection over changing to make things better. This person likes routine.

- **The Beaver**: An analytic-type person who is detail-obsessed. Often, this person carries a big fear of being incorrect, and so he or she may be slow to make decisions.

- **The Peacock**: A socializer-type person who loves talking about ideas with people. He or she is quick at decision-making and poor on follow-up.

Here's an example. When Alex was presenting to a group of people, he took into account their personality styles. He reached the engineer-type (Beaver) audience members by using his own acrostic P.R.E.S.E.N.T. to outline his material. These audience members appreciated his methodical approach.

He appealed to the relater-type (Dog) audience members by asking, "What do you hope or expect that I will talk about today?" Then he wrote down their topics and questions. Then Alex said, "During our time together, we will get to as many of these details as we can."

Finally, Alex appealed to the director-type (Lion) audience members by checking off the topics and questions as they were addressed. The director-type person appreciates that the meeting's progress is made clear.

Here is another example. John has a director (Lion) style, and he compensates for it. In the middle of a conversation with Susan, a relater (Dog), John slows down and asks gentle questions. He listens first.

On the other hand, when John works with Monica, an analyzer (Beaver), he might say something like, "Monica, write some notes on three alternative solutions to the problem we've been discussing. Then endorse one and tell me your reasoning when we meet on Friday." In this manner, John supports Monica's analytical personality style. And John supports his own director style that calls for brevity.

In your personal journal, write down your answers to these questions:

- Which personality style do I possess?

- How can understanding the different personality styles help me do better?

35

Open the Trigger-Sequence

When you think about self-discipline, do you cringe? Are you like many people who say they need to improve their self-discipline?

Discipline is important. In fact, it is crucial for creating the success you want.

> *Discipline makes the difference. Exceptions are what destroy people's dreams and keep them from being significant.*
>
> ZIG ZIGLAR

The idea is to make a commitment to yourself and keep it. If you decide to exercise 20 minutes a day and you keep that commitment, then you get a double reward. You gain the physical benefits and you feel great about yourself.

But wait a minute. Many people say self-discipline is difficult.

There is something that is better than self-discipline

The truth no one will tell you: The good news is that self-discipline does not have to be so hard. The real power is in a well-prepared Trigger-Sequence.

A Trigger-Sequence includes four things: a trigger, emotion, thoughts and behavior. So when I say open the Trigger-Sequence, I'm inviting you to take a look as if you're opening a box to look inside.

Here's a vivid example: Pets are often an important part of family life. When they pass away we feel we've lost a family member. When a friend's pet died, he fell into a pit of depressed thoughts and feelings. His beloved pet's death caused him to want to eat comfort food. The trigger was his sadness about the death. The next element was his desire for comfort food, namely his mother's special recipe of orange cookies.

I emphasize the need to prepare your Trigger-Sequence to work in your favor. In the Trigger-Sequence, a person can replace orange cookies with an orange.

My client Stephen has a Trigger-Sequence that holds him back. Every time he thinks about updating his résumé, he feels like a deflated balloon. All energy leaves his body. I guide him to change the Trigger-Sequence. He identifies ten energizing songs. Then he turns up his sound system and plays the energizing song – and only then works on his résumé.

Now his improved Trigger-Sequence is:

1. *Trigger* – Energizing music

2. *Emotion* – Excitement

3. *Thoughts* – I feel good.

4. *Behavior* – Revising the résumé.

How a Trigger-Sequence Works Better Than Discipline

The idea is that you prepare your Trigger-Sequence ahead of time to work naturally in your favor. Then, when the trigger shows up, you naturally go into a better place. You do not have to force yourself and practice onerous self-discipline.

Prepare your trigger-sequence

Here's how to prepare for painful blows. Pull out your personal journal and write about the following details:

1. Make a list of the times when you lost your discipline and turned to a harmful behavior for comfort, like eating fatty foods, talking in an irritable way or ignoring a deadline.

2. Identify a specific trigger that propelled you toward the harmful behavior.

3. Identify what good or neutral behavior you can use to replace the harmful behavior. You might identify something that can be easy to do: For example, choosing to drink a diet soda instead of overeating.

Bob Greene, the personal fitness trainer for Oprah Winfrey, points out that many people reach for food when they are really thirsty. I used this insight when I created a sign: "Only water: 9 PM – 6 AM." This was part of the process of when I shed 12 lbs. in 20 days. I drank six eight-ounce glasses of water a day. I prepared my Trigger-Sequence to avoid food when I really needed to be hydrated. This process really helped.

Identify a trigger, emotion, thought and behavior you want to modify.

How can you use the Replacement-Behavior method to your benefit?

36

Win

Have you ever heard someone say they're just not interested in competition? In years of coaching clients, I discovered that many people have allowed their lives to fall into a rut in which they cannot win. In this case, we're not talking about you winning and someone else losing. Instead, we're talking about you feeling good and bringing good results to your interactions with others. In this way, the other person wins, too.

However, some individuals stay in a rut in that they cannot win and have expectations out of alignment with what their actions are creating. For example, some people who want their lives to improve may seek comfort first. Improvements in life often require dedicated effort and hard work over a significant period of time. Temporary comfort may need to be sacrificed for long-term meaning and satisfaction. It's a good trade.

On the other hand, some people discover that excessive television viewing may prevent them from excelling at what they are working toward. Author Malcolm Gladwell reported that research suggests it may take 10,000 hours to become truly accomplished at something.

One client expressed her dismay. "I don't have that kind of time."

I told her to look at what she's been devoting her time to over the past 20 years. I pointed out that she had likely been in training for work that she hasn't yet considered. She talked about how she loves to host parties for her circle of friends. I told her to consider that her hosting skills make her a chef, a communications expert (to get people to attend) and even a project manager. Her response was, "I never looked at it that way."

The idea is to look at your life in new ways. Remember, some people allow their lives to fall into a rut in which they cannot win. Instead, learn to improve your situation. Make it a game you can win. An interviewer asked, "So what is winning to you?" I replied, "Personally, I like to lead projects that turn out successfully. I have developed skills for handling problems."

Imagination is more important than knowledge.

ALBERT EINSTEIN

A proactive use of imagination can help you plan for and overcome problems. First, start by imagining good outcomes and phenomenal outcomes. An old phrase worth remembering: Success is met expectations.

In essence, we seek to make sure appropriate expectations are fulfilled. So, identify who the stakeholders are, that is, those who will benefit from your project. I seek out my stakeholders and ask them questions to discover their expectations. I find it helpful to use my imagination and then gain knowledge to fulfill my targets.

Your imagination can help you save a dying business in this recession. However, your imagination needs to be focused on two important areas as noted by Brian Koslow:

> *The most profitable businesses are not necessarily those with the most skilled employees or the best products. They are the ones with the best marketing strategy and the best leadership.*
>
> BRIAN KOSLOW

In your day planner, write "best marketing strategy" and "best leadership," and put "next action" under each heading.

Dealing with Problems

The truth no one will tell you: Problems are not just difficulties; they can be indicators that something good is happening. In fact, an old phrase holds: Problems are landmarks of progress.

As mentioned earlier, Albert Einstein said, "You cannot solve a problem on the same level on which it was created." Using that thought as a springboard, I go over dilemmas with people I trust and identify things that I am afraid might happen. Then I figure out ways to avoid bad outcomes. I figure out ways to turn the situation around.

Like most consumers, I tend to make purchases from companies that used courtesy and care when correcting any problems I had. If your company is responsible for the problem

– like a late shipment – turn the situation into a chance to demonstrate how much you want to make amends with the customer. This action creates a new level of commitment in the customer. The customer has seen how you improved a tough situation, which encourages the customer's trust in your company.

Principle:

Problems are often hallmarks of progress – so use them as opportunities to stretch and rise to a higher level of success.

Power Questions:

What can you do related to "best marketing strategy"? Do you want to find books that can help you? What can you do related to "best leadership"? What books on leadership can help you?

Conclusion to Part VI

In this section, we have explored the S.U.C.C.E.S.S.—N.O.W. Process:

S – Start with a castle

U – Unwrap fulfillment

C – Change habits

C – Conquer fear

E – Enhance relationships

S – Show a personal brand

S – Stimulate productivity

N – Nurture yourself

O – Open the Trigger-Sequence

W – Win

We also learned to set reasonable criteria when strategizing on a goal and to use the R.E.A.C.H. Process:

R – Reduce risk

E – Expect results

A – Adjust to circumstances

C – Compensate for your own shortcomings

H – Hook your attention

In Part VII, we will discover how to make your impossible dreams come true. But first you need to uncover the obstacles that may be holding you back. Armed with new knowledge and methods, you'll leap forward.

Part VII

37

Make Your Impossible Dreams Come True

The D.R.E.A.M. Process

Why do some things we want seem impossible to obtain? Because we feel we have these Roadblocks:

1. No money

2. No contacts

3. No time

4. No personal energy

5. No personal discipline to overcome procrastination

I'll show how you can overcome each of these five roadblocks to making your dreams come true.

To Make Impossible Dreams Come True ...

First, realize that we create things twice: First in our mind and then in reality. If you cut off your thinking with a knee-jerk response like, "I can't do that. It's impossible for me," then you get the disappointing results made from that self-fulfilling prophecy. Instead, you need a better way of thinking and of strategizing.

I help my clients and audiences to overcome the roadblocks that keep their dreams from coming true. The truth no one will tell you: To break out of a rut, you actually need to make progress on parallel activities. That's the reason that I now present five powerful actions each of us can do to make our dreams come true. This is the D.R.E.A.M. process:

> D – Do something now
>
> R – Reach out by helping
>
> E – Empower your time plan
>
> A – Act and recover
>
> M – Measure progress

38

Do Something Now

To resolve Roadblock 1, no money, you need to get clever and find a way to take action now. This will show you and the world that you can do what you want to do. Begin on a small scale.

I had directed small films and won awards before I began raising funds for my first motion picture. I had built credibility so that investors would believe in me when the time came to approach them for money. I demonstrated that I could complete quality projects. I also learned by doing.

Before filmmakers Zucker, Abrahams, and Zucker (*Airplane, Naked Gun*) made feature films, they did live shows that were like plays. They started small with no money. Before Sam Raimi directed "Spider-Man 2," he began by making a short Super-8 film. He showed potential investors the film and raised the funds he needed to make his first feature film that he shot on 16-mm film.

> *You never suffer from a money problem,*
> *you always suffer from an idea problem.*

ROBERT H. SCHULLER

Do something now. Try something new. For example, as this is being written, there is a new trend: roach-coaches that serve high-end cuisine. These coaches are vehicles that normally provide fast food to workers on location. The trendy coaches are run by chefs who are becoming known and many are opening their own restaurants, which now have ready-made customers. The chefs gain customers through Twitter by announcing where and when their coach will be parked. It's become very popular and people are quickly becoming famous doing this. And the chefs are prospering without paying anyone rent.

The truth no one will tell you: You need to start right where you are. My client Miguel wanted to be an author-speaker. He went to Radio Shack and bought a $25 microphone and a $99 recorder. He recorded a speech with an audience of friends, and *boom!*, he had his first audio book. This was a start. Certainly, he will make better products as he earns more money.

As many of us are working longer hours just to keep our jobs, it may seem impossible to make a transition from something you do merely for rent money to work that provides you feelings of fulfillment. The solution is to start small.

> *Do what you can with what you have. When you have*
> *more, do more.*

TOM MARCOUX

Put this principle into practice: Find out the numbers. That is, find out what is the minimum amount of money you need to get started on a hobby that can turn into another source of income.

For example, let's use the Latte Factor, an idea devised by David Bach, author of *The Automatic Millionaire*. The Latte Factor refers to someone spending $5 a day on a latte when she could have saved the money to apply to a life-changing goal. If she had instead opted to save the money, in 60 days she would have $300.

Although it's true that she, like so many people, is addicted to coffee, I would have advised her to make coffee at home and then bring it to work in a thermos.

By the way, don't let limiting thoughts slow you down. Julia Child did not start to gain success as a popularizer of cooking French cuisine until she was 50 years old. She took a passion and transformed it into a new career.

The idea is to start where you are and use strategy.

Set Powerful Goals

To make your impossible dreams come true, you must go beyond setting goals that are merely average. You need to create goals that move you. These goals must be so compelling that nothing will stop you. The goals must be solid enough to override the tendency to procrastinate.

Researchers have noted that many people procrastinate because they do not have a big enough "why" to keep their goals on track. These people need to be more strategic about how they set up and work with their goals. My clients learn to put the Go into Goals.

My coaching clients use the following Turn Insights Into Action process.

Turn Insights into Action (Put the "Go" into Goals)

Write your answers to the following questions in your personal journal:

1. Quickly write out five possible goals in 20 seconds. Now review the goals and see which one jumps out at you. What goal inspires feelings in you? Identify a goal that you can accomplish this year.

2. When you achieve the goal, what will be new and terrific about your life?

3. How will you feel when you succeed? What will feel great? What pain will cease?

4. What would be a modest success? A good success? A spectacular success?

5. How will achieving this goal help make your lifetime goals come true?

6. What is the price you need to pay to achieve this goal? Are you willing to pay this price?

7. Rate the possibility that you will achieve your goal using a scale of one to ten, where one means almost no chance and ten means you will easily achieve it.

8. List three important sub-goals involved with your goal. Write a target date next to each sub-goal.

9. What obstacles stand between you and the successful completion of this goal?

10. What type of help do you need to get around the obstacles? Where can you get this help?

11. What can you do today to take a small step toward completing this goal?

12. Why is it absolutely important to you to achieve this goal? What makes it compelling?

Small steps bring surprise leaps.

TOM MARCOUX

When you focus your mind on strategies to achieve your goal, you feel the power to move forward faster. One goal that some job-seekers and certain business owners fail to set is to do something every week to grow and nurture your circle of contacts.

Now, Robin Jay shares a secret to nurturing your new relationships.

Secret Recipe for Building Relationships!

Robin Jay

One of the best-kept yet simplest secrets for building relationships is to find common ground! If you've ever heard me speak, then you know that I've spent entire hours discussing gardening in the desert soil (rocks), dogs & cats, vacations, and – I'm sorry to say – sometimes just being a sounding board for my clients to vent and release stress.

Finding common ground is critical to your success in business. If you are a woman, have you ever commented on a woman's shoes only to discover they are Jimmy Choo's and the next thing you know, you're off and running talking about the Choo's you own and how fab-u-lous they are?

Okay, maybe it wasn't shoes. Maybe it was a great, new vacation spot, a new restaurant, hit movie, or music. You never know what someone will want to talk about. I have found, however, that when two people really click, it's pure magic.

Being able to find that common ground is gold for a relationship. For some people, it's sports. They could talk about games, players, and teams endlessly. But, personally, I've discovered that there is not much else that binds people together like a love of dogs. If dogs are your passion, and your client feels the same way, look out!

Here is my newest passion: I've decided to give Georgie, my shih tzu, her own blog. I sent out this press release last night at midnight and already it's had more than 130 hits! That's incredible. The blog is www.WorldsMostBeautifulDog.com. Georgie is certainly beautiful; she has the longest black eyelashes and when we go for a walk, people stop me and ask if I glued them on! I tell them no, that she is simply a natural beauty. (That's the truth!)

Georgie announces her new blog!

So it begins. Tonight I'm going to set her up with her own Twitter page. The hardest part of all of this is that she's behind me now, snoring, while I'm typing away. Typical Diva!

Find those things that excite you and about which you are passionate and indulge them! When you have a lot of interests and can share them with others, finding common ground will become easier than you ever imagined!

Robin Jay is an award-winning author and professional speaker. Her first book, *The Art of the Business Lunch: Building Relationships Between 12 and 2* (Career Press), is currently available in twelve languages. She is a Business Relationship Expert who speaks on building productive, long-lasting business relationships. Robin is also an accomplished mentor and publisher.

www.RobinJay.com

Robin encourages us to search for common ground and then devote significant time and attention in your conversation to that topic. With my audiences, when I say do something now, I also mean do something this week to grow and nurture your circle of friends and colleagues. Remember, small steps bring surprise leaps forward. Your next opportunities will probably arrive via your network of contacts.

Set Up a Power-3 Action Plan

The Power-3 Action Plan helps you overcome procrastination. The plan is a strategic process to help you avoid the typical setbacks people have setting and achieving goals. Many people set goals that are too hard and unrealistic. Instead, we need to look deeper and make a better plan – one that identifies different levels of activity.

Here is an example:

Writing a book

Level I – Easy: 50 words a day

Level II – Stretch: 500 words a day

Level III – Overstretch: 3,000 words a day

When you begin the process to achieve a goal, start with Level 1 (Easy). You need some Immediate Victories to boost your morale and create momentum. Immediate Victories provide nutrients for your new habits and successful behaviors. For example, I began by running only ten minutes each morning. I benefited from my modest goal, and it only involved waking up a little earlier.

You might go into unknown areas when you start working on a new goal, which makes your morale a little fragile. Take care of yourself. That is, begin with Level 1. I call this the Easy-Part Start.

Later, build up to Level 2 (Stretch). For the time being, be sure to avoid Level 3 (Overstretch).

Here are steps you can take:

1. Identify three actions that will help you achieve your goal.

2. Select the action that is strategically best to begin with. Using the Power-3 Action Plan, break it down into three levels of activity. Choose to begin an activity at Level 1 (Easy).

3. Identify some Immediate Victories, that is, something small you can easily do. (Examples: buy a helpful

book, call for a catalog of evening college courses, start making the phone calls you need to make.)

4. Identify some Immediate Rewards and attach them to your Immediate Victories.

Here are examples of linking an action with an Immediate Reward.

- Buy a helpful book: I'll also pick up a DVD of my favorite movie.

- Call for a catalog of evening college courses: I'll go out to dinner right after I make the call.

- Start making phone calls: As soon as I finish, I'll call Susan to set up a date for Saturday.

The Power-3 Action Plan can be your springboard to action. Using the three levels helps you get discomfort out of your way.

39

Reach Out by Helping

To resolve Roadblock 2, no contacts, learn the essence of networking: helping people. To help people you need to be observant. For example, two days ago my father called me about a local news broadcast airing a segment entitled "Protect Yourself from Spyware." I saw the segment, took action with the information, and called my father about the successful outcome. Let's break this down into a pattern for successful networking.

- Observe some way to help a person.

- Contact the person with the helpful information.

- The recipient takes action with the information.

- The recipient reports on the outcome of the action taken.

As you notice, both people do their part. When someone in your network of contacts does you a good turn, be sure to report to them the outcome of the action you took with their information.

Someone new in an industry may question the need to contribute. Here's a powerful example showing the importance of networking. As a motion picture director, actors often ask to be cast in my films. What good turn would I favor? Movie directors and producers value good tips on fundraising and distribution. The actress who sent me e-mails about fundraising and distribution sources helped me a great deal. I remembered her for opportunities to audition and have subsequently cast her in four productions.

Prepare an Elevator Speech

An elevator speech is your expression of your personal brand in a mere 30 seconds. Many times, it is a way to tell people how you can help them or someone they know.

Here's an example from author Dan Kennedy: "I help people like you become the dominant force in their market for less that $1.75 per prospect."

Other examples include: "I help people like you triple their income and double their time off." "I develop high-end medical equipment for 20% less than what my competitors charge." "My travel agency specializes in unusual and exciting cost-effective adventures for young travelers."

Our goal is to come up with a phrase that gets people to exclaim, "Oh! How do you do that?"

I have a few different elevator speeches that I use for various occasions. Here's one example:

> *I'm Tom Marcoux, known as America's Communication Coach. I help people like you command the Wow! in your audience. When presenting, branding, or communicating one-on-one, my coaching helps you make people feel good and want to follow your lead. I help people like you break through obstacles. What's an obstacle for you – between where you are and where you ideally want to be?*

For added distinction, add a relevant question to the end of your elevator speech. The question is crucial because you are returning the metaphorical spotlight onto the other person. You make the person "the star."

Here is an example for a graphic designer:

> *What I'm best known for is asking helpful questions to make sure the client expresses exactly what she wishes in an ad. I implement the answers, and the client is satisfied. Is there a marketing campaign that your company has done that you personally like?*

Make sure that you have the benefits in your elevator speech like: "I'm best known for providing strong design concepts that make memorable brands and raise profits."

Now use the following format and write a rough draft of your elevator speech in your personal journal:

> I help ___ people like you, who are struggling with ____. Using my ____ (process/product) they get great results like ______. [Add a question here.]

Fine-tuning your elevator speech will take time and practice. Strive to find a smooth way to convey the great benefits you offer.

A definition of personal branding:

> *Personal branding is to express your authentic self so the listener feels the benefits you are offering, trusts you, and feels compelled to get involved.*

This ties in with reach out by helping. You must clearly and briefly express your personal brand so that the listener knows exactly what you're offering.

A brand is the shortest distance to trust. If you do not take conscious action to make a personal brand, other people will do it for you. For example, author Robin Fisher Roffer described how someone at a cocktail party introduced her: "This is Robin Fisher, the Sweepstakes Queen of Cable!" Robin expressed her horror. "I had been branded, and branded as someone I didn't want to be. I learned that if you don't brand yourself, someone else will."

Your Personal Brand Begins with S.K.I.L.L.

The truth no one will tell you: For you to derive fulfillment, your personal brand needs to reflect your deeply held personal desires, talents and skills. Your personal brand needs to reflect the inner you. It's true that many people first become interested in creating a personal brand as a means to gain more money. This situation works because your personal brand is a tool that helps you convince people that you're trustworthy and that you're offering a service or product that provides great value.

What convinces is conviction.

LYNDON BAINES JOHNSON

One way to develop conviction in yourself is to pull together the elements of your personal brand. Make sure to experience the value of what you offer; that means use the product that you sell or at least get testimonials from people who use it.

Then make the elements memorable to you so you can express them at any time. For example, I rehearse my "elevator speech" (30-second description of what I offer) at various times during the week.

Creating your Personal Brand is an inside job. You need to explore how you really feel. We will use the S.K.I.LL. process:

S – Surprise yourself

K – Kindle kindness

I – Include possibilities

L – Lead by helping

L – Leverage your way

Surprise Yourself

After a decade of teaching college classes, I can still recall that first year when a student made a comment that I will always remember. My student said in class, "I live to amaze myself." He explained that his instructors guide him and he improves his artwork so much that it comes out better than he first imagined.

> *Along these lines, realize that your*
> *personal brand needs to have an element*
> *that amazes and delights you.*

When we respond to people with patience, restraint and compassion, we become trustworthy to others, which is a powerful part of an effective personal brand. For your personal brand to be delightful to someone, it helps if you go through your daily life with poise and kindness. Authors Linda and Charlie Bloom show us how to make a shift to an empowering state of mind.

What Really Matters

Linda & Charlie Bloom

Unless you've been in a coma for the past few weeks (Oct. 2008) you've probably been inundated with news about the current implosion of the U.S. (and now world) economy. Inundated may be too mild a term. "Completely overwhelmed" may be more accurate. After 9/11, Americans were repeatedly warned to "be afraid, very afraid" and encouraged to go out and shop as an antidote to our fear and as an expression of patriotism. Given the tone and content of many of the conversations that I've had with people over the past few weeks, despite efforts on the part of national "leaders" to reassure us not to worry and that "help is on the way" if we just trust that wise minds are taking care of business, it seems like there's a greater inclination to "be afraid" than there is to shop. This isn't surprising since for most of us there seems to increasingly be less to spend and more to fear. Yet as President Franklin Roosevelt announced during the first depression, "the only thing we have to fear is fear itself."

While I've heard that quote hundreds of times over the years, it has only been very recently that I've given any serious thought to what it actually means. To fully appreciate these words they must be provided with some context. It was March of 1933, seventy five years ago, and Roosevelt was delivering his first inaugural address to the country. The nation was experiencing the worst financial crisis of its history. The depression had reached its depth. Credit wasn't just tight, it was unavailable. There were massive foreclosures. The unemployment rate was through the roof. Banks all over the country had failed (and there was as yet no FDIC), international tensions were unprecedented with Fascism on the rise in Europe. It was truly one of our darkest hours as a nation.

In his address, FDR's intention was not simply to inspire and reassure Americans that we could and would get through these terrible times, but to put things in perspective and provide a plan that would effectively meet the challenges of the day. But first he had to cool the flames of fear that four years into the crisis were burning nearly out of control. What he was referring to with his now-famous quote, was the "nameless, unreasoning, unjustified terror which paralyzes needed efforts to convert retreat into advance." When he spoke these words, Roosevelt was acknowledging that it isn't the current situation that is our greatest threat, but rather our emotionally-driven reaction to it that undermines our ability to clearly assess the situation with clarity. He was acknowledging that fear that is intensified by inflammatory words and threats, whether they come from others or from our own mind, serves only to distort our perception of the reality in front of us and inhibits our ability to respond effectively. In so doing, Roosevelt was making a critical distinction between worry and concern, the former referring to feeling threatened and anxious and the latter having to do with being engaged and interested in something of importance and relevance to one's life. In other words, concern is worry minus fear. Of course it's hard not to feel fearful when the ground beneath our feet (figuratively speaking) is quaking and threatening to collapse. Choosing not to feel afraid is often easier said than done. But Roosevelt did not admonish us not to fear. He merely reminded us of the dangers in believing everything you think or have been told. The appropriate response to fear is to examine it and question the assumptions that underlie it in order to respond to it in a way that addresses the concern that underlies it. When we just react rather than respond to fear, we usually amplify it and get caught in a self-fulfilling, repeatedly reinforcing cycle which often ultimately leads to irrational thinking and panic.

Roosevelt of course didn't put an end to the depression of the thirties with his historic address, but he did interrupt what was rapidly becoming a national hysteria that could have had unimaginable consequences without his eloquence, wisdom, and confidence in the human character.

There are many other brilliant insights that he offered in his address that have been largely forgotten, overshadowed by the "fear" quote, but it behooves us, particularly in some of these trying times, to recall them. Roosevelt went on to say that: "We face our common difficulties [that] concern, thank God, *only material things*" (emphasis added). These last three words to me are the most powerful of his entire speech, for in them is contained the essential understanding that reminds us all that as difficult as things are, and as demanding as our personal, national and global challenges may be, we are dealing with material matters that only partially impact upon our overall quality of life. This is of course not to say that such concerns aren't extremely serious and in need of being addressed and corrected as quickly and effectively as possible. It is simply to help us to put things in perspective and remember what it is in our lives that truly matters. What it is that has meaning and purpose for us. What it is that truly impacts upon the quality of our heart and soul, and what it is that ultimately sustains and nurtures us and those around us.

The word crisis in Chinese is composed of two characters meaning 'danger' and 'opportunity'. Sometimes it takes a crisis to shake us out of the complacency of sleep-walking through a life driven by a script of material concerns in which we have lost sight of the purpose that underlies our need for work, money, and possessions. We can forget that these things are not ends in themselves, but rather means to greater ends. We may fail to ask ourselves the questions that can reveal the deeper needs and longings of the heart that can easily become neglected in our endless quest for "success". But true fulfillment cannot come from material achievement alone. Although the body does require food to sustain itself, the heart cannot be filled by material accomplishment. There is a wonderful saying that you can't get enough of what you really don't need. Sometimes it takes a crisis to tell the difference between what you really need and what you merely want. Although Roosevelt didn't actually say that "This situation is a wonderful growth opportunity" (the New Age wouldn't come into being for another forty years!), he did remind us to look beyond the immediacy of our anxieties to the deeper lessons that might be contained within this crisis. He simultaneously acknowledged the seriousness of the situation pointing to the underlying conditions that had contributed to it and offered a powerful and practical response to it.

Roosevelt went on to state that "the rulers of the exchange of mankind's goods have failed, through their own stubbornness and their own incompetence, have admitted their failure, and abdicated. They know only the rules of a generation of self-seekers. They have no vision, and when there is no vision the people perish." The grave danger that he alerted the nation to was not a failure of the banking system. That was merely a symptom. It was a failure of imagination, an absence of vision that underlay the systemic breakdowns that inevitably ensued. He further offered the extraordinary perspective that "happiness lies not in the mere possession of money; it lies in the joy of achievement, in the thrill of creative effort" and to "realize as we have never realized before, our interdependence on each other".

In speaking of the inextricably interwoven nature of all of our relationships, Roosevelt reminded us that one of the "gifts" of this crisis was that it helped us to remember that our basic nature involves interconnectedness, and that when our lives are an expression of this truth, all difficulties become more workable. In acknowledging our common needs, interests and concerns, we become more able to operate interdependently with each other, other groups, and even other nations rather than reinforcing the illusion of separateness and the experience of isolation that fuels our sense of powerlessness and fear.

Roosevelt would deliver three more inaugural addresses until 1945 when he died in office. He has always been considered one of our three most respected and beloved Presidents, along with Lincoln and Washington. Before his tenure was over, Roosevelt would lead America out of two of the greatest challenges of its history: the depression and World War II. But perhaps his greatest accomplishment was in reminding Americans of what really mattered and inspiring them to find within their own hearts the strength, the spirit, the faith, and the love that honors our deepest longings and our true purpose. When we are connected to the truth of our heart and to the hearts of others, not only do we see what truly matters and what is needed to fulfill the challenges that we face, but we see that we have within ourselves the ability to meet these challenges successfully. We also see that we are not alone, and that in working together in partnership with others we are capable of far more than we can in isolation or separateness.

In ninety days we will be hearing the inaugural address of our next President [which was President Barack Obama]. May we be blessed with a leader whose wisdom, judgment, compassion and ability to inspire matches that of FDR's. But let's not forget that even great leaders need the support of their constituents. America's founders envisioned a true partnership between citizens and representative-leaders. Our current situation awakens us to the challenge of fulfilling their vision. Imagine the possibilities.

Linda Bloom, LCSW and Charlie Bloom, MSW have been married since 1972. Trained as psychotherapists and relationship counselors, they have been working with individuals and couples and facilitating group seminars since 1975. They have served individually or jointly as faculty at many learning institutes throughout the USA, including Esalen Institute, The California Institute for Integral Studies, the Institute of Imaginal Studies, John F. Kennedy University, The Crossings, Omega institute, The Institute for Transpersoanl Psychology, University of California at Berkeley Extension Program, Kripalu Institute, The Hoffman Institute, and the World Health Organization. They have offered seminars throughout the world, including China, Indonesia, Denmark, Sweden, India, Brazil, and many other locations. Their book, *101 Things I Wish I Knew When I*

Got Married: Simple Lessons to Make Love Last (New World Library) is currently in its thirteenth printing.

www.bloomwork.com

Linda and Charlie Bloom remind us of President Roosevelt's powerful comments: "Happiness lies not in the mere possession of money; it lies in the joy of achievement, in the thrill of creative effort." And, "Realize as we have never realized before, our interdependence on each other." These ideas are related to the powerful and benevolent essence of a good personal brand. How do you help, surprise, and delight your customer or co-worker? It begins with expressing your own natural brilliance in ways that delight and surprise you!

A delightful surprise provides you with energy. So it's crucial to reconnect with the positive energy so that you keep going forward through tough economic times.

In your personal journal, write down your answers to these questions:

- What have you done in life that has amazed you? (Examples: you spontaneously helped someone or began a new hobby that felt delightful.)

- What would you like to do that would amaze and delight you?

I have talked about surprising yourself. You can also use a delightful surprising story to help you get a job.

People really grasp an idea when it is clothed in a story. Many influential spiritual leaders spoke in parables, or stories. The best stories have compelling details like: "At Acme Company, I streamlined the AB procedures and saved the company 17% in costs."

The truth no one will tell you: For your story to be compelling, you need to provide:

- An attention-grabber

- Suspense and tension

- A release

Here's an attention-grabbing opener that I sometimes use: "When I was hanging on to the hood of a speeding truck by my fingertips, I wasn't thinking about whether my cameraman could get the shot. Instead, I was focusing on … "

That's the beginning of a story about the stunts I did when playing a leading role for a feature film that I directed.

For suspense and tension, provide specific details in which it appears that a good outcome will be impossible.

Here's an example: "The client changed the specs on us four times. My lead designer went home with the flu. And our deadline is less than 17 hours away."

To release tension, provide the triumphant ending when you and your team saved the day. For example: "Our deadline was less than 17 hours away. I called in the team and said, "We can do this. Everyone write down five ways to streamline this process right now. We will implement the best new ideas and get the project done on time." My co-worker Serena said, "I have never seen this happen so fast. Your leadership is terrific!"

The best stories end with a third party praising you. It sounds better than your own assessment. I emphasize to my clients and graduate students:

It's not real until you tell a story.

TOM MARCOUX

In your personal journal, write a draft of a story you can use in a job interview.

Kindle Kindness

If you want others to be happy, practice compassion. If you want to be happy, practice compassion.

THE DALAI LAMA

Kindness blesses both the giver and the receiver. With your personal brand, find something in what you offer that provides a kind service. If you sell cell phones, find ways to make your customer's life easier. Learn ways to explain the complicated service plans. Show how to download fun ringtones. Offer to transfer their phonebook from their old phone into the new one.

In your personal journal, write down how you can add kindness to what you're already doing in your job.

Include Possibilities

What does success require? We need to include possibilities for change and growth. People who complain a lot are resisting the natural changes that arise.

It is not necessary to change. Survival is not mandatory.

W. EDWARDS DEMING

They must often change, who would be constant in happiness or wisdom.

CONFUCIUS

Research reveals that millionaires are good at noticing a hunch and then taking action on it. As one put it: You only have to be right 51% of the time.

Therefore, in order to create the success and fulfillment you want, you need to consciously strive to be open to new experiences and insights.

Try an Experiment

When I work so hard that I become burned out, I know that it's time to try something new! I said to friends, "I am going to experiment with not touching a computer for 24 hours during the weekend."

The word "experiment" can be liberating. You do not have to commit to something. You can try it out.

- List some activities you can experiment with. Perhaps, you'll do your marketing calls as the first thing in the morning. Maybe you'll write a to-do list for your next day's work during the last 15 minutes before you leave the office.

- List the Ideal Results and Good Results that your experiments may yield.

Lead by Helping

Want to make more money? Here's the truth no one will tell you: The more you serve, the more money you will make.

For example, I often begin a conversation with a new person by asking gentle questions. I listen to his or her answers. Eventually, the person asks me about what I do. That's when I sprinkle in a brief detail about my personal brand. I then ask a question that returns the spotlight of the conversation back to the other person. Here's an example:

New person: So what do you do?

Taesha: I'm known as the Power-Presentation Coach. I help people like you persuade with ease and leap to the next level of success and fulfillment. I help people get past obstacles. So what's an obstacle that keeps you from where you want to be?

The point here is to be helpful. I often ask, "So, who's your ideal client?"

Every person can have a personal brand and can feel great about providing a service. Many people discover their calling, or what some people term "the path given by Higher Power." Here are important ideas:

Everyone can be great because anyone can serve.

MARTIN LUTHER KING, JR.

Let no one come to you without leaving better.
MOTHER TERESA

Love in action is the force that will set us free.
SUSAN TAYLOR

One spiritual book has a phrase: "I am here only to be truly helpful."

In your personal journal, write notes related to:

- How have you helped someone?

- List three times you felt terrific while helping someone.

Leverage Your Way

The process to making significant money through your personal brand is to identify ways you can use leverage. Leverage is devoting little effort and gaining a big result. Best-selling authors Mark Victor Hansen and Robert Allen identify the following Five Forms of Leverage in the business world:

1. Other People's Money

2. Other People's Experiences

3. Other People's Ideas

4. Other People's Time

5. Other People's Work

Some readers might wince at the idea of taking these elements from someone else. Here is the key idea: First identify a benefit for the other person so that he or she wants to participate with you. Make it a win-win interaction.

Here are my comments on Mark and Robert's idea:

Other People's Money – Rich people learn to borrow money appropriately. They see debt as leverage.

Other People's Experiences – Effective people study books and audio programs and learn from other people's mistakes to save personal time and effort.

Other People's Ideas – When you quote someone's ideas and give them appropriate credit, you are creating a circle of success.

Other People's Time – I benefited when I hired a computer expert to do something in three hours that would have taken me 20 hours.

Other People's Work – To function at your peak capacity, learn to delegate work. When you delegate, you free up your energy to express your natural brilliance.

Mark Victor Hansen and Robert Allen identify the following Six Forms of Maximum Leverage:

1. **Mentor** – Your mentor knows the shortcuts, the time-savers and the little tricks.

2. **Team** – Team members fill in the gaps in your skills sets.

3. **Network** – Identify the key contacts, the people who control huge networks of people.

4. **Infinite Network** – This is the spiritual connection, which includes serendipity.

5. **Tools and Skills** – Use computers, the Internet and e-mail for fast communications, fast calculations and fast decisions.

6. **Systems** – These are systematized, streamlined and organized processes for generating wealth.

Where does maximum leverage truly come from?

Maximum leverage comes from how you give feedback and how you receive feedback.

As the leader of my company, I need to carefully give feedback that encourages team members to improve their work, feel supported to take appropriate risks, and to tell me about problems that need to be solved.

How to give effective feedback

Many people are not trained leaders. I've often heard friends mention managers who make abusive comments, which drains away the employee's energy and commitment.

Clumsy managers say things like: "That's wrong. Why did you do that? I told you before not to do it like that."

> *People find it hard to hear you when their ears are stuffed with pain.*
>
> TOM MARCOUX

Instead, we need to practice methods to gently give feedback.

*Nothing is so strong as gentleness, and nothing is so
gentle as true strength.*

ST. FRANCIS DE SALES

Giving gentle feedback often takes practice. This extra effort
is tremendously worth it. You gain new leverage to create better
results.

A good director knows when to say yes.

STEVEN SPIELBERG

*A good director sets up an atmosphere in which there
is a lot to say yes to.*

TOM MARCOUX

Many times, when someone asks you for feedback, what they
really want (emotionally) is for you to agree with them. So you
need to tread lightly. People are emotionally vulnerable when
they ask for feedback. If you do not agree or point out flaws, the
person will feel disappointment on some level.

Here are three methods to help you give effective feedback:

1. Ask questions first and then listen carefully

Ask questions like:

- Who is this for?

- What are you aiming for?

- Is there an area you're concerned about?

Then let the person's responses guide your next comments.

2. *"Perhaps, you might add more of …"*

Find something that's working and then say, "Perhaps, you might add more of …" This ties into a principle I emphasize:

Talk about what works first before you talk about areas to improve. Make a friend.

Here is an example of giving gentle feedback:

"At the beginning of your speech, you were asking questions and looking directly at the audience. That was terrific. Perhaps you might want to add questions when you're talking about Step Three."

3. *"I'm wondering about …"*

Create a hypothetical opponent and then say, "I'm wondering about …" A hypothetical opponent is a rhetorical device that allows you to frame an idea to be "knocked down." Here is an example of how you can offer feedback using a hypothetical opponent: "I like your new marketing plan. I really think it will work on the coast … I'm wondering if people in the middle of the country will go for it."

Saying "I'm wondering …" makes a point without your appearing as a direct opponent of the creative person.

You can later say, "You might consider ___," which is better than saying, "You should do." The person who says "should" sounds like he is elevating himself and putting down the other person. This is a form of judging. Judging creates separation and not closeness. Don't do it. Instead, take a gentle approach with "I'm wondering … "

How to Effectively Receive Feedback

How do you respond to feedback so that a mentor or team member is eager to help you? You express how you are welcoming their ideas. Say things like:

- I'm glad you brought that up.

- That's important. I'm listening carefully to what you're saying.

- I'm going to think carefully about this.

- I'm not yet sure what to do about that. But I'm certain that looking at this detail can help us do better.

People who feel appreciated are great sources for your personal leverage!

Answer these questions in your personal journal:

- What can you do to gain a mentor? Can you hire an expert and begin an interaction? Can you seek out a seasoned member within your business community?

- What can you do to form a team? Who do you know would make a good founding member?

- What can you do to expand your network? How can you help people? Which people can you pull together?

- What can you do to experience a positive spiritual connection?

- What can you do to expand your skill set?

- How can you put some form of system in place?

40

Empower Your Time Plan

To resolve Roadblock 3, no time, you need to reserve time for the important things that will help you create the best results. I emphasize "empower your time plan," and *Dictionary. com* defines empower as "to equip or supply with an ability; enable."

The idea is to enable your time plan so that you can do the most good. Be sure to set aside time for yourself. You then can respond to people with: "I'd like to help with that, but I already have an appointment scheduled at that time." The appointment is with yourself!

You also need to become effective at saying No gracefully. The philosopher Chuang-tzu told the story of a master sword-maker who became effective at his art. The sword-maker said,

"I took all the energy that I did not give in other directions and put it in the direction of my art. This is the secret of my mastery."

The first part of saying No gracefully is to give yourself some think-space. That is, some time and space to think about the situation. To create think-space, you might answer an invitation with something like: "I'm not sure about that. I need to check my calendar. How about if I call you back this afternoon."

Or, in another situation, you might say, "Thanks for thinking of me. I'll have to say No at this time. Perhaps, we can brainstorm about someone who can help you with your project."

Another part of saying No gracefully is to offer a this-or-that possibility. For example, once when I was asked to serve on a committee, I responded, "We could do the meeting on the phone. Or, you could have the meeting and then talk to me about details during a ten-minute phone conversation. I do want to be supportive of this project." The idea is that I presented two choices, and the choices protected my time.

41

Act then Recover

To resolve Roadblock 4, no personal energy, you need to become skillful about replenishing your energy. To do this, learn the Activity-Recovery Pattern. First, identify your prime time. For me, a great time for writing is when I first get up in the morning. I am refreshed and excited by the new day.

Second, make sure to tackle your important tasks during your prime time. Perhaps your prime time is in the afternoon when you are most alert. If so, schedule your crucial team meetings to fall during that timeframe. If you need to devote prime time to writing a report, make an appointment with yourself. Place your cell phone into take-a-message mode.

Third, identify elements for your Low Mood First Aid Kit (which we discussed earlier). Your Low Mood First Aid Kit is a list of things you can do to raise your tone and energy level. Perhaps you will benefit from a walk, a brief phone call with a loved one or energizing music.

When I need to energize myself, I step aboard my exercise machine and call a close friend. It feels great to take care of my body, and my soul feels enriched, too.

Fourth, honor your natural rhythms. For example, my client Mary is a writer. She will write for one hour and then "it just doesn't feel like fun anymore." At that point, she will take a break. In college, I studied for 50 minutes and then took a ten-minute break to step outside and walk around the library building. In this way I could study for 12 hours a day.

It is crucial to get in recovery time every day. When you have enough rest, you will have a reservoir of patience. For example, one year I was teaching a particular online class. I witnessed a student making mean remarks about another student's posted comments. In reply, I wrote the following comment. I am glad that I had programmed in recovery time so I had the energy to write this message.

Hello,

This concerns the comment that upset Sophie. [I quoted a student who expressed her upset about an insult that was posted about her own posted thoughts.] This inspires deep sadness in me. Let's go gently here in this discussion area. Let's simply state an idea and leave it at that. Let's not push vigorously against anyone, any particular group or any particular idea. This posting board does not give us a chance to provide a comment in a gentle voice. So let's be gentle with our words.

Thank you all. Tom

It was important that I write a message that showed the path of light and compassion. I also avoided chastising the errant student.

To my relief, the troublemaker sent me an e-mail with the words, "I apologize."

Making sure that I had recovery time enabled me to under-react, or rather, respond to the situation with compassion and quiet strength.

Now, Aaron Parnell comments on recovery time as true recreation.

Thriving on Stress

Aaron Parnell

Thriving on stress to achieve vitality is like flexing a muscle.

Building and developing muscle tone requires that you spend time and attention to pushing your muscles to their maximum ability and to resting, relaxing and nourishing them. Then it makes sense to revive your ability to thrive on stress by having a system of nurturing which restores your ability to handle a maximum amount of stress.

To Thrive, You Must Recreate

Studies have shown that 62 percent of health club members go for the purpose of minimizing stress, and that number is growing daily. What my personal investigation has shown is that certain people seem to gravitate toward specific recreational activities consistently.

Many sales people tend to gravitate toward competitive activities (fast paced, high adrenaline) such as racquetball, tennis, basketball, and kick boxing. I have found that CEOs and general managers gravitated to strategy-dependent recreation, such as golf, billiards, tennis, marksmanship and chess.

Recreation is the key

When we recreate or play, our "healthy" hormone levels return to normal. Furthermore, the part of us that we hold back in a stressful situation has a chance to "come out," express itself mentally, emotionally, psychologically and physically.

The Main Five Reasons why you want to use recreation to thrive on stress:

1. It's usually easy to do

2. It's fun to "play"

3. It provides balance – Helps you "get a life!"

4. It gives you activities that help you spend quality time with friends and loved ones

5. It may add years to your life – with quality

TOP THINGS YOU CAN DO TO NEUTRALIZE STRESS – ALMOST ANYTIME

1. Deep breathe and do nothing

How: Sit quietly, eyes closed. Breathe deeply – in through your nose, then out through your mouth. Breathe deeply three to five times then normally for one minute or more, without responding to your surroundings. Repeat.

Benefits: Sends oxygen to your brain, nutrients to cells and helps clear your thoughts.

2. Drink ample amounts of water daily

How: Add two cups of water to every one cup of coffee, alcohol or soda.

Benefits: Makes body fluids flow better, gives more energy and increases flow; helps you sleep; organs work better; helps body release toxins and waste better; improves body's cooling system; lowers blood pressure.

3. Take a nap

How: As little as five minutes – no maximum (whatever your body says it needs, if time allows). Some people sleep in sets of two 4-hour naps every day. Go to a place you can rest, cover eyes or turn off lights (no light) and give yourself permission to go to sleep, set an alarm clock (place it across room if necessary so you get up when you need to).

Benefits: Allows your body to get deep sleep which has double or triple benefit of just closing or resting your eyes. Accelerates the body's restorative process. Adds an extra half hour of productive mental energy per five minutes of nap time. Lowers blood pressure.

4. Stretch

How: Nice upper body stretch – lock your thumbs and put arms above head way up high, don't bend back; reach arms down and back behind and reach up again (shoulder circles) – and try a backwards swimming stretch.

Benefits: Helps pump the lymphatic system; improves immune system function; helps pump body fluids; stimulates circulation of blood; helps lift rib cage so you take more air in per breath.

5. Play / have fun

How: Always have two or three things you can do with no warm-up and no prep (playing darts, Nerf basketball, reading "fun" stuff – anything you don't have to calculate or think about).

Benefits: Gives your mind a break from routine and time to refresh mental sharpness.

Aaron Parnell, "The Vitality Man," is one of today's top talents in the Vitality and Healthy Aging movement. Author of nearly 100 published articles, he has appeared on radio and TV across the nation. Aaron was one of 35 therapists chosen out of 2000 nationwide applicants for the first Olympic Sportsmassage team in Los Angeles. With over 20 years experience, Aaron is on a mission to help humanity thrive with vitality, fulfillment, and longevity. Performing some 300 interviews during the Olympiad, Parnell researched the thoughts, attitudes, and actions of world-class athletes. Using Reposturing Dynamics™, with a success-rate of nearly 100%, Parnell helps individual clients at his center in San Mateo, CA improve their posture, flexibility, sports performance, and eliminate chronic pain forever. He trains and certifies practitioners in this extraordinary technique in a State Registered 140-hour program. Parnell helps companies save money and maximize functional efficiency and workplace productivity.

www.aaronparnell.com

Aaron Parnell coaches us to devote time to recreation. This is better than a one-for-one benefit. I have noticed that when I have some rest and recreation, I return to work with three times the efficiency and effectiveness. It's worth it!

42

Measure Progress

To resolve Roadblock 5, no personal discipline to overcome procrastination, you need a strategic plan and a means to measure your progress. Researchers point out that procrastination is actually about anticipated pain. The truth is that we need a big enough *why* so that we will flow through anticipated pain. We need to set powerful goals.

We also need to make taking action (for our goals) into a game that we can win. When we vividly feel our progress, we create a good feeling that allows us to set aside the anticipated pain that fosters procrastination. *Keep Score and Achieve More.* That is, set up simple ways to achieve milestones. These milestones will provide you with energy and motivation. For example, when I write a book, I keep a log of how many words I write per day. A salesperson can keep a log of how many sales phone calls and closed sales she achieves.

To create a viable game, we need to set up appropriate measurements.

If you can't measure it, you can't manage it.

KEN BLANCHARD

Measurement is the first step that leads to control and eventually to improvement. If you can't measure something, you can't understand it. If you can't understand it, you can't control it. If you can't control it, you can't improve it.

H. JAMES HARRINGTON

Ken Blanchard has a story that illustrates the value of incremental measurement.

How do they train killer whales to jump over the rope at Sea World? Do they hang a rope 20 feet over the pool and then shout to the whale 'Up, up, up!' No. They start with the rope under the water. When the whale swims over the rope, it gets rewarded. Then the rope is gradually raised. Each time the whale swims over it, again, a reward is given. How often do you give a 'reward' to those with whom you work? Only when the final goal is reached or do you give praise along the way as incremental progress is made?

KEN BLANCHARD

A powerful way to measure progress is to use a Self-Leadership Chart™ in which you note activities you want to do on a daily basis. Here is an example:

Self–Leadership Chart™							
Reward I Will Give Myself for 7 Days of Progress: a new CD.	Mon	Tues	Wed	Thu	Fri	Sat	Sun
Check this chart	√	√	√	√	√	√	√
Exercise	√		√	√	√	√	√
20-minute walk with spouse	√	√	√	√	√		
Write 30 minutes on my book	√	√	√		√	√	√

The Self-Leadership Chart™ helps you overcome backsliding and replace undesired behavior.

Be sure to check the chart every day. This will keep the important tasks in your mind.

Principle:

To make significant progress, set up appropriate steps for incremental measurement.

Power Questions:

How can you measure your progress? What can you place in a Self-Leadership Chart™ to ensure that you make daily progress?

Conclusion to Part VII

We have covered the D.R.E.A.M. process:

D – Do something now

R – Reach out by helping

E – Empower your time

A – Act and recover

M – Measure progress

To make your impossible dreams come true, you need to take action in five areas as mapped out in the D.R.E.A.M. process:

1. Do something now

To resolve Roadblock 1, no money, you need to get clever and find ways to take action now. You need to show the world that you can do what you want to do. Begin on a small scale.

2. Reach out by helping

To resolve Roadblock 2, no contacts, learn the essence of networking: helping people.

3. Empower your time plan

To resolve Roadblock 3, no time, you need to reserve time for the important things that will help you create the best results. You need to say No gracefully.

4. Act then recover

To resolve Roadblock 4, no personal energy, you need to become skillful about replenishing your energy. Use the Activity-Recovery Pattern.

5. Measure progress

To resolve Roadblock 5, no personal discipline to overcome procrastination, you need a strategic plan and a means to measure your progress.

When you take action and use the D.R.E.A.M. process, you'll find that your momentum toward your dreams builds and builds. It becomes fun to see roadblocks dissolve and new opportunities open up.

The best to you.

Springboard to Your Dreams

Thank you for your attention and efforts.

We have focused on skills so that you can experience a nothing-can-stop-you year. When you employ the skills demonstrated in this book, you attract more opportunities. People cooperate easily with you and make decisions that are favorable to your dreams and goals.

Remember to return to these pages again and again to reenergize yourself. You will get more value each time you review the steps covered in this book – and take action!

Please visit me at TomSuperCoach.com to get free reports and my free e-newsletter, *Success Secrets*. I also work with clients one-on-one in-person and over the telephone, and I present workshops and speeches to associations and companies.

On the following pages, you will find special discounts, presentations, and empowering audio programs and books that will help you continue your education and expand your prosperity. The best to you,

Tom

Tom Marcoux
America's Communication Coach
Motion Picture Director & CEO, Tom Marcoux Media, LLC

Special Offer for My Readers

Bring Tom to your company, conference, or church and get a 10% discount on his fee. TomSuperCoach@gmail.com.

Tom's popular topics:

- Be Heard and Be Trusted
- Truth No One Will Tell You
- Nothing Can Stop You This Year!
- Power Time Management
- Double Your Sales in Half the Time™
- 10 Best Kept Secrets of Persuasion Masters
- Wake Up Your Spirit To Prosperity
- Say Yes to Yourself: Reduce Stress and Increase Ease
- Empower Your Personal Brand

To view a downloadable page of these topics, go to:

bureau.espeakers.com/simp/viewspeaker5261&multimedia

Don't miss a special offer for readers of *Truth No One Will Tell You* at:

www.TomSuperCoach.com/ReaderOffer.htm

Get FREE reports and an e-newsletter subscription, *Success Secrets* (a $195 value!). Also order books and audios, see list at front of book.

Glossary

Glossary

For easy reference, here are listed all the specially defined terms used in this book.

~~~~~~~~~~~~~~~~

Belly Breathing – An important tool to bring your focus back to yourself. To do this, breathe in through your nose and allow your belly to inflate to its fullest. Briefly hold in your breath, and then breathe out while your belly deflates. I've heard my audience members comment how this process releases stress from their shoulders, and that they felt calm and even hopeful.

Brand, Personal – This is what makes you unique and trustworthy to your listener. Your personal brand is the answer to the question, "What are you best known for?" The clearly expressed personal brand establishes
~~~~~~~~~~~~~~~~

credibility. It is also part of the process of rising to the QuickBreakthrough Level, on which you have rapport with people and can even get access to their intuition! Here are the six elements of your personal brand:

1. The answer to "What am I best known for?"
2. A story that moves emotions
3. A memorable phrase
4. A label
5. A sound bite
6. Develop a moniker

B.R.A.N.D. Process – To develop your extraordinary personal brand, learn to

B – Bring your best stories

R – Reveal overcoming a weakness

A – Announce your strengths

N – Notice your interviewer

D – Devote yourself to the job

Breathe in God™ Process – When you're feeling exhausted, remind yourself to say, silently, "breathe in God." Take in a deep breath, let your belly expand, and silently say "God" as you breathe in. Then say, silently, "Thank You" as you exhale. You'll find that you will start to relax.

Bring Calm Steps – Take the following steps to guide someone to be more cooperative, by bringing them to calm.

1. Release your own disquiet.
2. Breathe deeply before seeing or calling the person.
3. Match tone, volume and pacing.
4. In graduated steps, lower your tone and volume … and in graduated steps, slow down your pacing.

C.A.K.E. Process – It takes energy and insight to save a business. If you feel depleted of energy, please return to the feed your soul section in this book. The idea is to keep up your self-nurturing efforts while you go into action with the following methods.

C – Create community

A – Adapt

K – Keep learning

E – Encourage help

Catchphrase ➠ "Hook"

Charisma – A charismatic person expresses compelling messages – messages which have a powerful and irresistible influence. These messages overpower inertia, low moods, and procrastination.

Contraction – To contract is to pull back out of fear of being hurt. The problem is that contracting often hurts us. It can feel like we're missing out on fun or fulfillment. Contracting can lead us to resent our current circumstances and limitations. Contracting cannot be your sole stance in life. You need some "expansion" in your life.

Contraction ⸺➤ "Expansion vs. Contraction"

Courage – Ambrose Redmoon stated, "Courage is not the absence of fear, but rather the judgment that something else is more important than fear." I emphasize to my audiences – *Courage is easier when you're prepared.*

Dog ⸺➤ "Personality Styles, Four"

D.R.E.A.M. Process – To break out of a rut, you actually need to make progress on parallel activities. That's the reason that I now present five powerful actions each of us can do to make our dreams come true.

> D   Do something now
>
> R   Reach out by helping
>
> E   Empower your time plan
>
> A   Act and recover
>
> M   Measure progress

Easethrough™ – The next evolutionary step beyond a breakthrough. The idea of rising to the QuickBreakthrough Level includes the Easethrough,™ which is better than a standard breakthrough. A breakthrough implies resistance that one must push through. With the Easethrough,™ you neutralize any resistance. Benefits of the Easethrough:

- Save your energy
- Get the pain out
- Eliminate procrastination
- Have more fun
- Enjoy your daily life

Elevator Speech – An elevator speech is your expression of your personal brand in a mere 30 seconds. Many times, it is a way to tell people how you can help them or someone they know.

Emotional Leverage™ – This involves using your emotional buttons to move yourself to action. Many people procrastinate to avoid anticipated pain. The strategy is to get the pain out of the situation and thereby eliminate hesitation. That's when you experience an Easethrough.™

Empathy Switch, The – A process that helps us shift into a mode of connection.

1. Pause
2. Move your body to connect
3. Ask a question
4. Give a Reflective Reply

Engage – To win over or attract; to draw into; involve.

Expansion vs. Contraction – As used in this book, Expansion is a hopeful process of opening up to opportunity, while Contraction is a process of fearfully shutting down. Expansion is the voice of intuition and thus a hallmark of good ideas, contrasted with bad ones. While this distinction is not part of popular usage, it is established within the arena of positive psychology and opens the door to a life affirming perspective.

Expert – An empowering definition of an expert is someone who has devised a system that people like and use.

Goal, Effort – This is a goal defined in terms of the effort required, rather than the result desired. It is a goal harmonized with the perspective that a journey is its own reward. Effort Goals contrast with Result Goals. Effort Goals are much less likely to be met with frustration.

Effort Goals grow naturally from your values; that is, what is most important to you. To help my clients complete their Effort Goals, I coach them to use a Self-Leadership Chart.™ *Also* ⇒ "Goal, Result" and "Self-Leadership Chart."

Goal, Result – This is a goal defined in terms of the result desired, rather than the effort required. This is most people's paradigm of a goal. Result Goals contrast with Effort Goals. Result Goals can be frustrating, since outcomes are often not within our control. *Also* ⇒ "Goal, Effort."

Good Decision – Here are some hallmarks of a good decision:

1. It's timely

2. It's proportional (devoting too much time to trivial details can keep you from your real priorities)

3. It may be informed by the expertise of others

4. It feels "intuitively right" (For example, Walt Disney felt his vision of Disneyland was worth overcoming the objections of his wife, brother/business partner Roy and the board of directors. Walt had to cash in his life insurance policy to fund the initial stages of Disneyland.)

Good Story – Stories reach us on our subconscious and emotional levels, going around our natural resistance. For your story to be compelling, you need to provide:

- An attention-grabber

- Suspense and tension

- A release

Higher Power – This is a non-denominational designation for the theist presence in the universe, with no reference to any particular faith. Higher Power as referred to herein has the following characteristics: (1) compassion for the human condition, and (2) concern for the well being of individuals.

Hook or Catchphrase – Make your hook short, simple and articulate. Make sure it encapsulates the heart and soul of your goal. When you repeat it to yourself, make sure it brings up powerful emotions and gives you a strong sense of direction.

Journal of Victories and Blessings, Daily – To counteract feelings of underachievement and depression, keep a Daily Journal of Victories and Blessings. In it note down each day's joys and accomplishments, regardless of scale. This will promote feelings of gratitude and blessedness.

Journal, Personal – A vital record of your journey through this book. To get the most from this book, be sure to write down the answer to each exercise in your personal journal as you proceed.

Keep Score and Achieve More – Professional writers keep track of how many words they write each day. These top authors are engaging in a process I call Keep Score and Achieve More. Many authors accomplish their writing goal and then go on to enjoy the rest of day – guilt-free!

The point is to transform making progress into a fun activity. Keeping a daily word-count helps authors feel good and energized as they make progress on a daily basis.

L.A.U.G.H. – Each of the letters stands for one thing you can do immediately to keep your humor up when you are down. Allen Klein's acrostic is:

> L – Let Go
>
> A – Attitude
>
> U – You
>
> G – Go Do It
>
> H – Humor eyes & ears

L.E.A.D.S. Process – To thrive during a crisis, you need to lead yourself and others to calm.

> L – Listen
>
> E – Engage
>
> A – Act
>
> D – Decrease downers
>
> S – Shift to inner sources of happiness

Leverage – The process to making significant money through your personal brand is to identify ways you can use leverage. Leverage is when you strategically apply a small amount of effort for a big result. Leverage is a product of effective action. Bestselling authors Mark Victor Hansen and Robert Allen identify the following Five Forms of Leverage in the business world:

Other People's Experiences – Effective people study books and audio programs and learn from other people's mistakes to save personal time and effort.

Other People's Ideas – When you quote someone's ideas and give them appropriate credit, you are creating a circle of success.

Other People's Time – I benefited when I hired a computer expert to do something in three hours that would have taken me 20 hours.

Other People's Work – To function at your peak capacity, learn to delegate work. When you delegate, you free up your energy to express your natural brilliance.

Leverage, Maximum – Mark Victor Hansen and Robert Allen identify the following Six Forms of Maximum Leverage:

Mentor – Your mentor knows the shortcuts, the time-savers and the little tricks.

Team – Team members fill in the gaps in your skills sets.

Network – Identify the key contacts, the people who control huge networks of people.

Infinite Network – This is the spiritual connection, which includes serendipity.

Tools and Skills – Use computers, the Internet and e-mail for fast communications, fast calculations and fast decisions.

Systems – These are systematized, streamlined and organized processes for generating wealth.

Leverage Triangle™ – To create lasting change in your life, the kind that leads to fulfillment and success, you must use a stable process, one that can withstand resistance, doubt, despair, stress, obstacles and bad hair days. The beauty of The Leverage Triangle is that it allows you to change from a position of power, not weakness.

The three steps of this triangle are:

- Merge with your true self.
- Strategize how to proceed.
- Act according to your real goals.

Lion ⟹ "Personality Styles, Four"

Listeners, Effective – People trust and like individuals who listen well. The truth is that you need to be an effective listener, so that other people can feel that you truly heard them, opening the door to their truly hearing you in turn.

1. Turn your body so that your heart faces the other person's heart.
2. Lean forward.
3. Make listening sounds like "mm-hmm."
4. Mirror feelings by saying things like, "That sounds frustrating."

5. Confirm that you understand by saying, "So you want ______. Do I have that about right?"

Love Languages, Five – In his book, *The Five Love Languages*, Dr. Gary Chapman points out that each person has a personal "love language." If you speak the person's language, he or she will truly experience your gratitude.

1. Words of affirmation
2. Gifts
3. Quality time
4. Acts of service
5. Physical touch

Low Mood First-Aid Kit – This is a toolkit for coping when a crisis snatches away our external sources of happiness. The tools selected are those which connect us with our internal resources for self comfort.

Makeover, Six-Minute – A brief vacation (or quiet time that may include meditation or prayer) from problems that centers you and reaffirms your commitment to nonattachment.

Manipulation – Manipulation is a dark practice where someone selfishly focuses solely on their own benefit to the exclusion of concerns for the listener's welfare. *Also* ➠ "Persuasion vs. Manipulation."

Mission Caption – Some authors emphasize the need to write a mission statement. How many people have memorized their mission statement? Often a mission statement is several pages long.

We live on the QuickBreakthrough Level with the help of what I call the Mission Caption. It can appear like a caption below a photograph. It will help you gain access to your intuition.

Moniker – Monikers sound like:

- The go-to person for software , or
- The Tech Wizard of Department M2

A moniker can be a positive nickname. A moniker is helpful for your personal brand. To align ourselves for promotions and raises, we need to be careful about what moniker we get stuck with. We need to come up with a moniker before someone else applies a nickname to us.

Nonattachment – Nonattachment is the process of connecting with life as it is now, and rejoicing for anything that is positive. It is not being forced to let go of what you want nor a process of not getting involved. This is a process of backing off from demands in favor of having preferences. This is a softer, more flexible and freer way to live.

Nonresistance – Let's face it, often, one does not win by resisting. On the other hand, in aikido, one just guides the punch. You take the attacker in the direction that he or she was going. You don't stand in front – you step aside. The force goes past you. That is nonresistance.

Observer – Observe your thoughts and learn to step into the Observer – that part of you that is calm. People who meditate learn to observe their thoughts. The Observer doesn't get upset because the Observer is not identified with any particular part of you.

Peacock ⟼ "Personality Styles, Four"

P.E.C. ⟼ "Personaltainment Branding"

Personal Brand ⟼ "Brand, Personal"

Personal Brand P.R.O.C.E.S.S. ⟼ "Brand P.R.O.C.E.S.S."

Personal Journal ⟼ "Journal, Personal"

Personality Styles – The four archetypical personality types are:

> **Lion:** A hard-charging leader, who may be considered abrupt or bossy.

> **Beaver:** An analytical person, who likes tables, graphs and lots of details. This person wants to

> appear intelligent and makes decisions slowly due to a great fear of making a mistake.

> **Dog:** A supporter, who likes routine and cares about the feelings of others. This person may be slow to accept change.

> **Peacock:** An extrovert, who loves to stand out in a crowd and gain approval. This person may be ineffective when it comes to follow-up.

Personaltainment™ Branding – This is a powerful technique for structuring your services, interacting with the media, and creating a compelling Web presence. You focus on P.E.C.: personalized, entertaining, and connecting material.

Persuasion vs. Manipulation – It is critical to distinguish persuasion from manipulation. For this book, let us make the following distinction:

- **"Persuasion"** is helpful because we start with benefits for your listener in mind.
- **"Manipulation"** is a dark practice where someone selfishly focuses solely on his or her own benefit to the exclusion of concerns for the listener's welfare.

Platinum Rule – "Do unto others as they would like done unto them." Formulated by Dr. Tony Alessandra and Michael J. O'Connor.

Power-Three Action Plan – This plan helps you overcome procrastination. The plan is a strategic process to help you avoid the typical setbacks people have setting and achieving goals. Many people set goals that are too hard and unrealistic. Instead, we need to look deeper and make a better plans – one that identifies different levels of activity.

> Here is an Example, involving writing a book.
>
> *Level 1* – Easy: 50 words a day
>
> *Level 2* – Stretch: 500 words a day
>
> *Level 3* – Overstretch: 3,000 words a day

Power Communication – Tom Marcoux's unique method of coaching so that clients communicate effectively and listeners want to cooperate and support the clients' agenda. Methods include blending (an aikido concept) to eliminate resistance and conflict. Clients learn to use effective persuasive techniques to stimulate the listener's mirror neurons so that agreement is a natural result.

Power Questions – Power Questions are your inroad to your intuition. Through your intuition, you access a higher level of wisdom and knowledge.

Power Time Management – Tom Marcoux's unique method of coaching so that clients and audiences use their natural brilliance to get more done with less stress. Innovations including Time-Leverage™ and the Easethrough™ to help the individual let go of resistance, procrastination, and inappropriate behavior-patterns. Clients learn to rise to the QuickBreakthrough Level so that they create more fulfillment and attract more opportunities and success. *Also* ➠ "Time-Leverage," "Easethrough," and "QuickBreakthrough Level."

QuickBreakthrough Level – The empowered state of the QuickBreakthrough Level is one of heightened awareness and flexibility. When you are functioning on the QuickBreakthrough Level, you have the flow of:

- Intuition
- Cooperation
- Connection
- Creativity
- Integrity (wholeness)
- Excellent communication
- Effective action

At the QuickBreakthrough Level, you are free from distraction, pain, worry, limited thinking, judgments, and emotional baggage. You do not procrastinate. On the QuickBreakthrough Level, you have the full use of your resources and skills to gain the cooperation of other people.

React ➠ "Respond vs. React"

Respond vs. React – As used in this book, a Response is considered and reflective, while a Reaction is unconsidered and reflexive. While this distinction is not part of popular usage, it is established within the arena of positive psychology and opens the door to a life affirming perspective.

Resistance ⟹ "Persistence vs. Resistance"

Result Goal ⟹ "Goal, Result"

Rs, The Five – Of creating a community that wants you to succeed:

> 1. Reconnect Enthusiasm
> 2. Reward Them
> 3. Receive Praise
> 4. Repeat Updates
> 5. Realize Mutual Benefits

R.E.A.C.H. Process – To set reasonable criteria when strategizing on a goal, use the R.E.A.C.H. process:

> R – Reduce risk
> E – Expect results
> A – Adjust to circumstances
> C – Compensate for your own shortcomings
> H – Hook your attention

S.A.Y.—Y.E.S. Process – Many people use my strategies based on the S.A.Y.—Y.E.S. process:

> S – Step off the stage
>
> A – Accept better care
>
> Y – Yield to recovery
>
> Y – Yearn for energy
>
> E – Encourage your best
>
> S – Support your team

Science of Emotional Leverage™ – Based on numerous effective processes, the Science of Emotional Leverage is founded on: (1) letting an unhelpful neural pathway fade from disuse, (2) establishing empowering neural pathways, (3) using the TriggerSet Method,™ and (4) replacing undesired behavior. Replacing a behavior and replacing a neural pathway are effective methods for improving your life. A more extended discussion of these ideas is the planned subject of an upcoming book. *Also* ➠ "TriggerSet Method."

Self-Leadership Chart™ – Clarity helps you feul your progress, and this is motivating. You can use a Self-Leadership Chart to overcome backsliding and replace undesired behavior.

Self-Nurture Chart™– The Self-Nurture Chart helps plan your week to assure that you experience daily enjoyment in life without adding to your troubles through unnecessarily spending.

S.K.I.L.L Process – The S.K.I.LL. Process is used to create your Personal Brand, by exploring how you feel.

> S – Surprise yourself
>
> K – Kindle kindness
>
> I – Include
>
> L – Lead by helping
>
> L – Leverage your way

Soft Spot – How to avoid impulse purchases and handle your "soft spot":

1. Carefully choose your definition of success.

2. Have safety measures; for example, go shopping with a friend who tends to save money and is careful with purchases.

3. Replace troublesome behavior with helpful behavior; for example, take a walk in a park instead of a shopping mall.

4. Use a Self-Nurture Chart and make sure that you experience enjoyment (without spending money) on a daily basis.

S.O.U.L. Process – This four step approach is comprised of:

> S – Support yourself
>
> O – Open connection
>
> U – Unleash a plan
>
> L – Linger for touch

Sound Bite – A sound bite is the expression of your message boiled down to a simple, clear, hard-hitting point.

S.U.C.C.E.S.S.—N.O.W. Process – Here is a distillation of wisdom that has helped me accomplish so many of my dreams

> S – Start with a castle
>
> U – Unwrap fulfillment
>
> C – Change habits
>
> C – Conquer fear
>
> E – Enhance relationships
>
> S – Show a personal brand
>
> S – Stimulate productivity
>
> N – Nurture yourself
>
> O – Open the Trigger-Sequence
>
> W – Win

Support, Three Levels of – Facing your fears often involves gaining the insight and support of others. Sometimes we cannot get support from others at the time we need it. So, a good plan has three levels:

> *Level I* – Support that takes little or no energy. (Example: devoting time with a pet.)
>
> *Level II* – Support you can provide for yourself. (Example: taking a walk.)
>
> *Level III* – Support that arrives when you ask for help. (Example: phoning a kind friend.)

Time-Leverage™ – The process of reducing resistance and going into action quickly with the least energy required. In this way, Time-Leverage provides an Easethrough.™ With Time-Leverage, you neutralize your own resistance, a source of procrastination.

Time-Leverage is better than standard time management. This process uses your emotions as a fulcrum. That's how Time-Leverage gets you into action. Standard time management, using only a written list, does not give a person the energy to get into action.

Trigger-Sequence – Self-discipline does not have to be so hard. The real power is in a well-prepared Trigger-Sequence.

A Trigger-Sequence includes four things: a trigger, emotion, thoughts, and behavior. So when I say open the Trigger-Sequence, I'm inviting you to take a look as if you're opening a box to look inside.

Here is an example of a viable Trigger-Sequence:

1. **Trigger:** Energizing music
2. **Emotion:** Excitement
3. **Thoughts:** I feel good.
4. **Behavior:** Revising the résumé.

TriggerSet Method™ – This is a breakthrough process, because we rely on physiology instead of willpower. It goes as fast as:

Eyes see ⮕ Feeling in the body ⮕ Action!

For example, I have used the trigger of a portable sign that reads, "Only water 9 p.m. – 6 a.m." This is a positive trigger. It tells me exactly what the healthy thing is to do. It does not dwell on "food" or "hunger pains." When you are thinking clearly, set triggers so you will act automatically.

Truth No One Will Tell You, The – This concept encompasses four reasons people fail to express the truth:

1. They don't know the truth.
2. They don't want you to know the truth so they can exploit your weakness.
3. They care about you and want you to avoid getting hurt.
4. They can only guess about what is best for you because your inner truth is only revealed by your answers to effective questions.

T.R.U.T.H. Process – In order to do better financially, you need to stretch and take appropriate risks.

T – Transform to "Yes."

R – Run in better races.

U – Untangle from the money-for-time trade.

T – Take on risk.

H – Hone your persuasion skills.

Truth-Revealing Questions – Your inner truth is only revealed by your answers to effective questions:

1. What do you really want?

2. What do you want to feel?

3. Where are you grieving?

4. How can you take better care of yourself now?

5. Where are you "contracting"?

6. How can you have some "expansion" in your life?

T.U.R.N. Process – When it comes to debt, the target is to learn how to turn things around.

T – Talk

U – Understand

R – Right-size

N – Nurture

Victories ➠ "Journal of Victories and Blessings, Daily"

Write Down, Rip Up Method – This process begins when you write down the truth about what is bothering you. Then rip up the sheet of paper and place it in your pocket. Do not re-read your agitated comments – that would be like picking up the baggage all over again. Once the upsetting thoughts are down on paper and then ripped up, you will likely discover that you feel lighter and better.

Word Picture – A word picture creates an image with words, making your communication vivid.

Bibliography

Further Reading

The following list of books and audio programs provides the reader with select landmarks in the rich literary landscape which has informed this book. Enjoy!

~~~~~~~~~~~~~~~~~~~~~~

Adler, Bill ➠ Winfrey, Oprah & Bill Adler

Albom, Mitch, *Tuesdays with Morrie: An Old Man, a Young Man, and Life's Greatest Lesson*, 2002, 192p, Broadway, 978-0767905923

Alessandra, Dr. Tony, *Charisma: Seven Keys to Developing the Magnetism that Leads to Success*, 2000, 288p, Business Plus, 978-0446675987

________, *Non-Manipulative Selling*, 2nd Ed., 1992, 276p, Fireside; 978-0671764487
~~~~~~~~~~~~~~~~~~~~~~

__________, *The Dynamics of Effective Listening*, 2008, audio, 5 hours, 29 mins, Nightingale-Conant

Alessandra, Dr. Tony & Michael J. O'Connor, *The Platinum Rule: Discover the Four Basic Business Personalities and How They Can Lead You to Success*, 1998, 304p, Grand Central Publishing, 978-0446673433

Allen, Marc, *The Greatest Secret of All: Moving Beyond Abundance to a Life of True Fulfillment*, 2007, 128p, New World Library, 978-1577316190

__________, *The Type Z Guide to Success: A Lazy Person's Manifesto to Wealth and Fulfillment*, 2006, 160p, New World Library, 978-1577315407

Ash, Mary Kay, *Timeless Principles from America's Greatest Woman Entrepreneur*, 2008, 272p, Wiley, 978-0470379950

Bach, David, *The Automatic Millionaire: A Powerful One-Step Plan to Live and Finish Rich*, 2005, 272p, Broadway, 978-0767923828

Barron, David R. & Danek S. Kaus, *Power Persuasion: Using Hypnotic Influence to Win in Life, Love, and Business*, 2005, 108p, Robert D. Reed Publishers, 978-1931741521

Bauer, Joel et al., *How to Persuade People Who Don't Want to Be Persuaded: Get What You Want Every Time!*, 2004, 256p, Wiley, 978-0471647973

Bedell, Gene, *Three Steps to Yes: The Gentle Art of Getting Your Way*, 2002, 256p, Three Rivers Press, 978-0609807194

Ben-Shahar, Tal, *Happier: Learn the Secrets to Daily Joy and Lasting Fulfillment*, 2007, 224p, McGraw-Hill, 978-0071492393

Bettger, Fred, *How I Raised Myself from Failure to Success in Selling,* 1992, 192p, Fireside; 978-0671794378

Blanchard, Ken, & Sheldon Bowles, *Raving Fans: A Revolutionary Approach To Customer Service,* 1993, 160p, William Morrow, 978-0688123161

Bloom, Linda & Charlie, *101 Things I Wish I Knew When I Got Married: Simple Lessons to Make Love Last,* 2004, 256p, New World Library, 978-1577314240

Bowles, Sheldon, ⮕ Blanchard, Ken, & Sheldon Bowles

Byrne, Rhonda, *The Secret,* 2006, 198p, Atria Books, 978-1582701707

Campbell, Joseph, *The Hero with a Thousand Faces* (Bollingen Series, No. 17), 1972, 464p, Princeton University Press, 978-0691017846

Canfield, Jack & Mark Victor Hansen, *Chicken Soup for the Soul,* 2001, 480p, HCI, 978-1558749207

Carlson, Kristine, *Don't Sweat the Small Stuff for Women: Simple and Practical Ways to Do What Matters Most and Find Time for You,* 2001, 288p, Hyperion, 978-0786886029

Carlson, Richard, *Don't Sweat the Small Stuff – And It's All Small Stuff,* 1996, 272p, Hyperion, 978-0786881857

Chapman, Dr. Gary, *The Five Love Languages: How to Express Heartfelt Commitment to Your Mate,* 1995, 204p, Northfield Publishing , 978-1881273158

Churchill, Winston, *Never Give In!: The Best of Winston Churchill's Speeches,* 2004, 558p, Hyperion, 0786888709

Cialdini, Robert, *Influence: The Psychology of Persuasion* (Collins Business Essentials), 2006, 336p, Collins Business, 978-0061241895

Cohen, Alan, *Relax Into Wealth: How to Get More by Doing Less*, 2006, 240p, Tarcher, 978-1585425631

Collier, Robert, *The Secret of the Ages*, 2008, 164p, Wilder Publications, 978-1604591880

Confucius, *The Analects* (Oxford World's Classics), translated by Raymond Dawson, 2008, 160p, Oxford University Press, 978-0199540617

Covey, Stephen, *The 7 Habits of Highly Effective People*, 2004, 4p, FreePress, 978-0743269513

Cutler, Howard C., ➠ Dalai Lama, The, & Howard C. Cutler

da Vinci, Leonardo & Serge Bramly, *Leonardo: The Artist and the Man*, (Illustrated), 1995, 512p, Penguin, 978-0140231755

Dahlkoetter, Dr. JoAnn, *Your Performing Edge: The Total Mind-body Program for Excellence in Sports, Business and Life*, 4th Ed., 2007, 264p, Pulgas Ridge Press, 978-0970407986

Dalai Lama, The, & Howard C. Cutler, *The Art of Happiness: A Handbook for Living*, 1998, 336p, Riverhead, 978-1573221115

DeNoon, Daniel, "Health-Food-Store Safari," WebMD.com

Disney, Walt, *Quotable Walt Disney*, 2001, 272p, Disney Editions, 978-0786853328

Dyer, Dr. Wayne, *Inspiration: Your Ultimate Calling*, 2007, 272p, Hay House, 978-1401907228

________, *Your Erroneous Zones*, 1993, 320p, Avon Books, 978-0061091483

Einstein, Albert, *The World As I See It*, 2006, 128p, Filiquarian Publishing , 978-1599869650

Emerson, Ralph Waldo, *Emerson: Essays and Lectures: Nature: Addresses and Lectures / Essays: First and Second Series / Representative Men / English Traits / The Conduct of Life*, 1983, 1150p, Library of America, 978-0940450158

Fettke, Rich, *Extreme Success: The 7-Part Program That Shows You How to Succeed Without Struggle*, 2002, 288p, Fireside, 978-0743223140

Franklin, Benjamin, *Benjamin Franklin: Autobiography, Poor Richard, and Later Writings* (Library of America), J. A. Leo Lemay ed., 2005, 816p, Library of America, 978-1883011536

Gage, Randy, *Why You're Dumb, Sick & Broke ... And How to Get Smart, Healthy & Rich!*, 2006, 224p, Wiley, 978-0470049310

Gandhi, Mahatma, *An Autobiography: The Story of My Experiments With Truth*, 1993, 528p, Beacon Press, 978-0807059098

Gilbert, Bill ➠ King, Larry & Bill Gilbert

Gospe, Mike, *Marketing Campaign Development: What Marketing Executives Need to Know About Architecting Global Integrated Marketing Campaigns*, 2008, 176p, Happy About, 978-1600050770

Greene, Bob, *Get with the Program!: Getting Real About Your Weight, Health, and Emotional Well-Being*, 2003, 224p, Simon & Schuster Australia, 978-0731811892

Groppel, Jack L., PhD, *The Anti-Diet Book*, 1995

Hansen, Mark Victor ➠ Hayden, C. J., *Get Clients Now!*, 2nd Ed., 2007, 256p, AMACOM, 978-0814473740

Hendricks, Gay, *The Big Leap: Conquer Your Hidden Fear and Take Life to the Next Level*, 2009, 224p, HarperOne, 978-0061735349

Hepburn, Katherine, *Me: Stories of My Life*, 1996, 432p, Ballantine Books, 978-0345410092

Jampolsky, Gerald "Jerry," MD, *Love is Letting Go of Fear*, 25th Anniversary Ed., 2004, 144p, Ten Speed Press, 978-1587611964

Jay, Robin, *The Art of the Business Lunch: Building Relationships Between 12 and 2*, 2006, 254p, Career Press, 978-1564148513

Jung, Carl, *The Portable Carl Jung* (Viking Portable Library), Joseph Campbell ed.,1976, 704p, Penguin, 978-014015070

Kaus, Danek S. ⟹ Barron, David R. + Danek S. Kaus

Kaus, Danek S., *You Can Be Famous: Insider Secrets to Getting Free Publicity*, 2009, 176p, Robert Reed Publishers, 978-1934759110

Kawasaki, Guy, *The Art of the Start: The Time-Tested, Battle-Hardened Guide for Anyone Starting Anything*, 2004, 226p, Portfolio Hardcover, 978-1591840565

Keller, Helen, *The Story of My Life: The Restored Classic*, Centennial Ed., Anne Sullivan et al. eds, 2003, 352p, W. W. Norton & Company, 978-0393057447

Kennedy, John F., *Let the Word Go Forth: The Speeches, Statements, and Writings of John F. Kennedy 1947 to 1963*, Theodore Sorensen ed, 1991, 448p, Delta, 978-0440504061

King, Larry & Bill Gilbert, *How to Talk to Anyone, Anytime, Anywhere: The Secrets of Good Communication*, 1995, 224p, Three Rivers Press, 978-0517884539

King, Jr., Martin Luther, *A Testament of Hope: The Essential Writings and Speeches of Martin Luther King, Jr.*, James M. Washington ed., 1990, 736p, HarperOne, 978-0060646912

Kiyosaki, Robert T. & Sharon L. Lechter, *Rich Dad, Poor Dad: What the Rich Teach Their Kids About Money – That the Poor and Middle Class Do Not!*, 2000, 207p, Business Plus, 978-0446677455

Klein, MA, CSP, Allen, *The Healing Power of Humor*, 1989, 240p, Tarcher, 978-0874775198

Kushner, Malcolm, *Presentations for Dummies*, 2004, 384p, For Dummies, 978-0764559556

———, *Public Speaking for Dummies*, 2nd Ed., 2004, 288p, For Dummies; 978-0764559549

Lao-Tzu, *Te-Tao Ching – A New Translation Based on the Recently Discovered Ma-wang-tui Texts* (Classics of Ancient China), tranlated by Robert G. Henricks, 1992, 430p, Ballantine Books, 978-0345370990

Lee, Michael Soon, MBA & Sensei Grant Tabuchi, *Black Belt Negotiating: Become a Master Negotiator Using Powerful Lessons from the Martial Arts*, 2007, 224p, Amacom Books, 978-0814474617

Lee, Michael Soon, Ralph R. Roberts, & Joe Kraynak, *Cross-Cultural Selling for Dummies*, (Illustrated), 2008, 384p, For Dummies, 0470377011

Levinson, Jay Conrad, *Guerrilla Marketing: Easy and Inexpensive Strategies for Making Big Profits from Your Small Business*, 4th Ed., 2007, 384p, Mariner Books , 978-0618785919

Luskin, Dr. Fred, *Forgive for Good*, 2003, 240p, HarperOne, 978-0062517210

Luskin, Dr. Fred, *Forgive for Love: The Missing Ingredient for a Healthy and Lasting Relationship*, 2009, 240p, HarperOne, 978-0061234958

MacFarlane, Michael, *Share and Grow Rich: The Dottie Walters Effect*, 2007, 207p, Elevate, 978-1601940087

Marcoux, Tom, *10 Best Kept Secrets of Persuasion Masters*, Marcoux Media

————, *101 Acting Secrets: Tips from A Director for Your Acting, Auditions, Movie Roles, and Self-Promotion*, Marcoux Media, www.TomSuperCoach.com

————, *Be Heard and Be Trusted: How You Can Use Secrets of the Greatest Communicators to Get What You Want, 3rd Ed.*, 2009, Marcoux Media, 978-0-9800511-4-8

————, *Darkest Secrets of Persuasion and Seduction Masters: How to Protect Yourself and Turn the Power to Good*, 2006, 186p, Marcoux Media, 978-0-9800511-0-0

————, *Double Your Sales in Half the Time*, Marcoux Media

————, *Empower Your Personal Brand: Align Yourself for Promotions and Raises*, Marcoux Media

————, *How to Heal When Life's Too Much*, Marcoux Media

————, *Make Money through Products Power*, Marcoux Media

————, *Nothing Can Stop You This Year!: How to Unleash Your Hidden Power to Persuade Well, Get More Done, Gain Sudden Profits, Command Intuition, and Feel Great, 2nd Ed.*, 2010, Tom Marcoux Media, 978-0-9800511-5-5

————, *Online Secrets to Build Your Brand*, Marcoux Media

————, *Personal Branding*, Marcoux Media

________, *Power Time Management: More Time, Less Stress and Zero Procrastination*, Marcoux Media

________, *Say Yes to Yourself: Secrets to Overcome Stress and Change in Your Workplace*, Marcoux Media

________, *Secret Influence to Get You Out of Trouble: How You Can Restore a Personal or Business Relationship After You've Really Screwed Up*, 2008, 156p, Marcoux Media, 978-0-9800511-3-1, www.TomSuperCoach.com

________, *The Recession-Proof Cupcake: How to Feed Your Soul, Save a Business, or Get a Job in a Crisis*, Marcoux Media

________, *Truth No One Will One Tell You: How to Feed Your Soul, Save a Business, or Get a Job in a Crisis*, 2010, Tom Marcoux Media, 978-0-9800511-6-2

________, *Ultimate Make Money While You Sleep via the Internet System*, Marcoux Media, www.TomSuperCoach.com

________, *Wake Up Your Spirit to Prosperity for Couples!: 7 Secrets to Increase Wealth, Romance, and Anything You Want*, 2006, 150p, Marcoux Media, 0-9624660-6-9

________, *Wake Up Your Spirit to Prosperity!: 7 Secrets to Attract Wealth, Love, and Anything You Want*, 2006, 132p, Marcoux Media, 0-9624660-5-0

McWilliams, Peter, *Wealth 101: Getting What You Want-Enjoying What You'Ve Got*, 1999, 532p, Prelude Press, 978-0931580185

Melograni, Piero, *Wolfgang Amadeus Mozart: A Biography*, 2008, 316p, University Of Chicago Press, 978-0226519616

O'Connor, Michael J. *see* Alessandra, Dr. Tony & Michael J. O'Connor

Orman, Suze, *The Laws of Money: 5 Timeless Secrets to Get Out and Stay Out of Financial Trouble*, 2004, 352p, Free Press, 978-0743245180

Parnell, Aaron Lloyd U., *Living with Vitality – The Dynamic Power of Extraordinary Health*, 2007, 204p, PZQ Press Divison, 978-0615143323

Ragas, Matthew W. and B. J. Bueno, *The Power of Cult Branding: How 9 Magnetic Brands Turned Customers into Loyal Followers (and Yours Can, Too!)*, 2002, 224p, Crown Business, 978-0761536949

Reeve, Christopher, *Nothing is Impossible: Reflections on a New Life*, 2004, 224p, Ballantine Books, 978-0345470737

RoAnne, Susan, *How to Work a Room*, Revised Ed., 2007, 336p, Collins Living, 978-0061238673

Robbins, Anthony, *Awaken the Giant Within: How to Take Immediate Control of Your Mental, Emotional, Physical and Financial Destiny!*, 1992, 544p, Free Press, 978-0671791544

Robbins, Mike, CSP, *Be Yourself, Everyone Else is Already Taken: Transform Your Life with the Power of Authenticity*, 2009, 256p, Jossey-Bass, 978-0470395011

_______, *Focus on the Good Stuff: The Power of Appreciation*, 2007, 240p, Jossey-Bass, 978-0787988791

Roffer, Robin Fisher, *Make a Name for Yourself: Eight Steps Every Woman Needs to Create a Personal Brand Strategy for Success*, 2002, 224p, Broadway, 978-0767904926

Savage, PhD, Elayne, *Don't Take It Personally! The Art of Dealing with Rejection*, 2002, 242p, iUniverse, 978-0595255757

_______, *Breathing Room – Creating Space to Be a Couple*, 2001, 210p, New Harbinger Publications, 978-1572242210

Seid, Syndi, *Etiquette in Minutes,* www.etiquetteinminutes.com

Siddhartha, Guatama, *In the Buddha's Words: An Anthology of Discourses from the Pali Canon* (Teachings of the Buddha), Bhikkhu Bodhi ed., 2005, 496p, Wisdom Publications, 978-0861714919

Siegel, Dr. Bernie, *Love, Medicine and Miracles: Lessons Learned about Self-Healing from a Surgeon's Experience with Exceptional Patients*, 1990, 256p, Harper, 978-0060919832

Spielberg, Steven, *Interviews* (Conversations with Filmmakers Series), Lester D. Friedman & Brent Notbohm eds., 2000, 250p, University Press of Mississippi, 978-1578061136

St. John, Noah, *The Secret Code of Success*, 2009, 256p, Collins Business, 978-0061715747

Tabuchi, Sensei Grant *see* Lee, Michael Soon, MBA & Sensei Grant Tabuchi

Teresa, Mother, *Mother Teresa: In My Own Words*, edited by Jose Luis Gonzalez-Balado, 1997, 128p, Liguori Publications, 978-0764802003

Tracy, Brian, *Eat That Frog!: 21 Great Ways to Stop Procrastinating and Get More Done in Less Time*, 2nd Ed., 2007, 128p, Berrett-Koehler Publishers, 978-1576754221

Trump, Donald J., *The Art of the Deal*, 2004, 384p, Ballantine Books, 978-0345479174

Waitley, Denis, *The Psychology of Winning*, 1987, Nightingale-Conant, 0671520679, audio recording (also available in paperback)

Walters, Dottie & Lillet "Lilly" Walters, *Speak and Grow Rich*, 1997, 288p, Prentice Hall, 978-0735203518

Wattles, Wallace D., *The Science of Getting Rich*, 2008, 112p, Wilder Publications, 978-1604591903

Wieder, Marcia, *Making Your Dreams Come True*, 1999, 235p, Harmony, 978-0609606087

Williams, A.L., *All You Can Do Is All You Can Do, But All You Can Do Is Enough!*, 1997, 219p, Ballantne Books, 978-0449001103

Winfrey, Oprah & O, The Oprah Magazine, Editors of O, *Live Your Best Life: A Treasury of Wisdom, Wit, Advice, Interviews, and Inspiration from O, The Oprah Magazine*, 2005, 336p, Oxmoor House, 978-0848731052

_______ & Bill Adler, *The Uncommon Wisdom Of Oprah Winfrey: A Portrait in Her Own Words*, 2000, 290p, Citadel, 978-1559724197

Ziglar, Zig, *Goals – Set goals ... and reach them!*, 1988, Nightingale-Conant, audio recording

Index

Index

A

C

F

K

Kaus, Danek S. – xx, 132, 135, 136, 177, 182, XXXII, XXXVI

Kawasaki, Guy – XXXVI, LXV

Kay Cosmetics, Mary ➠ Mary Kay Cosmetics

Kay, Mary – 131, XXXII

Keep Score & Achieve More – X

Keller, Helen – XXXVI

Kennedy, John F. – 1, 50, 65, 277, 285, 286, XXXVI

Kindle Brand ➠ Brand, Kindle

Kinesthetic ➠ Preferred Input Style, Kinesthetic

King, Jr., Martin Luther – 200, 258, 348, XXXVII

King, Larry – XXXVI

Kiyosaki, Robert T. – XXXVII

Klein, Allen – xix, 112, 115, 116, XI, XXXVII

Kong Qiu ➠ Confucius

Koslow, Brian – 315

Kraynak, Joe – XXXVII

Kunst+Aventur – vi, LXIX

Kushner, Malcolm – 133, XXXVII

L

N

O

Y

Z

About the Author

Tom Marcoux
America's Communication Coach

Tom Marcoux helps people like *you* accomplish big dreams. As Tom says, "I help people like you *command the Wow!* in your audience. When presenting, branding, or communicating one-on-one, my coaching helps you make people feel good and *want* to follow your lead." Further, Tom helps people get more done and feel good doing it.

Tom is also a prolific author, including *Nothing Can Stop You This Year!*, he has published 10 books and 21 audio programs, with sales in 15 countries. These have included both fiction and nonfiction. Prominent among his publications is *Be Heard & Be Trusted,* 3rd Ed., which, in a prior edition, was a required textbook at Cogswell Polytechnical College. The Third edition features contributions by Jay Conrad Levinson, Guy Kawasaki, and Dr. Fred Luskin, among others.

When you want *to influence others*, join Tom's many clients who benefit from his secrets on branding. Tom is described as "the Personal Branding Instructor" by the *San*

Francisco Examiner. Helping people become more effective job candidates, he has presented to ProMatch, Project Management Institute and chapters of Experience Unlimited (affiliated with the California Employment Development Department).

Holding a degree in psychology, Tom is also a personal and professional coach and guest expert on TV and radio In addition to being featured in technology and communication magazines, he earned a special award at the Emmy Awards. For six years, he addressed the National Association of Broadcasters Conference in Las Vegas on topics like, "Online Secrets to Build Your Brand."

Tom is an award-winning speaker and corporate workshop leader (to professionals from IBM, Wells Fargo, Sun Micro-systems, and Silicon Valley Bank). He is a member of the National Speakers Association.

Tom is also a faculty lecturer in public speaking, science fiction and fantasy literature and cinema, and comparative religion at Academy of Art University. He has been a guest lecturer at Stanford University, DeAnza College, and California State University at Los Angeles, among others. In addition to traditional classroom forums, he teaches online and has authored several online courses. He also presents workshops to fellow faculty at the Academy of Art University's Teacher Conferences.

In a more artistic vein, Tom has written, directed, and produced feature films, including one that went to the Cannes Film Festival market, where it gained international distribution. He performed as an actor in feature films and commercials. Presently, he is leading teams working on book-film projects titled *Crystal Pegasus* (children's fantasy) and *TimePulse* (science fiction). In addition, his audio programs and audio novels often feature orginal soundtracks composed by Tom.

When you need to enthrall audiences or effectively communicate your message to the media, engage Tom as your media coach. Tom will clarify your message, build your confidence in speaking, and craft compelling sound bites and stories for the press. Tom will help you excel!

(415) 572-6609
TomSuperCoach@gmail.com
www.TomSuperCoach.com

Designed

and set by gBambo of the graphic
and cartographic atelier:

kunst**+aventur**

Named for the slim booklet *Kunst
und Aventur* (Art & Enterprise),
published in Strasbourg, France in
1440, in which Johannes Gutenberg
(*c.* 1398 – 1468), a German goldsmith,
unveiled his epochal mechanization
of printing, vastly accelerating the
pace of learning and human progress.

The text was set principally in Minion
Pro, Zapf Humanist, Poor Richard,
Fontin, and Gill Sans families. The
body font, Minion Pro, was designed
by Robert Slimbach based on classical
old style types of the late Renaissance.

The design was executed in Adobe's
excellent Creative Suite 4, including
Photoshop, Illustrator, and InDesign.

Photographic kit was a Nikon D70
DSLR fitted with a Nikkor ED AF-S
24-120mm 1.3-5.6 G VR lens.

Write kunst.aventur@gmail.com
about design inquiries large or small
and user feedback.
Enjoy!

Collophon

Get what you really want ...

use the methods found in Tom Marcoux's books!

For special discounts, order at:
www.TomSuperCoach.com/SpecialOffer.htm

For more QuickBreakthrough resources, see
www.TomSuperCoach.com